Policing Scotland

D0265700

Policing Scotland

edited by

Daniel Donnelly and Kenneth Scott

WILLAN
PUBLISHING

Published by

Willan Publishing
Culmcott House
Mill Street, Uffculme
Cullompton, Devon
EX15 3AT, UK
Tel: +44(0)1884 840337
Fax: +44(0)1884 840251
website: www.willanpublishing.co.uk
e-mail: info@willanpublishing.co.uk

Published simultaneously in the USA and Canada by

Willan Publishing
c/o ISBS, 920 NE 58th Ave, Suite 300
Portland, Oregon 97213-3644, USA
Tel: +001(0)503 287 3093
Fax: +001(0)503 280 8832
e-mail: info@isbs.com
website: www.isbs.com

© The editors and contributors, 2005

The rights of the editors to be identified as the authors of this book have been asserted
by them in accordance with the Copyright, Designs and Patents Act of 1988.

All rights reserved; no part of this publication may be reproduced, stored in a
retrieval system, or transmitted in any form or by any means, electronic, mechanical,
photocopying, recording or otherwise without the prior written permission of the
Publishers or a licence permitting copying in the UK issued by the Copyright Licensing
Agency Ltd, 90 Tottenham Court Road, London W1P 9HE.

First edition published 2005

ISBN 1-84392-125-1 paperback

British Library Cataloguing-in-Publication Data

A catalogue record for this book is available from the British Library

Project management by Deer Park Productions, Tavistock, Devon
Typeset by GCS, Leighton Buzzard, Beds
Printed and bound by T.J. International, Padstow, Cornwall

Willan Publishing are grateful to Strathclyde Police for permission to reproduce the image
appearing on the top right-hand corner of the front cover

Contents

Acknowledgements

The Editors acknowledge with thanks the work of all those who have contributed to this publication and who have helped to bring a long-cherished product to fruition.

First of all, to our fellow contributors who have managed to negotiate their way through tight deadlines and a host of other commitments to be part of this enterprise: to Alistair Dinsmor, Nick Fyfe, Alastair Goldsmith, Dale McFadzean, Joe McGallagly, Jim Pennycook, David Strang and John Vine.

Then, to a host of police friends and contacts who have very helpfully provided information, ensured that it was as current as possible, and have confirmed its factual accuracy.

Next, to some academic colleagues who have read and commented upon this work in whole or in part: to Dr Robert Corrins, Dr Jack Geekie, Professor Neil McKeganey, Ian Rennie and, above all, Professor Roy Wilkie.

Also, to those who work in a number of libraries who have been helpful in acquiring books and journals for us and for pointing us in the right direction when necessary: especially to Barbara Catt, College Librarian, deputy librarian John Burke and all the staff at Bell College Library; to Carole and Brian at Strathclyde Police Library; and to the library staffs at Glasgow Caledonian University and the University of Strathclyde.

Much of the initial research from which this book developed came from the *Policing Scotland* project which provided the basis of the creation of the Scottish Centre for Police Studies at Bell College. The financial support for this project was provided over a number of years by Bell College Research Grants Committee and that support is gratefully acknowledged.

Some of the material that forms the basis of Chapter 4 on 'Devolution, Accountability and Scottish Policing' by the Editors was originally published in papers in *The Police Journal* and *Policing Today*, acknowledgement to whom is willing given.

Many thanks also to Brian Willan and his team for all their support and assistance.

Any errors and shortcomings remain the responsibility of the Editors and Contributors.

Daniel Donnelly
Kenneth Scott
Scottish Centre for Police Studies,
Bell College,
Hamilton.

List of abbreviations

ACC	Assistant Chief Constable
ACMD	Advisory Council on the Misuse of Drugs
ACND	Afghan Counter Narcotics Directorate
ACPO	Association of Chief Police Officers
ACPOS	Association of Chief Police Officers in Scotland
ADAM	Arrestee Drug Abuse Monitoring
APS	Association of Police Superintendents
ASPS	Association of Scottish Police Superintendents
BCS	British Crime Survey
BCU	basic command unit
BTP	British Transport Polic
eCC	Chief Constable
CCT	compulsory competitive tendering
CCTV	closed-circuit television
CEMA	Customs and Excise Management Act 1997
CIB	Community Involvement Branch
CID	Criminal Investigation Department
CIDA	Concerted Inter-Agency Drugs Action
COPFS	Crown Office and Procurator Fiscal Service
COSLA	Convention of Scottish Local Authorities
CPD	continuous professional development
CPS	Crown Prosecution Service
DAT	Drug Action Team
DCC	Depute Chief Constable
DETR	Department of the Environment, Transport and the Regions
DTTO	Drug Treatment and Testing Order
ECHR	European Convention on Human Rights
FDCF	Force Drugs Coordinators' Forum
GAE	Grant-aided expenditure
HMCE	Her Majesty's Customs and Excise
HMCICS	Her Majesty's Chief Inspector of Constabulary for Scotland
HMICS	Her Majesty's Inspectorate of Constabulary for Scotland

IND	Immigration and Nationality Directorate
JP	Justice of the Peace
MDA	Misuse of Drugs Act 1971
MoD	Ministry of Defence
MOH	Medical Officer of Health
MP	Member of Parliament
MSP	Member of Scottish Parliament
NAO	National Audit Office
NCH	National Children's Homes
NCIS	National Criminal Intelligence Service
NCS	National Crime Squad
NIM	National Intelligence Model
NPM	New Public Management
OLR	Order for Lifelong Restriction
OSC	Office of the Surveillance Commissioner
PABS	Police Advisory Board for Scotland
PACE	Police and Criminal Evidence Act 1984
PIs	performance indicators
PMCA	Police and Magistrates' Courts Act 1994
PNB	Police Negotiating Board
PNC	Police National Computer
PSNI	Police Service of Northern Ireland
RIP(S)A	Regulation of Investigatory Powers (Scotland) Act 2000
RLO	Restriction of Liberty Order
SACRO	Safeguarding Communities, Reducing Offending
SACDM	Scottish Advisory Council on the Misuse of Drugs
SCCC	Standing Committee of Chief Constables
SCRA	Scottish Children's Reporter Administration
SCRO	Scottish Criminal Record Office
SCS	Scottish Court Service
SCS	Scottish Crime Survey
SDEA	Scottish Drug Enforcement Agency
SDEF	Scottish Drugs Enforcement Forum
SDMD	Scottish Drug Misuse Database
SHHD	Scottish Home and Health Department
SOCA	Serious and Organised Crime Agency
SPF	Scottish Police Federation
SPIS	Scottish Police Information Strategy
SPS	Scottish Prison Service
SSA	Scottish Strategic Assessment
SSG	Scottish Strategic Tasking and Coordination Group
STG	Scottish Tactical Tasking and Coordination Group
UKTA	United Kingdom Threat Assessment
UNODC	United Nations Office on Drugs and Crime
VIA	Victim Information and Advice
ZTP	Zero-Tolerance Policing

List of figures and tables

Table of statutes

Acts of the Scottish Parliament

List of contributors

Alistair Dinsmor is a former police officer and is now Secretary of the Glasgow Police Heritage Trust and curator of the Glasgow Police Museum.

Dr Daniel Donnelly is a former senior police officer with Strathclyde Police and is now Research Fellow in the Scottish Centre for Police Studies at Bell College, Hamilton.

Dr Nicholas R. Fyfe is Reader in Geography at the University of Dundee.

Dr Alastair Goldsmith is a Lecturer in the Scottish Hotel School at the University of Strathclyde.

Dale McFadzean is a Lecturer in Law at Bell College, Hamilton.

Joseph McGallagly is a serving police officer and a doctoral student at the Centre for Drug Misuse Research, University of Glasgow.

James D. Pennycook is a Lecturer in Law and Criminal Justice at Bell College, Hamilton.

Dr Kenneth Scott is Head of the School of Social Studies and Director of the Scottish Centre for Police Studies at Bell College, Hamilton.

David Strang QPM is Chief Constable of Dumfries and Galloway Constabulary and President of ACPOS in 2004–05.

John Vine QPM is Chief Constable of Tayside Police and was President of ACPOS in 2003–04.

Chapter 1

Introduction: policing Scotland

Daniel Donnelly and Kenneth Scott

Ask any Scottish police officer whether or not policing in Scotland is different from that in England and Wales and there is likely to be an almost intuitive, affirmative answer. Ask about the precise nature of these differences and how they have come about and the answer is likely to be less clear and, indeed, may be quite vague. Once the fact that Scotland has its own laws and legal system has been identified, it becomes more difficult to articulate specifically what it is about policing north of Hadrian's Wall that makes it peculiarly *Scottish*.

These are the issues which this book seeks to explore. Is policing in Scotland in any way different from that which pertains in the rest of the United Kingdom or not? If it is different, in what ways is it so and are the differences fundamental or are they merely an adaptation of a British model of policing to a specific locality? What are the main characteristics of modern policing in Scotland and how have these developed over the recent past to what they have become today? Is the Scottish police likely to generate its own models of policing for the future or will it simply copy what is done elsewhere?

The aims of this book are therefore threefold. The first aim is to fill a gap in the police studies literature because very little has been written about policing in Scotland. The second aim is to describe how Scottish policing works, not only for an academic audience with a comparative interest in such matters, but for the general public in Scotland who pay for and interact with this important public service. The third aim is to provide some analysis of policing in modern Scotland in the context of new and emerging ideas about the nature, purposes and methods of policing that are developing throughout the world and to determine how far Scottish policing is maintaining its own traditions and characteristics or is becoming a localised example of global trends.

The study of Scottish policing

The study of policing has been a growing phenomenon throughout the world in recent times. Police studies has emerged from a combination of academic disciplines which relates to the activities, individuals and organisations concerned with law enforcement, the investigation and prevention of crime, public order, and the processes of criminal justice within society. Academic research into policing in Britain is usually dated from the pioneering sociological study by Michael Banton (1964) entitled *The Policeman in the Community*. Since then the study of policing and the police has become an established field in its own right with its own issues and agendas. As well as a growing number of academic books, the range of specialist journals has continued to expand and there has been a significant increase in research into policing from both academic and public policy sources.

Policing in Scotland has received very limited attention within this expansion of police studies and police research. Many regular publications tend to be of an official or semi-official nature rather than studies carried out by independent researchers. Some of these originate with police organisations themselves, such as in the statutory annual reports required of each chief constable and of HM Chief Inspector of Constabulary for Scotland. Others are studies commissioned in the past by the Scottish Office and now by the Scottish Executive, for example through its Social Research Unit (www.scotland.gov.uk/socialresearch) and the Inspectorate of Constabulary has begun to engage in some research activity in support of its inspection tasks (www.scotland.gov.uk/hmics). However, because this kind of research emanates from government and requires co-operation from chief constables, there is a tendency for it to express the officially sanctioned views of the Scottish police tradition rather than providing any wider critical perspective.

Scottish universities and higher education institutions have paid relatively little attention to the police compared with other parts of the criminal justice system, although, as this volume demonstrates, that is changing. An honourable exception to this is the Centre for Police Studies at the University of Strathclyde, which in the 1970s and 1980s published primarily on police management issues (see Bradley *et al.* 1986). The director of the Centre, Professor Roy Wilkie, was also instrumental in developing management within the Scottish police service, especially through his contributions to the command courses for senior officers at the Scottish Police College over many years. He also promoted scholarship within the service itself by persuading a number of senior police officers to undertake postgraduate research degrees. One of these, who was a chief constable twice in Scotland, went on to publish his thesis as a textbook on police accountability (Oliver 1997), but it is concerned with Britain as a whole and contains limited, though insightful, references to the Scottish situation. The writings of another of the original Strathclyde group, Professor Neil Walker, have given due weight to policing in Scotland in terms of police culture (Walker 1994), general developments (Walker 1999) and the constitutional framework (Walker 2000), although he is probably best known for his work on transnational policing and police co-operation in Europe (for example, see Walker 2003).

The growth in academic studies of policing in the United Kingdom has contained relatively little description and even less analysis of Scottish policing. Most of the major works in the field deal with 'British' policing as a singular entity and even the delineation of the police in Scotland is variable. Some works, such as Benyon *et al.*'s (1995) review of police forces in Europe, clearly do recognise Scotland as a country apart in policing terms. Many careful studies of policing in Britain explain that their focus is really on England, or at most England and Wales; for example, Reiner's (1997) classic study of the politics of policing. In other cases the line that is followed is not to define the police jurisdictions being discussed at all (see Bowling and Foster 2002). Thereafter, it is assumed that there is a 'British' form of policing and the discussion deals solely with England without reference to other parts of the UK. There are some signs that this tendency is beginning to change and that police studies literature is at least identifying the possibility that Scotland is different. The otherwise comprehensive *Handbook of Policing*, edited by Tim Newburn (2003) directs its readers who wish to find out about Scotland to the work of Neil Walker (1999). In Leishman *et al.*'s (2000) review of core policing issues, Scotland receives little mention, apart from a chapter on drugs policing co-authored by a Scottish senior officer, but the point is usefully made in the introduction, with regard to the creation of new parliaments and assemblies in Scotland, Wales and Northern Ireland, that 'the implications of these developments for British policing are many and complex, not least the question of whether we can continue to use the term *British* policing in the same way ever again' (ibid.: 5). Against this background of relative neglect it is ironic that the pioneering work of Banton (1964) was written when he was a lecturer at the University of Edinburgh, and his book contains a detailed chapter describing a typical shift of police work in an unnamed Scottish city, which was almost certainly Edinburgh itself.

In one of the few published textbooks on the Scottish criminal justice system as a whole, Walker (1999) argues that:

> The policing of Scotland, like the policing of any territory with its own political and cultural identity, consists of a distinctive but broadly familiar set of social practices informed by a distinctive but broadly familiar pattern of historical development.
>
> (ibid.: 94)

One of the purposes of this book is to differentiate the 'distinctive' of Scottish policing from the 'broadly familiar' of policing in Britain as a whole and to seek to map the contours of the policing of Scotland in these terms. Some areas of difference in Scottish policing are well known: the separate legal system, for example. Some areas are beginning to emerge; for instance, the role of the Scottish Parliament and Scottish Executive in initiating their own devolved agendas and policies in relation to policing. However, many others are unexplored, such as how the police in Scotland deal with crime, the effectiveness of accountability mechanisms, evaluations of operational policing or the relationship between the police in Scotland and the people of Scotland. Within the considerable constraints of space, time and the existing knowledge base, *Policing Scotland* is an attempt to begin the process of describing and analysing these and many other topics that constitute the core of police work, activity and organisation in the northern part of the United Kingdom.

The Scottish public and the police

Without doubt what policing in Scotland does share with the rest of the United Kingdom is an adherence to the guiding principle of 'policing by consent'. This principle implies that policing is carried out on behalf of, and with the support of, the public. It finds embodiment in the idea that police men and women are not high-powered officers of the state, but are ordinary citizens armed with only a limited range of additional powers and subject to exactly the same rule of law as the rest of society. As a consequence the received wisdom is that police work can only be effective where it functions with the consent and co-operation of the general public.

In Scotland good relationships between the police and the public are accepted on both sides as crucial to the policing of the country. By and large, the Scottish public is highly supportive of the police, as shown in the outcomes of the Scottish Crime Surveys (SCS). The percentage of respondents saying that the police do a 'very good' or 'fairly good' job has never fallen below 70% since SCS began in 1982 (Hale and Uglow 2000; MVA 2000). This support is also present in situations where the public come into contact with the police. A consistent minimum of two-thirds of those surveyed in SCS who have reported crimes to the police have been 'very satisfied' or 'fairly satisfied' with the response (Hale and Uglow 2000; MVA 2000). Research carried out on the attitudes of victims of volume crimes in Scotland (Williams *et al.* 2004) showed that they were satisfied with the service the police had provided, including the time it had taken the police to respond. Where victims were critical of the lack of information about their cases, this was expressed in terms of frustration at the shortcomings of the wider criminal justice system rather than at the police as such. It is also true that Scottish police forces work hard to maintain the support of the public, partly through extensive involvement by police officers at all levels in a range of community meetings and activities, and partly through the development of media and information services aimed at keeping the public aware of what the police are doing.

Despite this level of interaction between the police and the public in Scotland, there is still a great deal about policing of which the public may not be aware. In 1990, at a time of considerable debate about police reform, the three police staff associations, representing chief constables, superintendents and the Police Federation, described a model of 'British' policing:

> That traditional British policing is relatively low on numbers, low on power and high on accountability; that it is undertaken with public consent which does not mean acquiescence but a broad tolerance indicating a satisfaction with the helping and enforcement roles of policing ... [It] is epitomised by the single constable, close to his [*sic*] community, patrolling his beat with the consent of the general public, armed only with his lawful powers and his use of discretion.
>
> (JCC 1990: 4)

This model, embodied in the popular television series of the 1950s, *Dixon of Dock Green*, has been subjected to critical scrutiny, particularly by Reiner (1995). He argues that it reflects a mythical form of policing from the past which does not relate accurately either to that past or to modern circumstances. However, it is probably a representation of policing which remains in public memory and against which contemporary police work continues to be judged.

It is, after all, only a small percentage of the population who have any extensive direct contact with the police. Like other modern organisations,

5

the Scottish police forces have learned the value of marketing themselves positively to their public and of presenting positive images about their work. The very real problems, tensions and dilemmas involved in policing in the 21st century are less likely to come into the public domain or to be the subject of informed public debate. In the first two election campaigns for the Scottish Parliament, in 1999 and 2003, law and order has been a significant issue on the agenda of the political parties competing for the electors' votes. Yet the only real reference to policing was in terms of which party would, in government, put more 'bobbies on the beat'. While this is obviously responding to an expressed public perception of what should be a key issue for the Scottish Executive, namely, providing funding for more frontline police officers, it is far from all that there is to the problems of policing Scotland.

Policing is a major public service in Scotland. It is funded almost entirely by the Scottish taxpayer through both central and local taxation and it is concerned with a range of issues which are of crucial interest to the people and communities of Scotland. How can crime rates be cut? What can be done about levels of violence in our society? How can our local areas be made safer? How do we protect communities from drugs and drug dealers? How do we deal with the risks all around us, from deaths on the roads to preventing terrorist attacks? These are all significant questions which involve the police. A major part of the purpose of this book, therefore, is to explain how those responsible for policing Scotland set about dealing with these issues. Our aim is to bring together information on what solutions to such questions have emerged so far and to contribute to informing the necessary public debate about how to tackle them in the future.

The nature of policing

In 1829 Sir Robert Peel presented his new Metropolitan Police as an instrument for controlling and preventing crime. The report of the Royal Commission on the Police in 1962 considered the basic task of policing to be 'the maintenance of the Queen's Peace'. In 1990 the strategic policy document produced by the chief police officers of England and Wales set out the policing function as one of public service provision, reassuring and helping the public, and responding to the public as customers and consumers of the service (ACPO 1990). The 1993 White Paper on Police Reform in England and Wales stated that the main job of the police was to catch criminals. It has been long realised that, both across societies and within a society that changes rapidly, there is nothing constant about the nature of policing and the range and variety of police duties.

In Scotland the cornerstone of modern policing is the Police (Scotland) Act 1967, which laid down the enduring purposes, principles and practices that underpin the workings of the Scottish police service and of individual police officers. Section 17 of the Act states:

(1)   ... it shall be the duty of the constables of a police force –
  (a) to guard, patrol and watch so as –
    (i)   to prevent the commission of offences;
    (ii) to preserve order; and
    (iii) to protect life and property.

The phrase 'guard, patrol and watch' has been ingrained on the hearts and minds of generations of Scottish bobbies and has become something of a mantra to express what Scottish policing is all about. However, over the past 30 years, and particularly in recent times, the limitations of this as a statement of purpose have become increasingly obvious:

- its focus on the individual constable
- its implication that foot patrol is the only policing method
- its emphasis on reactive policing
- the open-ended nature of the policing to which it refers, making it difficult to draw any boundaries at all around what the police are supposed to do.

Contemporary debates about the nature of policing have become widespread, not only in an abstract form, but very much in a way that has influenced the practice of policing around the world. Wright (2002), for example, has identified four key modes of policing practice.

1 Policing as peacekeeping is about the maintenance of order in society, not only in the negative sense of controlling disorder, such as in the miners' strike of 1984 or the poll tax riots of 1990, but also in the positive sense of promoting social order and liberty.

2 Policing as crime investigation focuses on the extent to which the police can control levels of crime through strategies of investigation and detection.

3 Policing as the management of risk is concerned with the application of the concept of risk to problems of crime prevention and community safety and to strategies of crime reduction.

4 Policing as community justice involves the balance between the use of traditional law-enforcement approaches alongside the role of the

police in partnership with others negotiating justice in a wide range of different types of communities, such as in restorative justice (ibid. 39–44).

The police in Scotland have not necessarily always been at the forefront of innovation in relation to new conceptions of policing, but they have undoubtedly been open to these new ideas and have been influenced by them. As a result, Scottish policing has undergone considerable change, partly because of the changing demands of the society that it seeks to serve, but also because of new ways of thinking about policing and of new strategies, approaches and modes of organisation that have emerged from the wider world of policing.

In Banton's account of police work in a Scottish city in the early 1960s, he reflects on the wide-ranging nature of police tasks:

> One of the most striking features of this account is the great variety of tasks performed by policemen. Another illustration of their range is that on top of a cupboard in the charge office stands a bird cage. In the streets near the station there are many tenement buildings, and in the summer months budgerigars regularly escape from them; when found they are brought into the station. The cage is often in use.'
>
> (Banton 1964: 49)

This indeed illustrates the very wide range of police work, but it also, in reflecting on the nature of policing some 40 years' ago, indicates how far the Scottish police service has travelled in policing the very different world of the 21st century.

Policing Scotland

In compiling this volume we have tried to bring together two main groups of contributors: those who study policing in Scotland and those who work in policing in Scotland. Their contributions are defined partly by the purposes behind this book, partly by the analysis that is beginning to take place of aspects of policing in Scotland, and, importantly, partly by the key themes and issues that are prominent in driving developments in Scottish policing.

The core of the book centres on four main sets of themes and issues. Firstly, we start with a straightforward description of basic factual information about policing in Scotland and how it is organised at both local and national levels. Then we look at a number of important contextual issues and how Scottish policing has been defined by its historical development, the impact of recent constitutional and political changes in Scotland, and the response of the Scottish police service to two important and challenging areas of management, the development of leadership and managing change. There follows an analysis of police operations in relation to four key problems in Scotland: crime and disorder; operational policing in the community; the relationship between drugs and crime and dealing with young people and youth crime. Two contributions look at the interaction between policing and the legal system: firstly, the role of the police in a criminal justice system which is very much in a state of flux; and secondly, in the potentially contentious area of the relationship between police powers and the implementation of the European Convention of Human Rights (ECHR). *Policing Scotland* concludes with some discussion about the possible future direction of policing in Scotland.

In drawing a final line for the present work in face of almost continuous changes and developments, it should be noted that all legislation, policies, strategies, events and information are described as at 31 January 2005.

References

Association of Chief Police Officers (1990) *Strategic Policy Document: Setting the Standards for Policing, Meeting Community Expectations*. London: ACPO.

Banton, M. (1964) *The Policeman in the Community*. London: Tavistock.

Benyon, J. *et al.* (1995) *Police Co-operation in Europe*. Leicester: University of Leicester Centre for the Study of Public Order.

Bowling, B. and Foster, J. (2002) 'Policing and the police', in M. Maguire, R. Morgan and R. Reiner (eds), *The Oxford Handbook of Criminology*, 3rd edn. Oxford: Clarendon Press, pp. 980–1033.

Bradley, D., Walker, N. and Wilkie, R. (1986) *Managing the Police*. Brighton: Wheatsheaf.

Hale, C. and Uglow, S. (2000) *The Police and the Public in Scotland: An Analysis of Data from the British and Scottish Crime Surveys 1982–96*. Crime and Criminal Justice Research Findings No. 33. Edinburgh: Central Research Unit.

Joint Consultative Committee (1990) *Operational Policing Review*. Surbiton: Joint Consultative Committee.

Leishman, F., Loveday, B. and Savage, S. (2000) *Core Issues in Policing*, 2nd edn. London: Longman.

MVA Ltd. (2000) *The 2000 Scottish Crime Survey: First Results* [accessed at www.scotland.gov.uk/socialresearch].

Newburn, T. (ed.) (2003) *Handbook of Policing*. Devon: Willan Publishing.

Oliver, I. (1997) *Police, Government and Accountability*, 2nd edn. London: Macmillan.

Reiner, R. (1995) 'Myth vs. modernity: reality and unreality in the English model of policing' in J. P. Brodeur (ed.) *Comparisons in Policing: An International Perspective*. Aldershot: Avebury.

Reiner, R. (1997) 'Policing and the police', in M. Maguire, R. Morgan and R. Reiner (eds), *Oxford Handbook of Criminology*, 2nd edn. Oxford: Clarendon Press.

Royal Commission on the Police (1962) *Report*. London: HMSO.

Walker, N. (1994) 'Care and control in the police organisation', in M. Stephens and S. Becker (eds), *Police Force, Police Service: Care and Control in Britain*. Basingstoke: Macmillan.

Walker, N. (1999) 'Situating Scottish policing', in N. Hutton and P. Duff (eds), *Scottish Criminal Justice*. Aldershot: Dartmouth.

Walker, N. (2000) *Policing in a Changing Constitutional Order*. London: Sweet & Maxwell.

Walker, N. (2003) 'The pattern of transnational policing', in T. Newburn (ed.), *Handbook of Policing*. Devon: Willan Publishing, pp. 111–35.

Williams, B. *et al.* (2004) *The Interface between the Scottish Police Service and the Public as Victims of Crime: Victim Perceptions* [accessed at www.scotland.gov.uk/socialresearch].

Wright, A. (2002) *Policing: An Introduction to Concepts and Practice*. Devon: Willan Publishing.

Chapter 2

The organisation of Scottish policing

Daniel Donnelly and Kenneth Scott

Introduction

The aim of this chapter is to provide a broad overview of contemporary Scottish policing. The most obvious features of any policing system are the types of structure which shape it and the ways in which it organises itself to carry out its stated functions. As in any public service, structure and organisation are key aspects of policing in Scotland because they relate to issues such as the nature of local and national organisation and the balance between them; the different roles carried out by people who inhabit the service and how these relate to each other; issues of governance, finance and purpose; and matters around quality and effectiveness and public satisfaction. A summary of essential facts and figures about the police in Scotland is provided in Table 2.1.

Police organisations in Scotland

The policing of Scotland lies primarily in the hands of its eight police forces whose diversity and differences reflect that of the country itself, as shown in Figure 2.1. At one extreme there is Strathclyde Police, which covers half the population and area of Scotland, including the large urban areas and small rural islands of the west of Scotland, and employs almost half of the country's police officers. At the other end of the scale is Dumfries

Table 2.1 Scottish police forces: facts and figures

Police Force	Local Authorities	Police Authority	Chief Police Officers	Civilian Executive (Directors/Heads of Service)	Police Strength* 31.03.04	Support Staff* 31.03.04	Population (approx.) 30.06.02	Gross Expenditure** 2002–03
Central Scotland Police	Clackmannanshire Falkirk Stirling Councils	Joint Police Board	1 Chief Constable 1 Depute CC 1 Assistant CC	Nil	760	319	280,000	£ 44m
Dumfries and Galloway Constabulary	Dumfries and Galloway Council	Single Police Board	1 Chief Constable 1 Depute CC	Finance Communications & IT	489	281	148,000	£ 27m
Fife Constabulary	Fife Council	Single Police Board	1 Chief Constable 1 Depute CC 1 Assistant CC	Finance Human Resources	980	411	351,000	£ 56m
Grampian Police	Aberdeen City Aberdeenshire Moray Councils	Joint Police Board	1 Chief Constable 1 Depute CC 1 Assistant CC	Corporate Services	1,338	654	523,000	£ 85m
Lothian and Borders Police	City of Edinburgh East Lothian Midlothian Scottish Borders West Lothian Councils	Joint Police Board	1 Chief Constable 1 Depute CC 2 Assistant CCs	Corporate Services Finance	2,748	1,149	888,000	£172m
Northern Constabulary	Highland Orkney Shetland Western Isles Councils	Joint Police Board	1 Chief Constable 1 Depute CC	Finance Human Resources	683	361	275,000	£ 52m

Strathclyde Police	Argyll & Bute, City of Glasgow, East Ayrshire, East Dunbartonshire, East Renfrewshire, Inverclyde, North Ayrshire, North Lanarkshire, Renfrewshire, South Ayrshire, South Lanarkshire, West Dunbartonshire Councils	Joint Police Board	1 Chief Constable 1 Depute CC 4 Assistant CCs	Finance and Resources Human Resources Information and Communication Legal Services	7,430	2,387	2,206,000	£444m
Tayside Police	Angus Dundee City, Perth & Kinross Councils	Joint Police Board	1 Chief Constable 1 Depute CC 1 Assistant CC	Corporate Services Human Resources	1,156	565	388,000	£ 75m
SCOTTISH TOTALS	32	6 Joint Boards 2 Single Boards	8 Chief Constables 8 Depute CCs 10 Assistant CCs	15 Civilian Heads	15,584	6,127	5,059,000	£955m

*Source: HMCIC Report 2003–2004
*Gross expenditure for financial year ending 31st March 2003

13

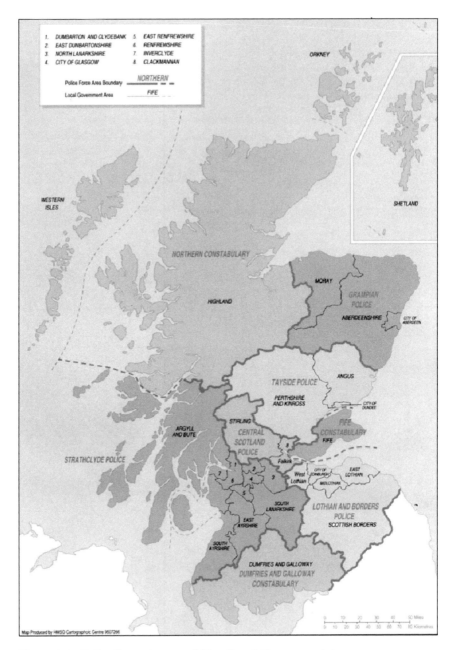

Figure 2.1 Police Force Areas and New Local Government Areas

and Galloway Constabulary, with fewer officers than one Strathclyde division, covering the largely rural southwest of the country, but with major transport links to both Northern Ireland and England within it. In between there lies a range of varying policing situations: Lothian and Borders Police with responsibility for Edinburgh, home of the devolved Scottish Parliament and Executive and an international gathering place; Northern Constabulary covering the extensive, but sparsely-populated lands of the Highlands and Islands with their particular communities and traditions; Grampian Police covering the northeast of Scotland with its unusual combination of protecting both offshore energy installations and the royal residencies on Deeside; and the band of forces covering north central Scotland – Tayside Police, Fife Constabulary and Central Scotland Police – with its mix of urban centres, suburban residential areas and rural hinterlands.

There is a further set of police organisations in Scotland. These are the central services which are associated with the provision of technical, scientific and training requirements to all Scottish forces. Under Section 36 of the Police (Scotland) Act 1967 the Scottish Ministers are empowered to establish common police services on a national basis. There are three such organisations that have been in existence for some time:

1 The Scottish Police College, based at Tulliallan Castle in Fife and popularly known by that name, provides the residential elements of probationer training for all forces as well as a range of specialist in-service programmes and rank-related management courses all the way up to a Scottish Command Course for potential chief officers.

2 The Scottish Criminal Record Office (SCRO) provides information to assist in, what its mission statement describes as 'the prevention and detection of crime'. This information includes fingerprint identification, criminal history information and a stolen-property database. It is also the home of Disclosure Scotland, the agency which vets job applicants, particularly those working with children and young people, for criminal convictions.

3 The Scottish Police Information Strategy (SPIS) aims to deliver and maintain 'a standard approach to development of new generation systems... to ensure the most cost-effective delivery of information services and to improve efficiency and exchange of information between forces and across traditional boundaries' (www. spis.police.uk), i.e. computer systems.

These common services are funded directly by the Scottish Executive, with some expenses being recouped from police authorities. Each service is managed by a centrally appointed director, which is a civilian post although police experience at a senior level appears still to be regarded as a significant factor in deciding on suitability. Each director is responsible to a board of management, which represents the interests of chief constables, other police professional bodies, and the Scottish Executive Justice Department. In only one case – the Scottish Police College – does the board of governors contain independent members.

The most recent addition to this corps of central services is the Scottish Drug Enforcement Agency (SDEA). It is also the most distinctive in that, in dealing with drug crime, it is the service whose work aligns most closely with frontline policing. Its director is equivalent to a deputy chief constable and CID officers seconded from local forces staff it. The managing board for SDEA is composed of the eight chief constables. To some extent the Agency replaced the Scottish Crime Squad, a co-operative effort by the territorial forces to tackle serious crimes wherever they happened in Scotland. To date, SDEA has been narrower in its approach, not only in concentrating on the supply of illegal drugs into Scotland, but also in its emphasis on gathering and disseminating intelligence in relation to such matters. The SDEA works very closely with UK police bodies such as the National Criminal Intelligence Service (NCIS) and external organisations such as HM Customs and Excise. It is intended that during 2005 the SDEA, in collaboration with the Scottish branches of these organisations, will head the Scottish dimension of the new Serious and Organised Crime Agency (SOCA) which the Westminster government is setting up.

A smaller presence is maintained in Scotland by a set of other police bodies, which are defined by their roles in relation to a number of public agencies. British Transport Police (BTP) is historically an amalgamation of various police forces which operated in connection with Britain's transport systems. Today the remit of British Transport Police is focused on the railways. It is quite close in structure and style to the public police, for example in shared training. Traditionally, one of the Transport Police's assistant chief constables is based in Scotland.

The Ministry of Defence (MoD) Police is primarily a patrolling force for installations owned by that ministry and, because of the state security aspect attached to that, tends to be routinely armed. In Scotland the main example of such an installation is the nuclear submarine base at Faslane on the Firth of Clyde, which regularly attracts demonstrations and protests by anti-nuclear campaigners. The remit of the MoD Police only runs on its own property, so while they would deal with any incursions by protesters, it is the local public police who are responsible for maintaining order on the roads outside.

The UK Civil Nuclear Constabulary is a small constabulary charged with protecting nuclear power stations. It has a presence at Dounreay Power Station in the very north of Scotland.

Police personnel

As with police forces in the rest of the United Kingdom, officers in the Scottish forces are divided into a number of ranks – probationary constable, constable, sergeant, inspector, chief inspector, superintendent, chief superintendent, assistant chief constable, deputy chief constable[1] and chief constable. On 31 March 2004 there were 22,674 people working within the Scottish police service – 69% (15,745) of this number were police officers, with the remaining 31% (6,929) being support staff. This includes those on central service and other secondments (HMCICS 2004a: 63).

Each force has a chief constable who is responsible for police operations in his/her force area[2] and who sets out the strategy for the efficient and effective use of police resources. Although police authorities appoint their chief constable, subject to approval by the Scottish Ministers, only the chief constable has the statutory authority to control, direct and instruct police resources in the enforcement of the law and general police functions as specified in the Police (Scotland) Act 1967. The only exception to this is the power of the Lord Advocate and the local Procurator Fiscal to instruct the police in relation to the investigation of crime.

Chief constables are significant figures within their own force and can be people of influence with the public in the area which their forces serve: 'the chief constable has sole overall responsibility for the efficient administration and management of police operations' (Scott and Wilkie 2001: 55). The whole tenor and approach taken by a police force to its tasks and priorities can change sharply with the appointment of a new chief. Equally, a chief constable's views on a wide range of matters will receive much publicity, especially in the local press and in interactions with other local decision-makers. All chief constables have come up through the ranks and have a varied background in policing. This range of experience is broadening with the increased number of appointments to Scottish forces of candidates from south of the border at chief constable level. As at December 2002 there were '10 of the overall total of 31 top positions (in Scotland) filled by officers from across the border' (Donnelly and Wilkie 2002: 20).

The factor of force size is a major determinant throughout the rank structure of what the job entails. Larger forces will have divisional commanders in the rank of chief superintendent, while in smaller ones it may be that a chief inspector or even inspector is in charge of policing in a geographical area. Key headquarters departments in larger forces are invariably led by a superintendent; in smaller forces, it may be an inspector or sergeant who is in charge of a similar department. Partly this reflects differing priorities in different forces as well as the scale of operations, but it does make it difficult to generalise across Scotland about the relationship between ranks and roles.

All entrants to the police in Scotland join as probationer constables. The probationary period lasts for two years. During this period probationers will spend some time receiving in-house training in their own force, undertaking residential elements of training at the Scottish Police College and working under the supervision of mentor constables in operational policing. There has been an increasing broadening of training approaches in the Scottish police service, with less reliance on didactic and rote learning and more exposure to a wider educational approach (Milne 2000: 42–44). Such an approach is certainly likely to be more successful with the increasing number of recruits who are mature and/or graduates. In the years immediately following the probationary period, officers can enter for the Police (Scotland) Examinations in crime, traffic and general police duties. Study for the examinations is entirely self-directed with no instructional support. These are still technically recognised as require-ments for promotion, but do not guarantee promotion. Consequently, there is a recognition that the 'promotion exams' have probably outlived their usefulness in their present format.

In recent times there has been some re-introduction of recruitment of police cadets in Scotland. Cadets were somewhat frowned upon and discouraged due to the opportunity cost to forces of fewer police officers on the street (HMCICS 1997, 1998). Under the Police Cadet (Scotland) Regulations 1968 chief constables can authorise the employment of police cadets in their force area. During 2003 the largest of the Scottish forces, Strathclyde Police, launched a major recruitment campaign for police cadets. The idea was to assist in the future employment of police personnel in the period from 2005 to 2010 when a significant number of Scottish police officers is expected to retire. It is widely expected that, due to demographic shifts, recruitment to the police service during this period will become more difficult as competition for human resources in both the private and public sectors increase. Strathclyde Police has adopted an innovative approach to its cadet recruitment programme by introducing a modern apprenticeship scheme of one to two and a half years' duration for persons between 16 and 18½ years of age. Participants in the scheme experience training programmes and modules which introduce them to core skills and competencies of probationary constables and experienced police officers. The cadet programme is also accredited by the Scottish Qualification Authority with the award of a nationally recognised certificate on successful completion of the scheme. At the present time only Dumfries and Galloway and Strathclyde Police employ police cadets, their total numbers being seven and 105 respectively (HMICS 2004a: 77).

Special constables are volunteers who work on an unpaid, part-time basis and while on duty they have the same powers as regular police officers. They have a key role to play in augmenting police resources on foot patrol, policing public order events, road traffic duty and administration duties within police offices. The 'Specials' have a significant contribution to make, in particular to rural policing, but unfortunately their numbers had been declining. New recruiting initiatives have changed this. The total number of special constables in Scotland on 31 March 2004 was 1,101 (HMICS 2004a: 77), an increase of 110 from the 2003 figure of 991. A breakdown of numbers in each force area is given in Table 2.2.

A number of thematic inspections carried out by HM Inspectorate of Constabulary for Scotland (HMICS 2002, 2004b) have examined the issues surrounding the recruitment, retention, deployment and training of special constables and have found there to be a lack of a corporate approach to these issues at both the national and local levels. However, chief constables have pledged their commitment to increasing the national complement of Specials by 500 officers by the year 2006, in acknowledgement of the valuable contribution they make to frontline policing throughout Scotland (HMICS 2004a: 65). One initiative successfully piloted in the Tayside and Grampian forces comprising a financial reward scheme whereby special constables are contracted to work for a specified number of days during the year for a fixed remuneration will be introduced throughout Scotland in 2005.

Table 2.2   Special constables by force area

Police Force	No. of Special Constables
Central Scotland	75
Dumfries and Galloway	116
Fife	109
Grampian	108
Lothian and Borders	267
Northern	53
Strathclyde	265
Tayside	108

Source: HM Inspectorate of Constabulary for Scotland 2004a.

Police organisation

The American academic David Bayley (1996) once asked the question: 'what do the police do?' In Scotland the key tasks in which the police are involved are extensive and wide-ranging, although they can differ in significant respects in detail from one force to another. They also require to be approached at different levels of complexity. Some activities are routine and frequent; others are major emergencies and are infrequent; some tasks require speedy responses; others involve long-term planning. The range and diversity of these functions are illustrated in Table 2.3.

Table 2.3   Police functions in Scotland

Operational Policing	Major Initiatives/Projects	Crime Investigation
Beat and Traffic Patrol	Licensing	Court Support
Internal Inspection	Serious Crimes	Stolen Vehicles
Witness Liaison	Fraud & Financial Investigation	Wildlife Crime
Nationality & Special Branch	Drugs	Informant Handling
Child Protection	Crimestoppers	Surveillance
Forensic Science Services	Road Crash Investigations	Road Policing
Provision of Air, Dog and Mounted Support		Emergencies Co-ordination
Underwater Search and Mountain Rescue		
Major Incidents	Counter-terrorism	Royal and VIP Visits
Major Event Co-ordination	Hostage/Crisis Negotiation	999 Emergency Call Management
Local Authority Liaison	Physical Crime Prevention	Race Issues
Architectural Liaison	Community Policing	Community Safety
Social Crime Prevention	Youth Issues	Drugs Awareness
Liaison with Business, Health Service, Voluntary Agencies, Local Groups		
Recruitment, Training and Personnel Management		Best Value
Computer, Radio and Telecommunications Services		Data Protection
Complaints and Discipline	Forward Planning	Legal Services
Statistics	Supplies	Vehicle Fleet
Property Services	Occupational Health and	Maintenance
Health and Safety	Welfare	Pipe Bands

Sources: Chief Constables' Annual Reports.

In general, police forces in Scotland tend to structure themselves along two main dimensions. Firstly, there is the physical distinction between headquarters and divisions. Headquarters is where the senior management of the force is situated and where matters relating to central strategic planning, central administration and central services are based. Divisions are geographical units that deal with policing in local areas. For example, Strathclyde Police has created nine large divisions, while Lothian and Borders has four. The balance between these two levels will vary across Scottish forces: some may be more centralised in retaining key functions at headquarters, some give greater devolution to divisions. It can also be difficult at times to draw clear lines between the two levels: a centrally devised and organised strategy will still require to be implemented at local divisional level, for instance.

Secondly, there is the functional distinction between general operations and specialist operations. The former relate to the routine tasks carried out mainly by uniformed patrol officers in the divisions. The latter refer to tasks which require specific training and experience. The 'traditional', broad specialisms include CID work and traffic, although not all forces have separate road policing departments. A whole range of newer specialisms has arisen in response to emerging additions to the policing agenda, such as child protection units, wildlife crime and liaison with local authorities, business and other agencies. Also, increasingly included under the specialism heading are those 'maintenance' functions which support the organisation and make it work effectively, especially in times of rapid change. These would include human resource management, training, health and safety, and organisational development. It is in many of these types of specialisms that police officers have been replaced by civilian support staff.

The specific structure of a force tends to emerge from the interaction of these two dimensions, physical and functional. Two detailed examples from Scottish forces are shown in Table 2.4.

Civilianisation

Police forces have employed civilian staff from time immemorial, normally in the capacity of minor clerical and administrative jobs. However, employing professionally trained civilians and substituting them in key roles hitherto occupied by sworn police officers are more recent phenomena. This expansion in civilianisation in the police service found its roots during the Thatcher era when the search for 'efficiency and effectiveness' and 'value for money' became key features of the public

Table 2.4 Examples of police force structure in Scotland

Central Scotland Police
OPERATIONS DIVISION (Chief Superintendent)
Includes all operational functions – 3 Area Commands (Superintendents)
12 Local Command Units (Inspectors)
Crime Management
Community Safety
Emergency Planning
Road Policing Unit & Support Services

CORPORATE MANAGEMENT DIVISION (Chief Superintendent)
Supports frontline services – Human Resources
Management Services
Professional Standards
Strategic Development

(*Source*: www.centralscotland.police.uk)

Grampian Police
DEPUTY CHIEF CONSTABLE
Responsible for – Corporate Communications
Human Resources, including Staff
Development
Professional Standards
Strategic Development

ASSISTANT CHIEF CONSTABLE
Responsible for
– Uniform Operations 4 Divisions/Command Areas (Chief
Superintendents)
– Operational Support (Chief Superintendent)
Traffic Department
Support Services
Operational Planning, including
Oil Liaison
Royalty/VIP
Control Room
– HQ CID (Detective Chief Superintendent)
HQ Squads
Forensic Laboratory
Community Development

DIRECTOR OF CORPORATE SERVICES
Responsible for – Corporate Services
Finance
Information Technology

(*Source*: www.grampian.police.uk)

---

sector, including the police service (see Home Office Circular 1983; Allan 1989, Audit Commission 1990).

The reality of having to account for resources in the Scottish police service in terms of value for money came in the form of Scottish Home and Health Department Circulars Numbers 3/1984, 2/1985, 5/1986 and 11/1993. These circulars made it clear that the period of rapid expansion in the number of police officers was drawing to a close, and forces would have to be more accountable for the effective and efficient use of all resources. During the previous years there had been a considerable rise in police expenditure and manpower and, following the Edmund Davies Inquiry (1978) into police pay and negotiation machinery, police salaries had improved substantially. Yet, over the same period, recorded crime had risen considerably. Local authorities were also beginning to express concern about how expensive police resources were being utilised at a time when the government was trying to drive down public-sector spending and local authorities were being hard-hit by cash limits on government grants. It was of no great surprise that central government started to ask what the public was getting for its money.

The initial reaction of the police service was one of unwilling acceptance of this approach, expecting the overall effect to be minimal. However, these circulars can now be regarded as landmarks in the development of police resource management and raised civilianisation high on the police agenda by linking future increases in police establishment to the civilianisation of posts 'which do not require the exercise of police powers or specialist police skills or experience and which could properly and more economically be filled by civilian staff' (SHHD 1984: 2).

By the mid-1980s there was a concerted attempt by the Scottish Office to speed up the civilianisation programme through a set of guidelines to police authorities and chief constables. The guidelines identified a large number of tasks as being suitable for civilianisation. The list included duties in connection with accounts, welfare, personnel records, statistics, scenes of crime, fingerprinting, photography, forensic examination, road safety, examination of vehicles, turnkey duties and computer maintenance (SHHD 1986: 2–3).

Despite considerable progress, a National Audit Office report entitled *Control of Manpower in Scotland* stated that further civilianisation of police posts could be made in the Scottish police service (NAO HC360: 1992). In 1993 the Scottish Office commented that only 70 per cent of key civilian posts identified by HM Inspector of Constabulary in the previous year had been filled (SHHD 1993: 1). Further guidance from the Secretary of State developed a three stage categorisation of police posts according to the degree of police or civilian involvement required (ibid.: 2). Category

A posts require police powers or experience and should be filled by police officers. These include CID, community policing, support group and drugs officers. Category B posts relate to community involvement, handling intelligence, control-room duties, warrants, and liquor licensing. These were identified as capable of being shared between police and support staff. Category C posts are normally jobs done by support staff only, such as administration and records, CID administration, IT, lost property, finance, wireless communications and vehicle workshops.

The extent of civilianisation in Scottish police forces is now considerable, with non-police officers constituting approximately one-third of the police workforce. In some of the common services this percentage is very much higher. For example, around 85% of the employees of the Scottish Police Information Strategy are support staff. This trend is partly to encourage police officers to focus on the specific duties for which they are trained, but it also recognises that a police force is in many respects no different from many other large work organisations in requiring specialist management and administrative support in order to operate efficiently.

In view of the militaristic tradition and hierarchical rank structures associated with the police, these developments do pose particular challenges for police management. In the past police managers have assumed that a fairly authoritarian leadership style would result in unquestioning obedience by those subordinate to them. In the new skill mix which the modern Scottish police organisation contains, not only do support staff often have greater expertise in their jobs than those in charge of them, but they are entitled to be treated in accordance with the principles of reasonable employment practice which prevail in other work organisations.

Governance

The chief constables of each of the eight Scottish forces, the local police authorities or joint police boards, and the Scottish Executive and Scottish Ministers share the responsibility for the delivery of police services to the Scottish people. All parties are governed by the Police (Scotland) Act 1967, as amended.

Responsibility for law and order in Scotland rests with the Scottish Executive and the Scottish Parliament, while the Westminster Parliament retains responsibility for national security, terrorism, firearms and drugs. One of the changes associated with Scottish devolution was the creation of a Justice Minister and Justice Department. The Department carries out the Scottish Executive's duties in respect of the administration of an efficient police service and the provision of other common police services in

Scotland. In addition, in partnership with local authorities and emergency services, the Department assists in the co-ordination, preparation and planning for civil emergencies in Scotland.

The Executive has the power to make regulations governing various aspects of the conditions of service of Scottish police officers. These include pay allowances and other related matters, which are subject to negotiation in the UK Police Negotiating Board (PNB), established in 1980, and on which Scottish police authorities are represented. In making regulations the Scottish Executive must take into consideration the recommendations of the Board and must consult it on draft proposals. The Board's membership comprises an independent chairman and secretary, representatives from the UK police staff associations, UK police authorities and government departments. Its remit is to consider and make recommendations to ministers on hours of duty, leave, pay and allowances, pensions, supplementary items such as clothing and equipment and to comment on draft regulations on any of these matters. That is why, on these issues of crucial importance to police officers, representatives of the Scottish staff associations can still be found lobbying the Parliament in London rather than in Edinburgh.

There is also a Police Advisory Board for Scotland (PABS), which covers matters other than pay and conditions. These include conduct and efficiency of police officers and advising the Scottish Ministers on general questions affecting the Scottish police. Its membership is made up of a ministerial chair, independent members appointed by Scottish ministers, staff association representatives and representation from the Convention of Scottish Local Authorities (COSLA). In addition to the Board's main remit it also receives and considers draft regulations on matters pertaining to the police service. PABS was established by the Police Act 1964. It is one of those bodies, common in UK public policy-making, whose influence is difficult to assess because its work is almost entirely unseen.

The Local Government etc. (Scotland) Act 1994 re-organised local government throughout Scotland with effect from 1 April 1996. Single-tier or unitary authorities replaced the regional and district councils and the governance of the eight Scottish police forces changed radically, from six regional police boards and two joint boards to six joint boards and two unitary ones. Two police forces, Dumfries and Galloway and Fife Constabulary, continue to be administered by the local authorities for their geographical areas. In the case of the other six Scottish forces, individual councils come together to exercise their duties through joint police boards. The eight police forces and their corresponding local authority area are shown in Table 2.1. The main responsibilities of the police boards include deciding on the force budget, providing the chief constable with the physical and human resources necessary to police the force area efficiently and effectively, and appointing senior officers of the rank of assistant chief constable, deputy chief constable and chief constable.

Unlike in England and Wales where the membership of police authorities is composed of elected members, magistrates and other appointments made by the Home Secretary, police boards in Scotland comprise of elected members only. In relation to joint police boards these representatives come from each council in the force area. Each unitary council is the police authority for its respective area and under the terms of an amalgamation scheme drawn up by the Scottish Executive most of the functions of the constituent authorities in respect of policing are delegated to the joint board. The amalgamation scheme includes the method by which the financial apportionment of the police budget between authorities is determined. Although the chief constable is accountable to the police authority or joint police board, the management and utilisation of both police and support staffs are under the direct control of the chief constable, thus preserving operational independence.

Police funding

Around 90% of the total annual police expenditure in Scotland comes from central government via a direct police grant, an indirect revenue support grant and non-domestic rate income. Local councils raise the other 10% or so from council tax and other income. The Scottish Executive's police grant contribution towards the revenue expenditure of police authorities is paid at 51% of net expenditure incurred by the authority up to a specified limit. The police grant is a specific grant that is dedicated to this one local authority service and cannot be used for any other purpose. The Scottish Executive decides on the total amount of police grant for the eight Scottish forces as part of the public spending review and the actual apportionment of the sum among each of the forces is decided after consultation with the Convention of Local Authorities (COSLA) and the Association of Chief Police Officers in Scotland (ACPOS). The police grant is income which is outside of the local authorities' own decision-making, unlike the raising of council tax, which is the main source of income available to them.

Grant-aided expenditure (GAE) represents the Scottish Executive's view of what needs to be spent by a local authority in order to provide a standard level of service. The GAE is an implied figure for specific services and is not spending-limited. Police authorities can decide independently on spending priorities within their own budgets, but any amount of expenditure higher than the implied figure from the Scottish Executive will not qualify for police grant. Police grant is set for the authority responsible for each police force, since police expenditure is incurred by the authority and not, in the case of joint police boards, the individual constituent councils. Joint police boards ratify the budget for their police forces, while the constituent councils raise the council tax to pay their proportion of the expenditure to the police board.

Police authorities have a principal responsibility to ensure that the chief constable is provided with sufficient financial resources to enable an efficient and effective police service within the command area to be maintained. The GAE is a key source of police funding and a new formula for distributing the GAE was ratified by the Scottish Executive in 2004 which aims to ensure local allocations are more closely related to local policing needs. Henceforth, a range of additional factors such as local crime, deprivation, rurality, city policing and population will be taken into account – unlike the previous incremental system which was less responsive to changes in local circumstances.

As the primary function of the police service is the delivery of operational policing, which necessitates a high number of police officers and support staff, a significant proportion of the police revenue budget goes towards the personnel costs, normally in excess of 85% of total budget. A typical revenue budget of a Scottish police force would cover pay and related matters, pensions, property costs, supplies and services, loan charges, common police costs, transport costs, administration costs and other ancillary costs.

Policing is very much a demand-led service which reflects the twin priorities of the public and of the government of the day. This is evident from the current impact of the 'war against terrorism' and the advent of newly available technological tools to aid the fight against crime. These additional workloads on an already overstretched police service are usually accompanied with extra financial costs and overheads not planned for in the police budget. Flexibility does exist in the current system of police funding to meet these supplementary costs and during each financial year additional funding can be provided by the Scottish Executive for specific expenditure relating to special projects or extraordinary demands managed by one or all of the Scottish police forces. For example, additional funding has been made available during industrial action by the fire service; for increased policing of ports to deal with drug trafficking; for the creation of a vulnerable persons' database; for a restorative justice project; and for the expansion of DNA testing. Additional funding requirements are also considered necessary for individual forces' commitments such as security arrangements for the Royal Family at Balmoral Castle, the costs of policing the Scottish Parliament, Royal and VIP visits, the Edinburgh Festival and other events in the country's capital city, and to meet the extra expenditure for policing major gatherings of international leaders, such as the G8 Summit at Gleneagles in Perthshire in 2005.

In view of the fact that Scottish forces are major owners of property, transport and equipment, capital investment constitutes a further significant feature of expenditure. Each of the eight forces, in collaboration with its police authority or joint police board, operates a capital programme to cover items such as replacement of buildings, minor and major maintenance, communication, IT and laboratory equipment, vehicle replacement, and other specialist equipment such as the introduction of the national Airwave Communication System which permits direct contact to be maintained between individual officers and their supervisors. A capital allocation from the Scottish Executive and capital receipts from local authorities fund such programmes.

Police associations

Three police staff associations represent the various ranks within the Scottish police service – the Association of Chief Police Officers in Scotland (ACPOS), the Association of Scottish Police Superintendents (ASPS) and the Scottish Police Federation (SPF).

A meeting of county chief constables in Scotland was held in Edinburgh on 28 September 1870, where it was decided to form a Chief Constable's Club with the aim of creating a forum for discussion of topics and issues of mutual interest. County chief constables were to be ordinary members, while chief officers of police of cities and burghs with a separate police establishment were eligible to become associate members. Chief officers had to wait until 1887 before all were treated equally and admitted to full membership of the club. Within a few years a committee was set up to address issues such as formulating a scheme for the introduction of superannuation, a Scottish police gazette, compilation of a police manual, pay scales and uniformity of dress. By 1920 it was agreed that the name of the club should be changed to the Chief Constables' (Scotland) Association. By 1991 the present title of Association of Chief Police Officers in Scotland had been adopted.

There are two distinct elements to the role of ACPOS. First, it is primarily concerned with the general welfare of its members, including salaries, pensions, conditions of service and chief officers' discipline. Second, its aim is fundamentally related to the operations, efficiency and effectiveness of the police service in Scotland. The executive level of ACPOS centres on a council comprising all chief constables, one deputy chief constable and one assistant chief constable, who represent the interests of their ranks. The function of the council is to agree broad policy issues affecting the police service in Scotland and to act in an advisory capacity to the Crown and Scottish Parliament. The routine work of ACPOS operates within a structure of nine specialised 'business areas' that deal with crime, general policing, information management, diversity, professional standards, personnel and training, road policing, financial management, and performance. Details of this structure are provided in Figure 2.5.

At first glance the ACPOS committee structure appears as a self-perpetuating bureaucracy and it is difficult to argue against this, especially when each Scottish force has its own local secretariat of officers and/or civilian staff feeding into the main central secretariat in order to keep up with the momentum of the ACPOS policy machine. In fairness to ACPOS, it has acknowledged the need for change and has moved towards replacing the committee system with 'business areas' with appropriate IT support. At its best the ACPOS decision-making machinery does try to take into account local, regional and national variations. Ultimately it is for each chief constable to decide on which policy to embrace in a force area and how it will be implemented. Sometimes there are instances when chief constables choose not to implement ACPOS policy at their own local force level for a variety of reasons. However, there is an increasing tendency for ACPOS, or at least its office-bearers, to be a major vehicle through which consultation and discussion take place with bodies such as the Scottish Executive and COSLA. It also tends to be the driving force behind Scotland-wide campaigns and strategies. Consequently, forces are more often than not tied in to national positions and policies through the representational processes of ACPOS.

The Association of Scottish Police Superintendents (ASPS) is a non-statutory body which represents all male and female police officers of the rank of superintendent and chief superintendent in Scotland. Records show the first reference to the rank of superintendent was in 1805 when the City of Edinburgh established a police force under an officer of that rank. However, it was not until the Police (Scotland) Act 1857 that the rank of superintendent received statutory recognition. By 1920 the Secretary of State for Scotland called a conference of superintendents and lieutenants for the purpose of choosing representatives for nomination to the Scottish Police Council that had been newly created and was the forerunner of the Police Advisory Board for Scotland.

The function of the Association is to consider and to bring to the attention of chief constables, police authorities, the Scottish Parliament and the Police Negotiating Board, matters affecting the welfare and efficiency of the service, with the exclusion of issues relating to discipline and promotion of individuals. An Executive Committee comprising representatives from the eight Scottish forces administers the Association. Normally, six meetings are held each year, including an annual conference at which a president, vice-president, honorary secretary and treasurer are appointed. These conferences are major showcase occasions for promoting

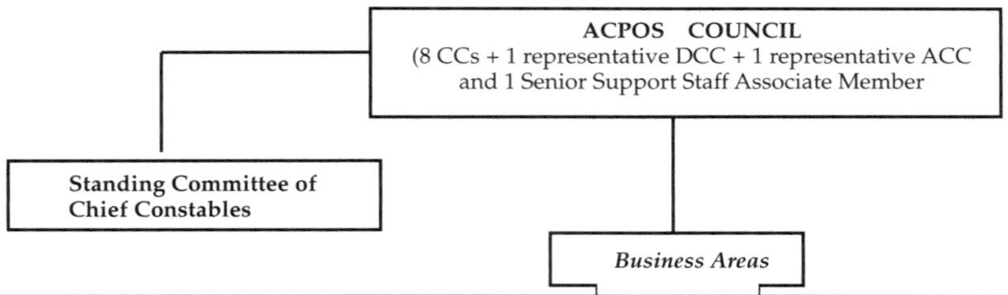

ACPOS COUNCIL
(8 CCs + 1 representative DCC + 1 representative ACC and 1 Senior Support Staff Associate Member)

Standing Committee of Chief Constables

Business Areas

Crime	General Policing	Information Management	Diversity	Professional Standards	Personnel & Training	Road Policing	Financial Management
Includes	*Includes*	*Includes*	*Includes*	*Includes*	*Includes*	*Includes*	*Includes*
Family Protection	Youth Issues	Mobile Information	LGBT Issues	Computer Use	HR Applications	Casualty	Best Value
Criminal Investigation	Search & Rescue	Radio Communication	Disability	Prof. Standards Unit	Accelerated Promotion	Road Users Information	Physical Resources
Counter Terrorism	Social Work Liaison	E-policing	Travellers	HMCICS Thematics	Senior Officers	Operational Policing	Finance Officers
Crime Management	Firearms	Data Protection	Race & Asylum		Personnel		
Violent Crime	Liquor Licensing	Freedom of Information	Gender		PNB Working Party		
Forensic Science	Custody Issues	Police National Computer & SCRO	Training		Training		
Training	ECHR	Airwave			Occupational Health		
Public Reassurance	Community Issues						
National Intelligence	Emergency Planning						
Crime Strategy	Football/Sporting Events						
Drugs	Missing Persons						
Serious & Organised Crime	Public Order						
Performance	Underwater						
Intelligence							

*A Business Area on Performance is still under consideration.

Source: Association of Chief Police Officers in Scotland, 2004.

Figure 2.5 ACPOS structure

the Association's views and are often attended by leading politicians. A small full-time staff carries out the day-to-day business of the Association. Similar to the other police associations, ASPS is actively involved in many areas of policing and is widely consulted on an extensive array of police-related topics. It also represents its members on many consultative bodies and committees, particularly with the advent of the Scottish Parliament. There are approximately 200 chief superintendents and superintendents in the Scottish police service, who normally carry out senior management roles in their force area, such as CID, traffic or operational commander or on secondment at central service.

The officers represented by ASPS are being given increasing responsibilities in their areas of command over large numbers of personnel with multi-million pound budgets. For example, a divisional commander in a large Scottish city division can be in charge of between 700 to 900 police and civilian personnel with a budget of around £30 million. Superintendents regularly take on roles as major incident commander or football match commander with crowds numbering up to 50,000 and detective superintendents continually find themselves in the role of senior investigating officers in complex and high-profile serious crime investigations and major incidents. ASPS has a key role to play in overseeing the welfare of its members in these situations and takes this responsibility seriously, including organising legal protection insurance cover against any claim or legal proceedings brought against the member while carrying out their official duties, especially in high-risk roles. Most ASPS members also find themselves increasingly vulnerable to complaints and claims of a non-operational, managerial nature, for instance in relation to equal opportunity issues, personnel and employment legislation.

New approaches to public management have placed the rank of superintendent in the 'hot seat' of police management in Scotland and with it come the stresses and strains incumbent on a senior manager in the public sector. The comment of one senior civil servant sums up their position: 'if it is the Chief Constables who put the show on the road, then it is the Superintendents who keep it there' (www.scottishpolicesupers.co.uk).

An Act of Parliament established the Scottish Police Federation (SPF) in 1919 to be the representative body or staff association for the ranks of constable, sergeant, inspector and chief inspector. Representation covers members' rights in welfare, conduct, discipline, efficiency and other related matters, but although the Federation functions as a quasi-trade union its members do not have the right to strike. In addition, police officers cannot be members of any trade union or of any association having as one of its objectives to control or influence police pay, pensions or conditions of service. Federation officials are regular members of a wide variety of committees and working groups where they play an active role in the proceedings or function simply as observers.

Federation representatives regularly act on behalf of their members at misconduct or discipline hearings and represent the Federation on working parties dealing with operational matters such as CS spray, body armour, firearms, training, working conditions and shift patterns. Federation branch members operate in all of the Scottish police forces and also oversee the rights of police cadets. Routine meetings are held at the local force level under the auspices of the Joint Branch Board, which comprises the Constables' Board, the Sergeants' Board and the Inspectors' Board, which also represents the rank of chief inspector. Representatives on each of these boards are elected every three years and meet quarterly, both as separate boards and together as the Joint Board. Discussion and debate centre on those problems and issues of most concern to the members. Matters are dealt with either locally or nationally by referral to the Joint Central Committee of the SPF. National policies are then formulated which give the Federation Executive the legitimacy to speak for the membership at national forums and at parliamentary committees of the Scottish Parliament. The SPF national president is frequently sought out by the news media for comment on a whole range of topical issues.

Under existing regulations, Federation funds can be used in the interests of members and the Federation, but cannot be used to support political parties, individual canvassing in an election or as contributions to trade unions or any group not associated with the police service. Funds are mainly used in the provision of legal assistance to members charged with certain offences while on duty and to meet other legal charges incurred by members in the course of their work. For example, the Federation normally meets a member's legal costs during the course of a criminal inquiry resulting from the death or injury to any person. However, a police officer involved in legal processes can apply to the police board or authority for legal assistance in certain circumstances and police authorities have the discretion to award financial support. A recent example of this was the case of the former police officer Shirley McKie, who was found not guilty of a charge of perjury in relation to a fingerprint found at a murder scene. The Strathclyde Police Board paid over £130,000 to Ms McKie in settlement of the costs incurred by her in defending the charge of perjury (*The Herald* 2004). Another invaluable function of the Federation is the assistance given to police officers who seek advice and guidance on claims for damages and injuries, such as criminal injuries, and on welfare issues. The SPF is also central to many initiatives relative to the well-being of its members that can range from the setting up and running of credit union schemes, insurance and convalescent homes for recuperating and retired police officers.

The SPF has over 15,000 members (400 part-time), which is approximately 98% of all police officers in Scotland, and is a strong voice on many matters related directly to policing, but also on wider issues affecting law and order, crime and punishment.

Her Majesty's Chief Inspector of Constabulary for Scotland

Her Majesty's Chief Inspector of Constabulary for Scotland (HMCICS) has a statutory duty under Section 33(3) of the Police (Scotland) Act 1967 to submit to the Scottish Ministers a written report on the state and efficiency of the police forces and common police services in Scotland after inspections have been carried out. An Assistant Inspector and a Lay Inspector assist the HMCICS. The Lay Inspector is employed on a part-time basis for three years and must be fully involved in inspections, but is particularly charged with looking at forces' handling of public complaints against the police. The first Lay Inspector was a journalist and broadcaster, who was followed by a senior churchman and a former director of education. The latest Lay Inspector, appointed in 2004, is a former local authority chief executive.

The main function of the Inspectorate of Constabulary is to promote police efficiency and effectiveness in the eight Scottish police forces. The system of inspection includes a primary inspection every five years, a review inspection and then a final visit, with reports being submitted after each inspection. A close examination of police performance is made, particularly at the review stage to ensure that the Inspectorate's earlier recommendations have been actioned. As Scotland has only eight police forces it means that each is subject to some form of inspection each year. Although the Inspectorate has no statutory power to enforce compliance with its recommendations, ministers and police boards can request reports from chief constables on matters highlighted during inspections and the HMCICS's reports receive wide public circulation, including to MPs, MSPs, sheriffs principal, chief executives of local authorities, staff associations, police-related organisations, public libraries, and, nowadays, on the Scottish Executive website (www.scotland.gov.uk).

In addition to general inspection reports, the Inspectorate regularly produces thematic reports on a wide range of topics, such as crime management and the use of police equipment. However, more recently, the Scottish Executive has shown a tendency to request special reports from HMCICS on subjects closely aligned to the development of government policy, for instance, race relations and community engagement. Although close relationships are still maintained between the Inspectorate and local forces, HMCICS also plays an influential role in advising ministers and police boards on the suitability of candidates for chief police officer posts in Scotland. The Inspectorate also advises the government on police matters in Scotland. However, these recent enhancements to the role of the Inspectorate suggest HMCICS 'is more firmly on the central government "side" of the relationship than merely an extension of police interests. In that sense its part in the overall central accountability process has grown significantly' (Donnelly and Scott 2002: 59).

Closely aligned to the Inspectorate's role is the review and audit of the Scottish police which is part of the remit of two bodies: the Accounts Commission for Scotland and Audit Scotland. The Accounts Commission is independent of both central and local government and is responsible for securing the audit of the 32 local councils and 34 joint boards. The Commission reports and makes recommendations to the Scottish ministers as well as to audited bodies, and can hold hearings. It also promotes best value, assists audited organisations to achieve economic, efficient and effective use of their resources and publishes performance information about local councils. Audit Scotland was set up by statute in April 2000 and provides services to the Accounts Commission and to the Auditor General, the Scottish Parliament's watchdog for ensuring propriety in the spending of public funds. Audit Scotland has two main roles: first, to carry out audits of particular public-sector bodies to ensure the highest standards of financial management and governance; and second, to carry out performance audits to ensure best possible value for money. Audit Scotland reports openly in the public interest and copies of reports are on its website (www.audit-scotland.gov.uk). The ubiquitous culture of inspection and audit means that some key area or other of Scottish policing is under scrutiny almost continuously.

Police complaints and professional standards

Scottish chief constables are responsible for dealing with complaints against the police in their own police areas. Police authorities have a statutory duty to keep themselves informed of the manner in which chief constables deal with complaints and local procurators fiscal are responsible for overseeing the more serious complaints against the police, normally of an alleged criminal nature. An inspection overlay exists in the form of HM Chief Inspector of Constabulary and associated HM Lay Inspector of Constabulary, who has a specific role in the area of overseeing complaints against the police. The Lay Inspector is a non-police officer, ideally placed to bring an independent and objective perspective into the monitoring of the complaints process.

There is no independent commission or organisation that oversees or investigates police complaints in Scotland. To date the involvement of the Procurator Fiscal in the more serious complaints is deemed to be a sufficient independent input into the system. In relation to the more minor complaints, if a complainer is dissatisfied with the way a force has dealt with the complaint, then HM Lay Inspector can refer the complaint to the HMCICS for re-examination. In the Chief Inspector's *Annual Report* for 2004 it is stated that the majority of complaints reviewed by the Inspectorate were found to have been investigated thoroughly and professionally and had reached impartial conclusions. Nevertheless, the independent investigation and oversight of police complaints remain key issues with the Scottish Parliament. In recognition of this the Scottish Executive has announced its commitment to introducing an Independent Police Complaints Body in Scotland within the lifetime of the present Parliament.

In the past the major arguments against a fully independent police complaints system in Scotland have rested on a lack of independent non-police investigators and the view that the police itself is best placed to identify malpractice in its own ways of working. This defence of current practice has now been greatly weakened by the large number of other nations that have developed systems of independent civilian oversight. In particular, the introduction of the Police Ombudsman in Northern Ireland and the launch in April 2004 of the Independent Police Complaints Commission for England and Wales, which specifically debars individuals with a police background from certain senior posts, have shown Scotland to be increasingly out of step in a UK context.

The burgeoning performance culture associated with the modernisation of policing generates increasing pressures on Scottish police organisations and their members to achieve results. In this climate there is an obligation on those who oversee policing to ensure that all staff have sufficient support and guidance within an ethical environment. Arguably, the police service is in the unique position that individual discretion tends to increase the further down the organisation one goes (Muir 1977). This leads to demands from society for the highest standards from individual police officers, including fairness, impartiality and integrity leading to self-control, tolerance and appropriate use of language and behaviour. Such issues were in the mind of the Royal Commission into the Police in 1962 when it commented that 'the police should be strong and effective in preserving law and order and preventing crime – but it is equally to the public good that police powers should be controlled so as not to interfere arbitrarily with personal freedom' (ibid.). Such concerns have recently led to the introduction of a code of ethical practice governing all police and support staff in Scotland (ACPOS 2003).

In addition, the Scottish police service has acknowledged that human rights in an ethical working environment are central to the acceptability of policing in the 21st century. In reality it would be difficult to envisage a successful police force whose members did not subscribe to this philosophy as it focuses on professional conduct and behaviour, and the maintenance of standards and good policing. To achieve these aims ACPOS introduced a Professional Standards unit in 2003 to complement its 'ethical code' and ensure that implementation of the code is constantly monitored across the service. To this end, each of the eight Scottish police forces is committed to maintaining professional standards through developing a culture of integrity, ethical and professional standards among police and support staff.

Conclusion

At the time of the Royal Commission in the early 1960s there were 33 police forces in Scotland, 9,000 police officers, 1,162 civilian support staff, two Scottish forces had no policewomen, and there were no traffic wardens employed in Scotland, compared to 1,800 south of the Border (Wilkie 1992: 250–51). Times have changed: Scotland now has fewer police forces, more officers and support staff than ever before, a variety of auxiliary wardens, and a considerable array of technologies that could only have been dreamed about in 1962. The existing police structure and organisation have withstood all the changes associated with police reform and modernisation over the past 40 years, and has served the Scottish community well in doing so. However, recent police reforms, devolution, constitutional adjustments and future challenges mean that the police organisation is struggling to maintain the level of service expected by the Scottish people. Substantial modifications to the existing organisational structure appear inevitable.

Recent years have witnessed a distinct move towards centralisation of police functions in Scotland (Scott 2003). A review of common police services may continue this trend by incorporating some existing local functions into the national level. Central government already controls police pay, conditions of service, discipline regulations, police funding, audit, performance management criteria, inspection, and exercises its right to approve senior appointments. Since devolution the Justice Minister has played a key role in setting national targets and objectives, probably more so than any Scottish politician in the past. The current drive for best value, efficiency and effectiveness, and overall strategic planning has to be seen not only as good management practice, but also as a key centralising process. The tension lies, on the one hand, with the important call from local communities for a greater say in how they are governed and policed at their own level and, on the other, with the political rhetoric which talks centralism rather than localism. All indications are that this route of devolved decision-making at the local level is being encouraged, while simultaneously the Scottish Executive is increasingly proactive in exercising co-ordination and control (Donnelly 2004: 27).

The structure and organisation of policing in Scotland have to find a way of steering a steady course through these countervailing tendencies, to balance operational efficiency and financial effectiveness with delivery of a wide range of services at the appropriate geographical level. The challenge is both to operate efficiently as large and complex organisations and to function effectively as the police, which meet the Scottish public's expectations and requirements.

Notes

1 In the Police and Magistrates' Courts Act 1994, following the recommendation of the Sheehy Report into Police Rewards and Responsibilities, the rank of depute chief constable was discontinued and officially forces were supposed to adhere to the clumsy mechanism whereby one assistant chief constable was 'designated' as deputy. Most Scottish forces openly used the old terminology and under the Criminal Justice (Scotland) Act 2003 the rank was formally restored.

2 There has never been a female chief constable in Scotland. Strathclyde Police appointed the first female assistant chief in 1998. As at January 2005, the two senior women police officers in Scotland are the depute director of the Scottish Police College (who holds the rank of assistant chief constable) and an assistant chief in Central Scotland Police.

References

Allan, D. L. (1989) *How Do the Police Measure Up? – A Study of Efficiency and Effectiveness in the Police Service*. University of Strathclyde, Glasgow: Unpublished MPhil thesis.

Association of Chief Police Officers in Scotland (2003) *Statement of Ethical Principles and Code of Ethical Practice*. Edinburgh: ACPOS.

Association of Chief Police Officers in Scotland (2004) *Annual Report 2003–2004*. Edinburgh: ACPOS.

Association of Scottish Police Superintendents website: www.scottishsupers.org. uk

Audit Commission (1990) *Effective Policing – Performance Review in Police Forces*, Paper No. 8. London: HMSO.

Audit Scotland website: www.audit-scotland.gov.uk

Bayley, D. (1996) 'What do the police do?', in W. Saulsbury *et al.* (eds), *Themes in Contemporary Policing*. London: Police Foundation/Policy Studies Institute, pp. 29–41.

Bradley, D., Walker, N. and Wilkie, R. (1986) *Managing The Police: Law, Organisation and Democracy*. Sussex: Wheatsheaf.

Donnelly, D. (2004) 'A national service', *Police Review*, 12 November: 26–7.

Donnelly, D. and Scott, K. B. (2002) 'Police accountability in Scotland – (2) New accountabilities', *The Police Journal*, 75: 56–66.

Donnelly, D. and Wilkie, R. (2002) 'Scottish colonisation', *Police Review,* 110 (5703): 20–21.

HM Chief Inspector of Constabulary for Scotland (1997) *Annual Report 1996–97*. Edinburgh: HMSO.

HM Chief Inspector of Constabulary for Scotland (1998) *Annual Report 1997–98*. Edinburgh: HMSO.

HM Inspectorate of Constabulary for Scotland (2000) *A Fair Cop ? – The Investigation of Complaints Against the Police in Scotland*. Edinburgh: HMCICS.

HM Inspectorate of Constabulary for Scotland (2002) *Narrowing the Gap – Police Visibility and Public Reassurance: Managing Public Expectation and Demand*. Edinburgh: HMCICS.

HM Chief Inspector of Constabulary for Scotland (2004a) *Annual Report 2003–04*. Edinburgh: HMCICS.

HM Inspectorate of Constabulary for Scotland (2004b) *Local Connections – Policing with the Community*. Edinburgh: HMCICS.

Home Office (1978) *Committee of Enquiry on the Police – Report on Negotiating Machinery and Pay*, Cmnd 7283. London: HMSO.

Home Office (1983) *Manpower, Effectiveness and Efficiency in the Police Service*. Home Office Circular: No 114/83.

Milne, B. (2002) 'Higher learning', *Policing Today*, 3(1): 42–44.

Muir, W. K. (1977) *Police – Streetcorner Politicians*. Chicago: University of Chicago Press.

National Audit Office (1991) *Promoting Value For Money in Provincial Police Forces*. London: HMSO.

Royal Commission on the Police (1962) *Final Report*, Cmnd 1728. London: HMSO.

Scott, K. (2003) 'Smash and grab: centralisation in Scottish policing', *Holyrood*, 100, 1 December: 24–5.

Scott, K. and Wilkie, R. (2001) 'Chief constables : a current "crisis" in Scottish policing?', *Scottish Affairs*, 35: 54–68.

Scottish Home and Health Department (1984) *Manpower, Effectiveness and Efficiency in the Police Service*. SHHD Police Circular No 3/84.

Scottish Home and Health Department (1985) *Manpower, Effectiveness and Efficiency in the Police Service – Objectives and Priorities*. SHHD Police Circular No 2/85.

Scottish Home and Health Department (1986) *Civilianisation in the Police Service.* SHHD Police Circular 5/86.

Scottish Home and Health Department (1993) *Civilianisation in the Police Service.* SHHD Police Circular 11/93.

Wilkie, R. (1992) 'The organisational structure of the police', in C. Pollitt and S. Harrison (eds), *Handbook of Public Services Management.* Oxford: Blackwell.

Chapter 3

Scottish policing – a historical perspective

Alastair Dinsmor and Alistair Goldsmith

Introduction

The history of the police in England and Wales is well chronicled by many writers (Radzinowicz 1948–1969; Reith 1956; Tobias 1972, 1979; Critchley 1978; Emsley 1991; Reiner 1992; Rawlings 2002). Unfortunately, the same cannot be said for the history of the Scottish police, as little published historical work exists and 'the dearth of serious historical investigation and analysis hinders attempts to account for this early development' (Walker 2000: 152). The purpose of this chapter is to give some insight into the history of Scottish policing in general from the early 19th century to the mid-20th century, seeking to identify the roots of any distinctive features that may be discerned. In particular, special attention will be paid to the Glasgow Police as a case study in the origins of the police in Scotland and its historical development.

The 'new police' in England and Wales was introduced at the beginning of the 19th century, at a time when the government regularly called in the military to maintain public order, in what were turbulent times. Rawlings (2002) neatly lists a sequence of public order events which covers the last quarter of the 18th century through to 1829, when the 'new police' was introduced in London, and is reproduced in Table 3.1.

As a consequence of the fears generated by these political, radical and public protests, the installation of a system of preventative policing became a priority. Unfortunately, when the Metropolitan Police Act 1829

Table 3.1 Background to the 'new police'

- End of convict transportation to the colonies in the 1770s
- Gordon Riots, which lasted for five days in 1780
- Rise in radicalism linked to American and French Revolutions
- Napoleonic War (1793–1815): food riots, poor relief and disruption of trade
- Luddite disturbances and demonstrations against the Corn Laws in 1815
- Riots in Manchester's Spa Fields and rural East Anglia in 1816
- Blanketeers march from Manchester in 1817 demanding political reform
- Peterloo massacre in 1819 after political demonstration
- Cato Street conspiracy to assassinate members of the Cabinet in 1820
- Riots among poor woollen workers in 1820
- Queen Caroline riots in London in 1820–1821.

(Rawlings 2002: 106)

---

introduced the new policing system it led to suspicion and unease among the populace, who viewed the 'new police' as an extension of the executive, ever fearful that it could develop into a police system similar to that on the continent, with its over-centralisation, linkage to the state, political and militaristic control, remoteness from the community, and low level of consent and legitimacy (Stead 1983: 44–53; Horton 1995: 8).

The reforms of the police in England and Wales began in 1829 and continued until the mid-1850s. Miller (1989) describes the concept of the so-called 'new police' as a response to a growing crime rate and charts the stormy passage of legislation at the time. This resulted in the emergence of a vigorous style of policing orientated towards crushing the criminal element thought to be sweeping the country. 'It signalled a decisive shift in the basis of the social order away from consent towards force' (Miller 1989: 48).

Origins: the 'new police' in Scotland?

The emergence of the police in Scotland differed in a number of respects from developments in its southern neighbour. Scottish policing emerged from the 1800s and developed over two centuries amidst ongoing political and social reform, industrialisation, urbanisation and technological innovation. The rationale behind the introduction of early police forces in Scotland seems to have been at variance with the emergence of policing in England. There was 'a much broader concept of policing for the public good, the public interest, or public happiness as opposed to concern to avert the ills to come or the maintenance of order' (Carson and Idzikowska 1989: 270–271). This view is further reinforced by reference to Erskine's comment in the late 18th century that the 'laws of police are calculated for providing all the members of the community with a sufficient quantity of the necessaries of life at reasonable rates, and for the preventing of dearth' (Erskine 1773). Policing in Scotland was seen as a proactive deterrent to criminal activity rather than a reaction to problems of order after the event, as suggested by the advent of the Metropolitan Police.

In a comprehensive examination of early policing in Scotland, Carson (1984) argues that Scotland began to develop locally funded police systems relatively early. Constabularies were established by Act of Parliament, for example, in 1800 in Glasgow, 1805 in Edinburgh, 1806 in Paisley, 1811 in Perth, 1818 in Aberdeen and 1824 in Dundee, while in London not until 1829 (Carson 1984: 210–211). In addition, a number of *ultra vires* forces without benefit of parliamentary sanction had been established, in Greenock from 1800 and in Forfarshire in the 1820s. In 1833, the first general Police Act was passed to enable Royal Burghs, Burghs of Regality and Burghs of Barony to establish a system of police. An Act of 1847 gave authority to the magistrates and burgh councils to convene a meeting of occupiers of premises of the yearly value of £10 to consider and determine whether the provisions of the 1833 Act should be adopted in whole or in part. No mention is made in either of these two Acts of the rank to be held by the officer in charge of the police, but an Act of 1850 gave power to the local commissioners to appoint a superintendent of police, who was empowered to appoint constables and to arrange for the distribution of these officers within the burgh. The superintendent, who can be seen as the forerunner of the later chief constable, was also empowered to remove constables from office at pleasure. It was not until the Police (Scotland) Act of 1857 that the Secretary of State for Scotland made rules and regulations compelling all towns, burghs and county areas to establish police forces. The Act also introduced the post of Her Majesty's Inspector of Constabulary for Scotland (HMICS).

By 1859 the first HMICS, John Kinloch, was publishing his first assessment of the police in Scotland and pointed out how greater efficiency could be achieved through amalgamation. At that time 32 counties and 57 burghs maintained separate police forces. Many took the opportunity to upgrade, expand, amalgamate and mature as a result of the powers vested in them by legislation. Greenock and Paisley were identified as 'completely re-organising their whole police establishments' (HMIC 1859). Other forces were seeking to be model employers. '[The] cities of Edinburgh, Glasgow and Elgin, and the boroughs of Arbroath, Leith &c., by increasing their former rates of pay, so as to place them on an equality with the best paid county constabularies, thus inducing highly respectable men to enter the police service' (ibid.). Nevertheless, the converse was also in evidence. For example, in Maybole in the county of Ayr 'the police consists of a superintendent and one constable, and is inefficient in numbers and discipline' (ibid.: 52). In Adrossan, the HMICS had heard informally that there was a policeman, but on inspection, this person could not be found! The middle ground was occupied by organisations of varying size and degrees of enthusiasm, and in many instances HMICS was impressed. In others, he recommended amalgamation into larger units on the grounds of economy and efficiency. The City of Glasgow Police, at 704 officers in 1859, was the largest force in Scotland. Kinloch reported that 'a police force was established in Glasgow many years before the Metropolitan police was formed in London in 1830 by Sir Robert Peel, and has ever been found a useful and efficient force' (ibid.: 43).

Over succeeding years a great deal of legislation placed enormous responsibilities on the police in Scotland with a widening range of crimes being identified and law-enforcement tasks being promoted.

- The Prevention of Crime Act 1871 redefined police authority at a national level, strengthening and deepening police powers of registration, arrest and conviction in relation to criminals.

- The Immoral Traffic Act 1902 attempted to curb the activities of those living off the immoral earnings of others.

- The Motor Car Act 1903 amended the Locomotives on Highways Act 1896, the precursor of the road traffic legislation of later years.

- New ground was broken in 1901 with the Youthful Offenders Act, which consolidated the Industrial Schools Act 1866, parts of the Summary Jurisdiction Act 1879 and the Probation of First Offenders Act 1887 in dealing with juvenile offending.

- The Summary Jurisdiction (Scotland) Act 1908 reviewed the court system for the trying of offenders.

- The concept of releasing young offenders with all its supervisory implications was instituted with the Probation of Offenders Act 1907.

- The Criminal Law Amendment Act 1912 reconciled the legislation encompassed in most previous Acts.

These Acts of Parliament were contrived with application on a national basis in mind, but were not easily and immediately applicable to the operational police role.

Rapid industrial change impacted greatly on Scottish society and the fact that Scotland was still mainly a rural economy in the early part of the 19th century accentuated the extent of the transformation. With the subsequent growth in population and movement of people from villages to towns and the developing urban sprawls came the acute problem of vagrancy and its perceived link with crime. The resultant fears that this phenomenon would adversely affect the economic opportunities of the time led to the gradual extension of the police into the rural areas (Carson 1984: 207–232). This produced a large increase in the establishment of the police by the mid-19th century and the burgeoning economy not only helped to fund additional police, but also gave justification to its rapid expansion across Scotland by the end of the century.

Constitutionally, since the Act of Union 1707 Scotland had 'maintained a relatively autonomous social and political system, notably through the preservation of indigenous Scottish traditions in key areas, such as, law, religion and education and through the development of devolved administrative authority in the nineteenth and twentieth centuries' (Walker 2000: 151). The Scottish experience of policing was founded on different concepts of the responsibilities inherent in a police function. Far from being a 'new police' in the English sense, early Scottish forces were seen as developments which formalised established systems based on the ancient system of watching and warding. Most of the many Police Acts 'can be broadly characterised as generic, having more to do with issues such as paving, lighting and cleanliness than with the problem of order associated with modern police' (Carson 1984: 211). Pasquino (1978) observed that, by giving the police authorities responsibility in previously unregulated domains, 'a new power base was established on a very practical basis' (Pasquino 1978: 211). This established a fundamental difference between Scottish and English policing in the first half of the 19th century. In England the introduction of formal policing was seen almost as an extension of a standing army (Storch 1976: 481), whereas the Scottish experience suggests that there was less suspicion on the part of the populace that the constabulary were associated with any political agenda. 'There was no dramatic divide which separates the old from the new, and indeed, residues of "the old" carried over far into the era of more contemporary police arrangements' (Carson 1984: 211).

In rural Scotland during the first half of the 19th century, however, the development of policing showed a more negative aspect: that the police were effectively to blame for the 'suppression of alternative means of subsistence' to a substantial proportion of the population (Carson 1985: 8). For example, traditional practices regularly carried out by the labouring classes, such as grazing cattle on public highways, pilfering wood, street gambling and begging, became illegal. Although not a primary reason for the introduction of the police, such actions did bring them into confrontation with the people. Chief officers of police regularly cautioned their men not to be seen as the landlord's gamekeeper in relation to poaching and to use discretion at all times. The responsibility for keeping the peace which had previously been dealt with by the military authorities increasingly became a police prerogative. Although the option of calling in the military was still available, the police were cautious about invoking such a decision. In 1894 the chief constable of Ayrshire commented that 'military aid should never be thought of or taken into account, much less called into requisition, until the civil authority has exhausted every other lawful means to preserve the peace' (Chief Constable of Ayrshire, 6 July 1894).

In England and Wales, Storch (1976) found a somewhat different police role being adopted. In a pre-industrialised society, local gentry exercised a degree of moral as well as actual control over the populace within each fiefdom. The growth of conurbations and the disappearance of 'older and more personal lines of authority and deference' (Storch 1976: 496) created a vacuum that was filled by a surrogate institution such as the police. The police became a 'bureaucracy of official morality' (op. cit.) produced to fill this vacuum and to act as a lever of moral reform of the industrial city's inner core. In other words, the policeman would take on the responsibilities of a local squire in the policing and control of those in his area of operation. Extrapolate this proposition through a hierarchy of officers, senior officers and police commissioners and the influence of a police institution, sanctioned by Parliament, became manifest.

The more cautious approach on the part of the police in Scotland helped to cultivate better relations with the community. As a consequence, communities became more comfortable with the idea of a permanent police presence in their midst and, more intriguingly, communities themselves became instrumental in helping to shape and develop the police organisation through the medium of consensus and utilisation of the available police services. In other words, members of the community began to seek help and advice from the police by reporting crimes and incidents, but more importantly they also expected police action and results. This could be taken as an embryonic sign of community-style policing and of a police service being held accountable by the community.

Origins: the birth of Glasgow police

The history of policing in the city of Glasgow deserves particular attention because such a large proportion of the Scottish population lived within the city boundaries during the 19th century. In 1831 Glasgow had a population of 202,426 out of the Scottish total of 2,365,807 and by 1901 the figures had risen to 622,372 and 4,472,103 respectively (Population Census 1901).

A police force had been established in Glasgow in February 1779 (Renwick 1912: 544, 545–547, 589) and James Buchanan was appointed Inspector. Its first year was obviously a success as, on 12 April 1780, Inspector

Buchanan was re-commissioned by the city council. Unfortunately, in 1781 it would appear that the force collapsed through lack of finance because it was not supported by a rating system. Following this attempt, the city council set up a 'committee of council' in 1788 to consider again the appointment of an inspector of police, his powers and other relevant details. The committee of six produced an innovative report which laid down for the first time the foundations of a disciplined, preventative and proactive police force for the city. The report recommended that the council should appoint an 'Intendent of Police' and eight uniformed police officers, who would also wear numbered badges with the word 'Police' inscribed thereon. They would swear an 'oath for the faithful execution of their duty' and lodge £50 for 'their honest and faithful behaviour' during the time they were in office. Their duties were to include:

- patrolling the streets to detect and prevent crimes during the day, the evenings and at night
- detecting house and shop breaking and theft by pocket picking
- searching for stolen goods and detecting resetters (receivers) of stolen goods
- gathering information on crimes, convicted persons and the public houses they frequented, and recording it in a book for the purpose
- suppressing riots, squabbles, begging and singing songs
- apprehending vagabonds, vagrants and disorderly persons
- controlling carts and carriages.

(Glasgow City Archives 1788: 142)

It can be seen that the committee, while responding to the problems observed in the city at that time, were laying the foundation for the establishment of a police force with duties recognisable as duties of today's police service, not least by focusing on both environmental nuisance and unacceptable behaviour. It is interesting to note that Patrick Colquhoun, a merchant baillie on the magistrate courts of Glasgow, was a merchant councillor at the time of the establishment of the policing system in the city. In later years he was to be the author of the *Treatise on the Police* of the Metropolis of London (1797) that influenced the setting up of the Metropolitan Police. In his Treatise Colquhoun gave examples of what he saw as the objectives of preventative policing, and they included many of the key points in the 1788 Glasgow committee's report (Babington 1969: 183).

In order to overcome the problem of finance, the committee suggested that the many Trades Houses could meet the cost of the police force from their coffers and maintain the payments until they obtained an Act of Parliament empowering the council to levy a rate for that purpose. When the council received the report on 19 February 1789, the main change instigated was that the force should be under the direction of the Lord Provost, three baillies and nine commissioners and that the commissioners would be elected annually from the traders and merchants of the city. The idea of having the police controlled by this wider group of people and not, as in England, by a magistrate in his police office, was ahead of its time and is the basis of the local government-based police board system still in use in Scotland today. On 30 June 1800 the Glasgow Police Act received the Royal Assent.

The origins of policing in Glasgow were founded basically on altruistic and parochial principles. The system of enfranchisement of voters and the election of a police board were liberal in concept and recognised the importance of the contribution of an active, committed, able and erudite section of society whose interests were provincial. The growth of the towns heralded the increasing influence of an emergent, politically aware and educated middle class who were enjoying increased prosperity, and who demanded a greater say in their destiny. Formalised solutions had to be found to this challenge. The impetus for change was generated by certain sections of the populace rather than by central government. Policing systems in Scotland were not imposed in the early 1800s; it was more a case of the Scots seeking permission to establish police organisations of their own devising. Nevertheless, as the population had expanded in the emergent industrial areas, anxieties had also grown over the condition of the environment and public behaviour. For example, Smout (1986) cites Simon Tremenheere, Ministering Commissioner, as late as 1844 discussing the problems in Lanarkshire where 'the low animal habits of the uneducated or demoralised receive little check or rebuke from a superior presence' (Smout 1986: 9). Devine (1994) concurs that the decision to form a police force in Glasgow was 'an attempt to improve the city's response to the growing problems of public order and deterioration in urban amenity' (Devine 1994: 185).

When the Metropolitan Police Act 1829 created the Metropolitan Police almost 30 years later, it was seen as a reaction to the deteriorating situation in London, where the control of crime, drunkenness and rioting were beyond the competence of the existing system of watchmen. The emergence of a structured policing system in Glasgow and other Scottish cities in the late 18th and early 19th centuries reflected more the inadequacy of the local authorities to control the social problems associated with the changes in population demographics. The conflicts in Glasgow with the 'moribund and unreformed burghal authorities' in the first 20 years of the 19th century suggest an autonomous police system with unprecedented power, even if its success was variable (Devine 1994: 188).

The preventative role of the police

Throughout the 19th century the police were portrayed as part of the progress towards more economic and efficient government and an improved civilisation through their preventative role in urban society. For example, 'while policing was as much a way of regulating working-class life in the nineteenth century as partial enfranchisement, trade union legislation, compulsory mass education, the licensing laws and sanitary legislation, it was different in being self-motivated' (Fielding 1991: 48). In this historical perspective the police in the early Victorian era are depicted as facilitating the ongoing social reformation and improving conditions within the cities, that is, the fight against poverty, disease and crime which was a concern of emerging middle-class liberalism (Smith 1985: 23–29). Police of a century ago had to contend with diseased animals and diseased members of the public, smallpox was rife and officers' duties extended to running the fire service and manning soup kitchens (Police Review Centenary Edition 1993: 21). Attempts were made in Scotland to incorporate elements of control of public health through the legislative system. Under the Police Act 1800, responsibility for cleansing of public places and the removal of filth was vested in the police authorities whose somewhat limited resources had the greatest difficulty in maintaining even the most modest of standards, and successive Police Acts of 1807, 1821, 1830 and 1837 continued to contain this provision *de facto*. However, there was no mechanism of enforcement to compel proprietors or the local authority to adhere to the regulations.

The Glasgow panorama in this respect was particularly acute and the pervasive sanitary problems of the city were well recognised. In 1818 Dr Robert Graham, Regius Professor of Botany at Glasgow University, described an expedition into the city of Glasgow with one of the district surgeons, a certain Mr Angus. Having examined the degree of squalor and filth in which he found the inhabitants, he interviewed the 'proprietrix' of a lodging house of the most 'wretched kind'. Concerned 'lest we cause some enquiry to be made to the Police', she intimated that 'each family had "a bed" and seldom had any guests to sleep on the floor' (Graham 1895: 13). This reference to the police instances the powers vested in the constabulary by the Police Acts to inspect ticketed houses for overcrowding. Dr Graham continued that 'the police can and ought to do a great deal. They can compel the removal of the dunghills; they can renew the pavement in the closes, or, they may put drains in them; they can compel the cleaning of the closes by the inhabitants themselves, which can be no difficult task, as almost everywhere there is one, and sometimes two water-pipes in these places' (ibid.: 14).

The 1843 Police Act introduced the appointment of an Inspector of Cleansing with powers 'to make regulations for the purpose of disinfection and otherwise promoting the health of the inhabitants' (Russell 1895: 24). Although a 'Committee on Nuisances' had been appointed in 1857 as a result of a Nuisance Removal Act of the previous year, when public health was distinguished as a responsibility of municipal government, it took further police legislation, the Glasgow Police Act of 1862, to establish a sanitary committee chaired by Mr Ure, and the choice of Dr William Gairdner as the first Medical Officer of Health (MOH). Checkland and Lamb (1982) attest to Gairdner's commitment to the fighting of endemic disease in the city and the use of some form of 'authority' to address the problems of epidemic and squalor. Nevertheless, they make the point that at the time 'the police were the only enforcement officers available to the civic authorities' (Checkland and Lamb 1982: 4).

Nor should it be assumed that as separate departments of cleansing, street repair and public health were instigated, the police withdrew from all involvement. Operational officers continued to have responsibilities for inspections of markets, lighting of stairs, granting of licences to sell liquor or run a taxi and so on. In the *Chief Constable's Criminal Returns for 1907* statistics show 'the number of complaints made to the Water Commissioners by the police of water running to waste; the number of reports made to the Gas Committee relative to the escape of gas; and the number of reports made to the Master of Works, of streets, pavements, &c. being out of repair' (Chief Constable's Criminal Returns 1908: 63). The theme of the 'intrinsic welfare of the inhabitants' and the maintenance of a 'common good' are still identified both in the legislation and police role. Whether it was the building of a tramline, the regulating of carpet beating on Sundays, examination of contaminated foodstuffs or inspecting ash pits, the police continued to be fully involved in 'quality of life' issues and local control and inspection.

Additional refinements of these functions were introduced by the Police Acts of 1866 and 1890 and the Confirmation Act of 1904 and further established the influence and power of the policing system. The powers were wide-ranging, under the designated responsibilities of a group of specialists including a master of works, a number of medical officers, and one or more surveyors. Special officers included an Inspector of Fires, Inspectors of Nuisances, Inspectors of Common Lodging Houses, an Inspector of Sewers, an Inspector of Cleansing and an Inspector of Lighting (Checkland and Lamb 1982: 7). While these appointments were fundamental to the legislation, they were also fluid and could be amalgamated or changed as the situation demanded. Power was vested in the police board and the chief constable could designate police officers to these duties if he so wished. Checkland and Lamb (1982) emphasise that, as with all police legislation in Scotland, this 'was more of a continuum rather than a sharp break with earlier legislation'.

The squalor of the expanding Victorian city throughout the 19th century was characterised by successive outbreaks of disease and epidemic. Before the Police Act 1866, the constabulary had a duty of 'inspection and report' as to the level of cleanliness enjoyed in the city by its inhabitants (Crowther and White 1988: 13). Diagnostics were not included in the police training. However, the police surgeon and his district surgeons were trained, and initial reports were passed to them for investigation and diagnosis. Sometimes this was too late. For example, the cholera outbreak in 1832 killed more than 3,000 people in Glasgow. The lack of civic arrangements to deal with the crisis resulted in vociferous complaints that developed into a public health lobby demanding more rigorous powers of sanitary control for local authorities (City of Glasgow 1857: 7).

The police function, despite its experiments and recommendations in the area of public health, remained one of containment and control within the restrictions of the resources available and the requirements of the local and national law. Societies and organisations existed for the succour of the poor, the ill-housed, the feckless and the unemployed. The police offered no proactive or reactive method of solving the social problems of the time. Nevertheless, successive chief constables were not above commenting and drawing the attention of the municipal hierarchy to specific, chronic problems. The combination of MOH and Police Surgeon in the police system was a powerful force that continued into the 20th century. White concluded that the Scottish 'medical policeman' proved very hard to dislodge (White 1994: 159).

Generally, having accepted at an early stage the financial implications of having police forces, the reaction from most sections of the Scottish populace was favourable and, as policing developed, senior police officers became respected members of the community. Chief constables, in exercising executive control over their organisations, had considerable influence over many aspects of local governance in the light of the diversity of their responsibilities. Far from being servants of a committee, successive chief constables were involved in planning and policy formulation at the local authority level. The process begun by the Glasgow commission was not only significant in creating one of the earliest and most extensive police organisations, the longer-term products of its labours proved it to be 'an innovative body whose initiatives did much to create a new range of public services in the expanding city' (Devine 1994: 188).

Police development: the rise of professionalism

As the 19th century wore on, the development of policing in Scotland moved in the direction of a drive by the police service for a professional identity within the context of continuous change. The police officer was not only at the heart of a turbulent society, s/he also had a significant role to play in that society as the century unfolded and the 20th century dawned. Indeed, there were similarities with the working-class majority which was finding its own identity and role at the same time. Both had similar aspirations and ambitions for themselves and their families and all were caught up in the dynamics of the political and social reform of the period.

The policeman's lot

The view of Her Majesty's Inspector of Constabulary in 1857 was that the police should be clothed, paid and housed in accordance with their station in society, and in 1891 the Ayrshire Police Committee considered that proper housing was important for officers 'as it raises their social position among those with whom they have to deal' (Carson 1985: 13). Bureaucratic control from the centre increased, and the 'respected policeman carried the values of the "centre" to the populace. The policeman became the intermediary to make these values palpable in daily life'. Public co-operation was essential to the execution of police duties, and consequently the development of a 'respectable and respected' police service in Scotland was in the interests of both parties. By the end of the 19th century the police records 'are absolutely littered with requests from local inhabitants to have a constable located in their town or village' (ibid.: 14). Finally, Carson (1985) eschews the more sinister connotation associated with 'surveillance' as a prime role of policing and concludes that 'the growth of Scottish policing in the nineteenth century legitimised the policeman as the personification of panopticism' (ibid.: 15).

By the start of the Great War in 1914, such had been the improvement in the quality of policing that the extent of public support was broadened considerably (Taylor 1998: 105). However, there was a degree of political and industrial unrest in Britain during the war years. This was controlled by a weakened and ageing police force, itself in a state of unrest due to depleted numbers, increased workloads, longer hours and poor pay. Sporadic, often unrelated, public protests took place throughout Britain for many reasons. These included demonstrations on pay, working conditions and food shortages. Many believed that a Bolshevik Revolution was the challenge to be met (Englander 1991: 126).

The police were not immune to this unrest. The National Union of Police and Prison Officers (NUPPO), an illegal union formed in 1913, called a UK-wide strike in July 1919 that lasted two days. Technically 45,000 of the country's 60,000 police were eligible to strike, but in reality only some 2,482 (including 72 prison officers) came out. The call was virtually ignored in the county forces in Scotland and a Scottish police union, formed in 1919, folded within months. Morrison, a founder member, recalled that senior officers adopted draconian behaviour towards those officers considering membership of the Scottish Police Union and orders were issued to members that they would be required to resign from the police service or face dismissal if they insisted on joining or maintaining their membership. There was a 'determined purge of union activity' (Scottish Police Federation 1969: 17). However, this did not prevent the statutory establishment of the Scottish Police Federation in the same year (ibid.: 15–16). Although the establishing of the Federation gave police officers representation, those who had campaigned up to 1919 were conspicuous to all and singled out. In 1967 C. H. Rolph wrote, 'I can remember when Police Federation representatives were marked men. To the senior officers they were crypto-commies, agitators and mikers. To the rank and file they were harmless asses elected as Federation representatives unopposed because everyone thought the whole thing a farce anyway' (Rolph 1967: 23). Nonetheless, the strike of 1919 caused considerable discomfort in the higher echelons of government. Gordon (1980) observed that only weeks before the 40 hours' strike, the Secretary of State for Scotland agreed to the demand of a minimum £3.00 per week for constables and a pension after 26 years. Gordon suggests, without substantiation, that this 'no doubt helped to ensure the loyalty of the police' (Gordon 1980: 26). For whatever reason, the tiny numbers involved in the strike indicate clearly that, despite the discontent felt nationally, the ultimate sanction of striking was not supported by the vast majority of police officers in Scotland.

The strike was instrumental in the formation of a committee under the chairmanship of Lord Desborough (Home Office 1919). The report prepared by the Desborough Committee considered the status of constable, the need to standardise police pay and conditions of service, and formed the basis of the Police Act 1919. The Committee's recommendations greatly accelerated the professionalism of the police. These included improvements in pay, hours of work, holidays, pensions and force structure as well as recognising the Police Federation to represent the interests of officers in matters regarding conditions of work and individual grievances. The Committee found that many married policemen had to rely on charity, take on extra work or use up army gratuities to make ends meet. A big increase in the cost of living during the First World War had left many poverty-stricken. At the beginning of the war the top rate of pay for a constable was 40 shillings a week. This rose to 48 shillings by the end of 1917, which was the level of a labourer's pay. Over the same period, however, the wages of engineering workers more than doubled to as much as 67 shillings per week. The Desborough Committee made it clear that police pay should no longer be set at the level of labourers. It standardised pay scales nationally, for constables beginning at 70 shillings per week and rising to a maximum of 95 shillings after 22 years. A constable of police now commanded wages at the higher end of the employment scale and earned a maximum well in excess of many skilled workers. On the other hand, the Home Secretary was given powers to regulate pay and conditions of service and the Police Council was established as a central consultative body on regulations. At the Council's first meeting, representatives of the Home Office, local authorities and policemen of all ranks hammered out the Police Regulations in only four days of meetings. These established universal standards for most conditions of service, including a standard code of discipline and provision for standard emoluments, such as free accommodation. This effectively put the service on the levels of pay and conditions equivalent to semi-professional men and the 'pull' of other employment decreased as wages and conditions of work improved. Not surprisingly, the report was 'favourably received by a vast majority of police officers' (Grant 1973: 70)

The police wage situation remained fairly stable during the 1920s and 1930s, but came to the fore again during the post-1945 era when it was evident that police wastage was unacceptably high. This resulted in the government setting up a committee in 1948 under Lord Oaksey to consider police conditions of service, principally in relation to recruitment and wastage. The committee's report in 1949 stressed the negative impact of the expanding number and complexity of police duties, together with increasing crime levels. This resulted in a recommendation for a fairly substantial wage increase, which the government accepted. However, the effect of this was temporary, and successive reviews by the Police Council in 1951 and 1953 failed to resolve the problem of maintaining police strengths, particularly in the large towns and cities of Scotland, as well as other parts of the United Kingdom.

As early as 1945, the difficulty of channelling police recruits to where they were needed most was recognised and Scotland was divided into recruiting districts to allow an even spread of manpower. It was also felt that in order to avoid the pitfalls of 1919, when large numbers were recruited, and consequently retired en masse in 1949, post-war recruiting should be spread over a number of years. It was hoped that this would also allow the recruitment of the best candidates, from men in the later demobilisation groups of HM Forces. The Western District Recruiting Board, for example, recruited for Glasgow and the surrounding county forces. Candidates gave the names of three of these forces in order of preference in which they would be willing to serve. They were then posted to the forces most in need of recruits. One of the key elements was the training scheme operated by the Glasgow Police Training School, which was the training base for all forces within the recruiting district. Similar schemes were successfully operated in the other five districts of Scotland. In 1947 the Scottish Police College was set up at Whitburn, West Lothian to replace the regional training centres at Glasgow, Edinburgh and Aberdeen, and a formal Scottish training scheme was established under the direction of the Scottish Office.

The 1960 Royal Commission again examined, *inter alia*, the whole question of police pay and conditions. It was meant to deliver on broad principles of policing. However, not only did the Commission give its first priority to pay, the formula it delivered was translated into pay rises of 40%. While the recommendations of the Commission were accepted and significant pay awards made, they did not provide a long-term solution to the problems of remuneration and the retention of experienced officers. Despite improved recruitment, wastage remained high and chief constables and staff associations widely articulated the serious concerns of the Scottish Police Service in its manpower crisis. It was not until the Edmund Davis Enquiry and Report (Home Office 1978) that these issues were resolved, and then only pending the next recruitment crisis facing the police service in Scotland and elsewhere at the turn of the 21st century as a result of demographic changes in society and large-scale retirements from the service.

Police work

Two images of the police emerged over the late 19th and early 20th centuries. First, the working class viewed the police with some hostility, as they arrested vagrants and the socially less well-off in the community. Second, the supposedly law-abiding working class and middle class looked upon the police as the peacemakers, to whom they could go for help and advice, the 'Dixon of Dock Green' type who saw children across the road, gave directions, chatted to the crowds at football grounds and controlled traffic. This homely image of the police officer on the beat, although causing some scepticism among some contemporary police commentators, did give a very public and social dimension of the police officer of the times. It is fair to assume that in the 1930s and 1940s the majority of the population in Scotland held the police in high regard.

Evidence also suggests that patrol officers found themselves spending more time away from crime prevention and patrol duties. For example, the increased use of motor vehicles by the public required a higher level of police supervision and traffic control. The Road Traffic Act 1930 required a specialist department, a traffic department, to be set up in most of the larger forces, while the smaller forces trained individual specialists. This move towards a more mobile form of policing also benefited from the development of radio communication.

The changing patterns of community life also impacted on the beat officer's role. This has been highlighted by Emsley, who pointed out that 'during the inter-war years particularly, the working class more and more found their leisure away from the street – in their own homes with radios and gramophones, in cinemas, dancehalls, and stadia for professional football and greyhound racing' (Emsley 1995: 140). The rise in personal transport and the increased pressure on the police to give a more rapid response to incidents of reported crime meant many officers had to patrol in police vehicles, which reduced the number of beat officers in the community. This led the police to change its approach to general policing in the 1950s and 1960s, with the assistance of technology, specialisation and mobility (Weatheritt 1987; Brown and Iles 1985; Fielding 1995).

The role of the police in the control of public order continued. For example, during the Depression years of the 1930s the activities of the National Unemployed Workers Movement occasioned a succession of demonstrations throughout the country. Gordon (1980) comments on one such incident that started in the early evening of 1 October 1931 when police baton-charged and deployed mounted officers when attempting to ban a demonstration through Glasgow city centre. Such was its violent nature that questions were asked in Parliament and recriminations continued for some months. *The Glasgow Herald* reported an exchange in the House of Commons instigated by Mr Buchanan, the Labour Member for Gorbals. Complaining about the huge number of police used during unemployment demonstrations, he suggested that 'given the liberty, the unemployed were as capable of conducting themselves in a decent fashion as were other sections of the community. The presence of large numbers of police on either side of the group was intimidating and unnecessary' (*The Glasgow Herald*, 3 May 1932).

The development of the Scottish police throughout the 20th century can be seen against a backdrop of massive social and technological changes. These had a twofold effect on the police. Firstly, it increased the police workload through the complexities of the modern environment; for example, the expanding working-class criminality, continuing industrial conflicts, and political unrest and dissent. Secondly, and conversely, the modernity with its new inventions, systems and techniques was seized upon by the police in an effort to improve its organisational efficiency and effectiveness. These included, for example, telephones and communication improvements, motor vehicles and new transport facilities, scientific aids and modern detection methods. The new 'professional policeman' was a far cry from the standards of his counterpart in the previous century. As Grant reminds us: 'In 1847 during a six month period 173 men, including 86 Irish, joined the Glasgow force, although 106 were dismissed in the same period – 71 for being drunk on duty, 11 for being absent without leave, 20 for being worn-out and unfit for further service, and 4 for assaulting prisoners' (Grant 1973: 24). The Scottish police officer had come a long way.

Police development: the Glasgow revolution

The political and social complexities of the post-First World War period created new difficulties for the police and these challenges had to be met in an atmosphere of deepening financial gloom. Recruitment problems had to be balanced against the changing nature of crime and the limited resources available to fight it. Glasgow's Chief Constable Andrew Donnan Smith addressed the problem in 1930. As an increase in police numbers was out of the question, Smith had to maintain the efficiency of the force with the existing manpower at his disposal. The restructuring of the constabulary's operation included changing the divisional boundaries by increasing the size of the inner divisions by about one-sixth, with proportionate decreases to the outer ones. Manpower numbers were left unchanged in each division. The result was that the outer divisions, which were becoming more populated with new housing schemes being built, had more officers available than before. Introducing new beats and restructuring hours of duty made further improvements. In addition, police on pedal cycles became commonplace in semi-rural areas 'to facilitate the surveillance of the outlying districts' (Smith 1931: 12), covering an equivalent of four or even five traditional beats. Smith reported that this innovation showed early signs of promise, with a noticeable reduction in housebreaking incidents and vandalism in gardens.

Smith was succeeded by one of the best known of the city's chief constables, Sir Percy Joseph Sillitoe, who took up post in December 1931. What can only be described as a revolution in the City of Glasgow Police followed his appointment. Major restructuring of the service at the most senior levels of command; streamlining the effectiveness of the policeman in the front line, with the use of new technology including, wireless, teleprinter and innovative photographic techniques; improved training at all levels in diverse skills; the foundation of specialist units, for example, the traffic department; and the improvement of the police box system, helped to combat rising crime.

The cause of equality was pushed forward in 1932 in the wake of the Police (Women) (Scotland) Regulations coming into force. The regulations formalised the entry qualifications, rank structure, rates of pay, duties and career progression for female officers. Promotion to the ranks of sergeant and inspector became open to women constables. Although the Regulations specified that patrol duties were a part of policewomen's work, female officers were seen as most valuable in relation to criminal investigations dealing with incidents involving women and children. There were less than 20 policewomen in Scotland in 1932, eleven of whom were in the City of Glasgow Police. They did not wear a uniform, a modest clothing allowance was paid, and on marriage or re-marriage they were required to resign their appointments.

Sillitoe considered the organisation of the Glasgow force to be too unwieldy, with too many divisions and a top-heavy management with too many years' service, causing promotional bottlenecks. New approaches to operational matters were incompatible with the fragmented organisation of the force, and increasing crime levels and cumbersome lines of communication also contributed to a need for considerable revamping. *The Police Review* intimated in January 1932 that a competition was to be run in which all officers of whatever rank or status were invited to make their own suggestions as to the improvement of the police service in the city. '1,300 men, i.e. more than half the force, have already applied to headquarters for the requisite city maps to be used in conjunction with the competitive plans of reorganisation.' This appeal to the grass roots for advice was also seen as a morale-boosting exercise. 'Where there is genuine co-operation between the higher and lower ranks there will be found the best possible kind of discipline' (*Police Review and Parade Gossip*, 22 January 1932: 31).

A constable, William Radcliffe of Central Division (later Assistant Chief Constable), won the coveted five guineas' prize with suggestions for the reorganisation of the force, including the reduction of the number of divisions from eleven to seven. Sillitoe commented that the several hundred schemes submitted by officers showed a very healthy feeling throughout the whole force, demonstrating the keen interest that there was, coupled with the desire to help in reorganising this police force to the best advantage of the community. By the end of the summer 1932, Sillitoe was in a position to report and make recommendations to the city council. In his statement to the council, Sillitoe referred to those officers who had submitted suggestions. They 'have every reason to hope and expect by their initiative and merit the chance of well-earned promotion' (*Police Review and Parade Gossip*, 28 October 1932: 304). Sillitoe achieved the streamlining of the Glasgow force and waste of personnel and materials was reduced. Old equipment was upgraded and new equipment installed.

Although considerable savings were achieved by the restructuring exercise, significant investment was also made in new equipment, motor vehicles, wireless installations, police boxes and teleprinter communications. After the expansion of the Glasgow city limits in 1935, a more stable force was emerging and officers tended to remain in post longer. Sillitoe's examination of the problem had been meticulous and his findings were far-reaching, not only in implication for the City of Glasgow Police, but also as a model to be studied throughout Scotland and the rest of the UK.

Conclusion

This chapter indicates the nature of Scottish policing and its institution compared to its counterpart in England and Wales against the backdrop of the early histories of policing. The piece mainly highlights the non-crime role of the police and how the relationship between police and the community in Scotland was founded on a policy of 'public good'. History shows that the close links between the police and the community were strengthened incrementally as police professionalism advanced in the late 19th and 20th centuries. It provides some insight into how and why the modern Scottish policing model, with its close public ties, has come about. As Das accurately points out: 'history helps in appreciating the contemporary developments of the police' (Das 1994: 419).

References

Babington, A. (1969) *A House in Bow Street*. London: Macdonald.

Bailey, V. (ed.) (1981) *Policing and Punishment in Nineteenth Century Britain*. London: Croom Helm.

Brown, D. and Iles, S. (1985) *Community Constables – A Study of a Policing Initiative*, Research and Planning Unit Paper, No. 30. London: Home Office.

Bunyan, T. (1977) *The History and Practice of the Political Police in Britain*. London: Quartet.

Butler, D., Adonis, A. and Travis, T. (1994) *Failure in British Government – Politics of the Poll Tax*. Oxford: Oxford Paperbacks.

Carson, W. G. (1984) 'Policing the periphery: the development of Scottish policing 1795–1900 (1)', *Australian and New Zealand Journal of Criminology*, 17(4): 207–232.

Carson, W. G. (1985) 'Policing the periphery: the development of Scottish policing 1795–1990 (2)', *Australian and New Zealand Journal of Criminology*, 18(1): 3–16.

Carson, W. and Idzikowska, H. (1989) 'The social production of Scottish policing 1795–1900', in D. Hay and F. Snyder (eds), *Policing and Prosecution in Britain 1750–1850*. Oxford: Oxford University Press.

Checkland, O. and Lamb, M. (eds) (1982) *Health Care as Social History – The Glasgow Case*. Aberdeen: Aberdeen University Press.

Colquhoun, P. (1797) *A Treatise on the Police of the Metropolis of London*. London.

Critchley, T. A. (1978) *A History of Police in England and Wales*. London: Constable.

Crowther, M. and White, B. (1988) *On Soul and Conscience – The Medical Expert and Crime, 150 years of Forensic Medicine in Glasgow*. Aberdeen: Aberdeen University Press.

Das, D. K. (ed.) (1994) *Police Practices – An International Review*. London: Scarecrow Press.

Devine, T. M. (1994) 'Urbanisation and the civic response: Glasgow 1800–1830', in A. J. G. Cummings and T. M. Devine (eds), *Industry, Business and Society in Scotland since 1700*. Edinburgh: John Donald.

Emsley. C. (1983) *Policing and its Context 1750–1870*. London: Macmillan.

Emsley, C. (1991) *The English Police – A Political and Social History*. Hemel Hempstead: Wheatsheaf.

Emsley, C. (1995) 'Preventive policing – the path to the present', in J. P. Brodeur (ed.), *Comparisons in Policing – An International Perspective*. Aldershot: Avebury, pp. 135–144.

Emsley, C. and Weinberger, B. (eds) (1991) *Policing Western Europe: Politics, Professionalism and Public Order, 1850–1940*. Connecticut: Greenwood Press.

Englander, D. (1991) 'Police and public order in Britain 1914–1918', in C. Emsley and B. Weinberger (eds), *Policing Western Europe: Politics, Professionalism and Public Order, 1850–1940*. Connecticut: Greenwood Press.

Erskine, J. (1773) *An Institute of the Law of Scotland*. Edinburgh.

Fielding, N. G. (1991) *The Police and Social Conflict*. London: Athlone Press.

Fielding, N. G. (1995) *Community Policing*. Oxford: Clarendon Press.

Fine, B. and Millar, R. (eds) (1985) *Policing the Miner's Strike*. London: Lawrence and Wishart.

The Glasgow Herald, 3 May, 1932.

The Glasgow Herald, 22 October, 1932.

The Glasgow Herald, 18 December, 1932.

Gordon, P. (1980) *Policing Scotland*. Glasgow: Scottish Council for Civil Liberties.

Goldsmith, A. (2002) *The Development of the City of Glasgow Police 1800–1939*. University of Strathclyde, Glasgow: Unpublished PhD thesis.

Graham, R. (1895) 'Description of expedition into Glasgow City', in J. Russell *The Evolution of the Function of Public Health Administration*. Glasgow.

Grant, D. (1973) *The Thin Blue Line – The Story of the Glasgow Police*. London: John Long.

Her Majesty's Inspector of Constabulary for Scotland (1859) *Annual Report for the Year Ending 15 March 1859*. Edinburgh: HMSO.

Home Office (1919) *Desborough Committee of Enquiry into Policing in England, Wales and Scotland*, Cmnd Nos. 253 and 574. London: HMSO.

Home Office (1949) *Oaksey Committee on Police Conditions of Service*, Cmnd 7674. London: HMSO.

Home Office (1962) *Royal Commission on the Police Final Report*, Cmnd 1728. London: HMSO.

Home Office (1978) *Committee of Enquiry on the Police (Edmund Davis Enquiry) – Report on Negotiating Machinery and Pay*, Cmnd 7283. London: HMSO.

Horton, C. (1995) *Policing Policy in France*. Dorset: Policy Studies Institute.

Miller, W. (1989) 'Party politics, class interest and reform of the police 1829–1856', *International Review of Police Development*, 10(1): Spring.

Morris, T. (1989) *Crime and Criminal Justice since 1945*. Oxford: Basil Blackwell.

Pasquino, P. (1978) 'Threatrum politicum: the genealogy of capital, police and the state of prosperity', *Ideology and Consciousness*, No 4, cited in W. G. Carson (1984) 'Policing the periphery: the development of Scottish policing 1795–1900 (1)', *Australian and New Zealand Journal of Criminology*, 17(4): 207–232.

Police Review *100 Years of Service, 1893–1993* (Centenary Edition), 3 January 1993.

Police Review and Parade Gossip, 22 January 1932.

Police Review and Parade Gossip, 28 October 1932.

Radzinowicz, L. (1948–1969) *A History of English Criminal Law, Vols. 1–4*. London: Stevens.

Rawlings, P. J. (2002) *Policing – A Short History*. Devon: Willan Publishing.

Rolf, C.H. (1967) *Police Review*.

Reiner, R. (1992) *The Politics of the Police*, 2nd edn. Hemel Hempstead: Harvester Wheatsheaf.

Reith, C. (1956) *A New Study of Police History*. Edinburgh: Oliver and Boyd.

Renwick, R. (ed.) (1912) *Extracts from the Records of the Burgh of Glasgow with Charters and Other Documents, Vol. V11. 1760–1780*. Glasgow: Scottish Burgh Records Society.

Russell, J. (1895) *The Evolution of the Function of Public Health Administration*. Glasgow.

Scottish Police Federation (1969) *Scottish Police Federation Golden Anniversary Brochure*. Edinburgh.

Scottish Population Census 1901. Edinburgh.

Smith, A. D. (1931) *City of Glasgow Police Criminal Returns 1930*. Glasgow.

Smith, P. T. (ed.) (1985) *Policing Victorian London*. Connecticut: Greenwood Press.

Smout, T. C. (1986) *A Century of the Scottish People 1830–1950*. London: Fontana.

Stead, P. J. (1983) *The Police of France*. London: Macmillan.

Steedman, C. (1984) *Policing the Victorian Community – The Formation of English Provincial Police Forces 1856–1880*. London: Routledge and Kegan Paul.

Storch, R. D. (1975) '"A plague of the blue locusts": police reform and popular resistance in Northern England, 1840–1857', *International Review of Social History*, 20: 61–90.

Storch, R. D. (1976) 'The policeman as domestic missionary: urban discipline and popular culture in Northern England, 1850–1880', *Journal of Social History*, 9(4): 481–509.

Taylor, D. (1998) *Crime, Policing and Punishment*. London, Macmillan.

Tobias, J. J. (1972) *Nineteenth-Century Crime – Prevention and Punishment*. Devon: David & Charles.

Tobias, J. J. (1979) *Crime and Police in England 1700–1900*. Dublin: Gill & Macmillan.

Walker, N. (2000) *Policing in a Changing Constitutional Order*. London: Sweet & Maxwell.

Weatheritt, M. (1987) 'Community policing now', in P. Willmott (ed.), *Policing and the Community*. London: Policy Studies Institute, pp. 7–20.

White, B. (1994) 'Training medical policemen: forensic medicine and public health in nineteenth century Scotland', in M. Clark and C. Crawford (eds), *Legal Medicine in History*. Cambridge: Cambridge University Press.

Chapter 4

Devolution, accountability and Scottish policing

Daniel Donnelly and Kenneth Scott

Introduction

The Scotland Act 1998 came into effect in May 1999 with the first elections to a Scottish Parliament and with it the creation of Scotland's devolved form of government, the Scottish Executive. As an undisputed area of domestic governance, Scottish policing now became a devolved matter subject to the will of the politicians in Edinburgh rather than in Westminster.[1] This significant change in the constitutional landscape of Britain has had important implications for policing in Scotland. The devolution settlement has had an effect on the composition of the tripartite partnership of central government, local government and the police. It has also arguably changed the balance of influence within that partnership towards the institutions of central government and has raised in a new way issues about the relationship between the police and politics at both national and local levels. Because the tripartite system provides the framework for police accountability as well as describing how the police are administered, these changes have also created new questions about the ways in which the police in Scotland are held publicly to account. In this chapter three particular aspects of these issues will be considered. Firstly, the new political context in which Scottish policing has to operate will be described in terms of the constitutional changes that devolution has brought about. Secondly, the topic of accountability will be explored in relation to changes to the tripartite system and the move towards performance management mechanisms. Then, thirdly, some emerging issues that arise from the constitutional and political changes that have occurred and which relate to policing and police accountability will be discussed.

The new political landscape

The Scottish Parliament

There is little similarity between the new Scottish Parliament in Holyrood and its counterpart in Westminster. The Scotland Act never intended the Parliament to be a miniaturised version of the House of Commons. The idea is to do political business in a pragmatic and democratic Scottish style. It aims to be a user-friendly Parliament that is open and transparent. The present presiding officer, George Reid MSP, who has experience of both Holyrood and the House of Commons, has stated: 'there is no more trailing around the lobbies, in division after division, at an hour when decent citizens are in their beds. Decision time at Holyrood, with electronic voting at five o'clock, takes no more than ten minutes – after which three quarters of its members can go home to their families and constituents' (Reid 2002: 29). Nearly 40% of the membership are women, the highest of any Commonwealth legislature, and with the European-style 'hemicycle' seating chamber the intention is to avoid the confrontational party environment in which business is done.

The Scottish Parliament was reconvened on 12 May 1999 after being adjourned on 25 March 1707 and four key principles laid the foundation for the new Parliament:

1 It should symbolise the sharing of power between the people of Scotland, the legislators and the Scottish Executive.

2 The Scottish Executive should be accountable to the Parliament, and the Parliament and Executive accountable in turn to the people.

3 The political process should be accessible, open and responsive, and encourage participation and scrutiny of policy and legislation.

4 The process should promote equal opportunities for all.

These principles form part of the Scottish Ministerial Code agreed by the Scottish Executive. The new electoral system is based on proportional representation and gives the Scottish people 129 Members of the Scottish Parliament (MSPs), 73 of whom are elected from 'first past the post' con-stituencies, with the remaining 56 from 'regional list' seats covering eight regional areas corresponding to Scotland's original European Parliament constituencies. List MSPs are therefore superimposed on to the areas of responsibility of constituency MSPs, which can lead to duplication and conflict at times as constituents may approach either type of MSP, or both, to represent them on a particular issue. Although such a system enhances citizen representation, it is almost inevitable that it means more politicians involved in local issues, such as policing. MSPs are elected for a fixed term of four years so there has already been a second round of Scottish Parliament elections in 2003.

The result of the first Scottish Parliament elections, with a 60% turnout, was that no single party had an overall majority. Six parties were represented in the new Parliament and 'Labour's traditional grip on Scottish politics was broken, a development which made some Labour activists less than enthusiastic about devolution' (Peele 2004: 400). Labour formed a coalition Executive with the Liberal Democrats. The second elections to the new Parliament in 2003 'marked a new stage in the evolution of Scotland's devolved system of government and exposed difficult inter-party divisions. Although Labour and the Liberal Democrats remained the key partners in the coalition process, it took nine days to reach an agreement' (ibid.: 411). Proportional representation for local government elections by 2007 was one of the main concessions by Labour, much to the angst of many of their party members and councillors who saw this as a further weakening of Labour's political influence in Scotland. In a reciprocal gesture, the Liberal Democrats accepted Labour's flagship policy on 'youth crime'. Another important feature of the Scottish Parliament is the emergence of groups representing smaller political parties, such as the Greens and the Scottish Socialists, as well as single-issue candidates. 'After the 2003 elections Holyrood emerged as the "rainbow" Scottish Parliament. There are now 17 MSPs who are either representing independent or minority parties – a rise of 14 from the first parliament' (Goldberg 2004: 1).

One of the central principles adopted by the Scottish Parliament is its promise of a more 'open' and 'transparent' government that is 'answerable', 'liable' and 'approachable'. One way of achieving this has been through the creation of strong parliamentary committees. As part of the intention to establish 'a Scottish political system different in its priorities, processes and culture from Westminster' (Hassan and Warhurst, 2001: 213), the Parliament has set up cross-party committees which are wide-ranging in their roles. There are seventeen parliamentary committees that in many respects are seen as the 'driving force' of the Parliament. Eight of the committees are mandatory – Audit, Equal Opportunities, Europe, Finance, Public Petitions, Procedures, Standards and Subordinate Legislation. The remaining nine are subject committees, which can be modified or amended at each parliamentary session. Justice falls into this category and, because of the amount of business relating to this area, there are now two Justice Committees in operation.

Committees not only shadow the work of a particular ministerial department, they have a part to play in initiating as well as scrutinising legislation and in conducting enquiries into subjects of their own choosing. All public sector agencies have therefore come to expect an increase in parliamentary scrutiny and monitoring to ensure that satisfactory standards and levels of service are being maintained. Already representatives of police organisations such as ACPOS and ASPS have been invited on a number of occasions to appear before committees of the Parliament, although not in relation to any particularly contentious policing issues as such. The political and popular importance of law and order, however, suggests that it is only a matter of time before MSPs begin to scrutinise core elements of policing itself more thoroughly. It is worth noting that the Justice Committees are amongst the busiest in the Parliament dealing with a wide array of subjects, many of which impinge on policing or on which the police are expected to have a view. The legislative programmes of the Parliament have also included a significant number of Bills of this type. Table 4.1 lists a selection of policing-related Acts that have been passed by the Scottish Parliament.

In addition, there is a mechanism whereby the Scottish Parliament may pass over to Westminster the right to legislate in its stead through what is called a Sewel motion. This has been utilised on a number of occasions where, for instance, the British Parliament is planning legislation similar to that which would be appropriate to Scotland. Thus, unnecessary duplication of enactments can be avoided. Some of these have related to matters in which the Scottish police have an interest, such as firearms. There are also reserved topics on which the Scottish Parliament has no say and which the Scotland Act specifically retains to the Westminster Parliament because they affect the integrity of the UK as a whole. These include policing-related matters such as drugs, anti-terrorism measures and the investigatory and enforcement activities of the Department of Social Security and HM Customs and Excise.

The Scottish Executive

Devolution did not in principle change the constitutional position of policing in Scotland, which is still governed by a tripartite system involving the chief constable, the local authority and, now, the Scottish Parliament. Traditionally, policing has been a local service, locally delivered and locally accountable. In creating a Scottish Executive, the Scotland Act 1998 did not specify what ministerial portfolios there should be. Instead, powers and duties which previously had been the remit of the Secretary of State for

Table 4.1   Policing-related Acts of the Scottish Parliament

Mental Health (Public Safety and Appeals) (Scotland) Act 1999
Bail, Judicial Appointments etc. (Scotland) Act 2000
Ethical Standards in Public Life etc. Act 2000
Regulation of Investigatory Powers (Scotland) Act 2000
Police and Fire Services (Finance) (Scotland) Act 2001
Protection from Abuse (Scotland) Act 2001
Salmon Conservation (Scotland) Act 2001
Transport (Scotland) Act 2001
Criminal Procedure (Amendment) (Scotland) Act 2002
Freedom of Information (Scotland) Act 2002
Protection of Wild Mammals (Scotland) Act 2002
Scottish Public Services Ombudsman Act 2002
Sexual Offences (Procedure and Evidence) (Scotland) Act 2002
Commissioner for Children and Young People (Scotland) Act 2003
Criminal Justice (Scotland) Act 2003
Dog Fouling (Scotland) Act 2003
Local Government in Scotland Act 2003
Mental Health (Care and Treatment) (Scotland) Act 2003
Protection of Children (Scotland) Act 2003
Antisocial Behaviour etc. (Scotland) Act 2004
Criminal Procedure (Amendment) (Scotland) Act 2004
Local Governance (Scotland) Act 2004
Vulnerable Witnesses (Scotland) Act 2004

Scotland were transferred to the Scottish Ministers collectively. The architect of the devolutionary settlement and initial First Minister, the late Donald Dewar, included a Justice Minister in his Executive with responsibility for, among other things, the police. British constitutionalism in the past has deliberately avoided a 'police' ministry of the type commonly found elsewhere in Europe. Scotland's Justice Department should not be seen as unduly contrary to this, not only because of the traditions of policing here, but also because of the somewhat loose collection of responsibilities which the Justice Minister and Department oversees. These include the fire service, land reform, freedom of information and prisons as well as the police, but do not include issues of national security, which are reserved to the Westminster Parliament.

In the life of the new Scottish Parliaments there has been more discussed about Scottish policing than during any other parliamentary term in Westminster, partly due to the high priority given to law-and-order issues and the amount of legislation and policy initiatives in that area. One example of this is the number of consultation exercises carried out by the Scottish Executive. Consultation is an important aspect of the Executive's work. The aim is to provide opportunities for those who wish to express opinions on a proposed area of work to do so in ways which will inform and enhance that work. Consultation exercises can take many different forms, such as written papers, public meetings, focus groups and surveys. Table 4.2 shows a selection of topics on which the Executive has sought, and received, a view from Scottish police organisations since devolution.

Table 4.2   Police-related consultative papers from the Scottish Executive

Stalking and Harassment	Complaints Against the Police
Victim Statements	Electronic Tagging of Offenders
Private Security Industry	Proceeds of Crime
Freedom of Information	Social Exclusion in Scotland
Alcohol Abuse	Review of Mental Health
Local Government Commission	Domestic Abuse Strategy
Vulnerable Witnesses	Human Rights in Scotland
Scottish Refugee Integration	Speed Limits
Rehabilitation of Offenders	Decriminalising Parking Enforcement
Community Planning and Best Value	Tackling Religious Hatred
Child Witness Support	Anti Social Behaviour
Hate Crime	Protecting Children from Sexual
Reducing Re-offending	Harm
Review of Marches and Parades	Protection of Emergency Workers
Summary Justice Review	Unauthorised Camping Gypsies and
Review of Prostitution	Travelling People

Policing and Politics

The Westminster Government has implemented a major movement of police reform in the past six years directed at the police service in England and Wales. Table 4.3 summarises some of the most important changes introduced by the Home Office since 1999.

   While politics in a devolved Scotland has diverged distinctly from south of the border in some areas such as care for the elderly, higher education tuition fees and the running of the health service, this is a much more extensive and comprehensive programme than has been attempted in relation to policing. It does not mean, however, that the police in Scotland have been untouched by the more vigorous approach which politicians have taken in recent years and in several respects there has been a much greater interaction between politics and the police now than was true when Westminster politics dominated the scene. How to handle politicians is becoming more important than ever before for senior police officers.

   The relative lack of Scottish parliamentary legislation or indeed policy-making aimed directly at the police should not hide the fact that Scottish ministers, politicians and political commentators are much more critical

Table 4.3   Home Office Police Reform Programme 1999–2005

Operational policing

Community Safety Accreditation Schemes	Enhanced Anti-Social Behaviour
Citizen-focused Policing	Orders
Increased delegation to Basic Command Units	Street Crime Initiative
Neighbourhood Wardens and Street Wardens	Increased police numbers

Enable chief officers to designate police authority support staff as community support officers, investigating officers, detention officers or escort officers in order to support police officers in tackling low-level crime and anti-social behaviour

Planning and standards

Introduction of National Intelligence Model	National Policing Plans
Police Reform Delivery Plan	National Centre for Policing
Statutory Codes of Good Practice	Excellence
New Independent Police Complaints	Police Science & Technology
Commission	Strategy
Early departure or suspension of chief	Police Reform legislation
constables	

Powers to remedy a police force judged to be Inefficient and Ineffective by HMIC

Resources

Retention of officers beyond 30 Years	National Recruitment Standards

Recruitment of foreign nationals as police officers
Enable recruitment of non-police officer to post of Director-General, NCIS
Establishment of the central Police Training and Development Authority

---

than in the past and are more open in the demands that are being made on chief constables and their forces.

- In February 1998 an article in *The Scotsman* argued that chief constables were public servants and must be reminded of that fact more frequently. 'They cannot be allowed to be a law unto themselves' (*The Scotsman* 1998).

- In May 2001 the Justice Minister publicly directed the police to increase the detection of racist incidents and drug seizures.

- In May 2003 the First Minister told the ACPOS annual conference: 'People tell me there's no point 'phoning the police because they cannot do anything, they don't have the powers and the laws to back them up. Or they take too long to come and when they do, they stay in the car and don't get out' (McConnell 2003).

- In October 2003 police forces were told to tackle people's 'fear of crime' rather than putting more officers on the street.

- On several occasions during 2004 the First Minister called chief constables to meet with him to discuss significant issues of law and order of concern to the Executive.

- In January 2005 the First Minister, commenting on new ACPOS guidelines on minor complaints, said that he wanted the police to ensure that anti-social behaviour legislation is observed in spirit and to the letter, where people find they are being terrorised by relatively low-level intimidation.

This 'hands-on' approach by Scottish politicians is not universally appreciated. A former chief constable, Ian Oliver, who was closely involved in the police opposition to the Conservative government's attempts at reform in the 1990s, has been outspoken on the inappropriateness of mixing of politics and policing:

> Telling officers how many criminals to arrest is not the function of a minister of state. When this becomes a habit, it is a danger to the public, the politician and the police. The number of dealers arrested cannot be dependent on the ballot box … [Now] politics is infecting the police like Aids.
>
> *(Sunday Herald* 2001: 6)

More recently, police concern over the legislation establishing the new Serious and Organised Crime Agency (SOCA) led to the Association of Scottish Police Superintendents writing to the Executive to say that senior officers were uneasy about Scottish Ministers being involved in setting SOCA's priorities because of the political control of operational policing which that implied (*The Herald* 2005: 6).

With most parts of Scotland only a few hours away from Holyrood, there is no doubt that the geographical proximity of MSPs to their constituents impacts on the responsiveness of the Parliament and Executive to voter concerns. Consequently, some of the more contentious issues that affect Scottish society have been taken on board by the Executive as a result of public and media pressure directly on ministers or through MSPs in committee or on the floor of the Parliament. There have been a number of examples of these traditionally thorny issues which can produce crime and public disorder taken on by the Executive.

Prostitution – An expert group on prostitution was set up by the Scottish Executive in 2003, under a retired senior police officer, to review the legal, policing, health and social justice issues surrounding prostitution in Scotland and to consider options for the future. This review came in the wake of concerns in some parts of Scotland about the setting up of tolerance zones for prostitutes.

Sectarianism – Following the efforts of a Liberal Democrat MSP, Donald Gorrie, and a number of anti-sectarian organisations, a cross-party working group on religious hatred was set up to look at this issue, which has become particularly, but not exclusively, associated with two leading Scottish football clubs. The working group reported that there were strong arguments for legislation, but that these should not overshadow the need for changes in practice, culture and attitudes to combat religious prejudice on a wider front.

Marches and parades – An independent review of marches and parades was established under a former chief constable of Strathclyde Police, Sir John Orr, to examine the procedures for authorising public marches and parades. Parades, especially those associated with political groups, such as the British National Party, and quasi-religious organisations, such as the Orange Order, have been seen as sources of much tension and disruption in some parts of Scotland. Implementation of the report's recommendations will follow after a period of public consultation (Scottish Executive 2005).

Problems such as these are far from being solved in Scotland, but at least there has been a demonstration of political will on the part of both ministers and parliamentarians to try to tackle these concerns. There is also an expectation that the police will show commitment to enforcing these policies in the community.

The changing face of accountability

The 'new' tripartite system

The tripartite partnership of central government, local authority and chief constable has served policing and society in the UK well since it was established as the standard form of police accountability by the 1962 Royal Commission on the Police. In Scotland police accountability has run on parallel lines to the system in England and Wales, with due recognition of the differences inherent in Scots law and tradition. From their inception police forces in Scotland were closely tied to the elected structures of local government. At central government level, while the Secretary of State for Scotland had certain formal powers with respect to the police, especially with regard to senior appointments, there was hardly any discussion at Westminster about policing in Scotland. The chief constable had a key constitutional role to play in the tripartite system, having 'sole overall responsibility for the efficient administration and management of police operations' (Scott and Wilkie 2001: 55). This position was reiterated over time to such a degree that 'legal judgements, political statements and academic commentary have served to reinforce the doctrine of constabulary independence to a point where any doubts about its validity have been dispelled' (Oliver 1997: 20).

Police authorities and accountability

Since the 1990s, however, it can be argued that the differences have widened and that the tripartite systems north and south of the border have become more divergent (see Donnelly and Scott 2002a). One major change came at central government level in May 1999 when the growing movement for Scottish devolution came to fruition in the creation of the Scottish Parliament and Executive, as described above. The second major change came at the local level when the Conservative government declared its intention of replacing the system of regional and district councils with 32 single-tier (or unitary) local authorities. The population range covered by these councils varies considerably, with seven of them catering for populations of under 100,000. As the running of large services such as the police and fire brigades would not be cost-effective for smaller councils, the Local Government etc. (Scotland) Act 1994, which effected local government reorganisation, enabled some services to be made available on a joint basis. Technically, each unitary council is a police authority in its own right, but the governance of the eight police forces changed dramatically, from six regional police boards and two joint boards to six joint boards and two unitary ones. Dumfries and Galloway and Fife Constabularies continued to be administered by their own local authorities, but the complexity of the new situation was particularly acute for Strathclyde Police, which now found itself serving twelve unitary councils represented in a single joint board. Joint board 'committees' were not entirely new to Scottish local government, but they were the subject of much criticism.

> The smaller councils tend to feel dominated by their larger colleagues, they tend to be officer-led rather than member-led and since their members are appointed by the councils and are not elected, they lack democratic legitimacy and direct accountability to the electorate.
> (McFadden and Lazarowicz 2002: 83)

For most chief constables it was viewed as a mixed blessing: a wider range of political interests to keep satisfied, but probably more scope for developing their own priorities.

A police authority's relationship with its tripartite partners differs greatly north of the border where the significant legislative changes contained in the Police and Magistrates' Courts Act (PMCA) 1994, the Crime and Disorder

Act 1998 and the Police Reform Act 2002 were more peripheral or did not apply at all. These Acts introduced radical change to the management and organisation of policing and to the relationships between the police, elected members and the Inspectorate. Consequently, the roles and responsibilities of the police authorities and their respective chief constables in England and Wales are laid out clearly and unambiguously in statute. This is not the case in Scotland, where there is a feeling of ambivalence and lack of transparency surrounding the traditional system and the positioning of new players in the 'game', such as the Parliament and Executive, the expanding role of HM Inspectorate, and the burgeoning audit machinery in policing.

This is reinforced by the 'compliance culture' which Jones and Newburn (1997) identified in the post-PMCA authorities in England and Wales, where 'members find it extremely difficult or simply do not wish to challenge the chief constable or senior officers' (1997: 208). Nonetheless, this study did suggest that, for example, in relation to the preparation of policing plans, authorities wished to be involved at an early stage rather than merely redrafting the chief constable's original version and that most authorities had in varying degrees increased their levels of influence and effectiveness compared with their predecessors. There has as yet been no similar research on boards in Scotland, but Vestri and Fitzpatrick's (2000) survey of local councillors provides some indirect insights. In particular, among policy priorities policing was nowhere to be seen. One might speculate that this is because much depends on being one of the chosen few nominated by a council to a joint board, or because of an awareness that councillors' powers are limited in the tripartite system. Unfortunately, this does little to strengthen the local government component of that system. Another indicator of the police board's weak position is highlighted in the selection procedure for depute and assistant chief constables. It is technically the role of the authority or board to appoint these officers, but in doing so it is unlikely to ignore the views of the chief constable. 'The way the tripartite system works is that the key players are central government officials and chief constables with the local police board largely providing the rubber stamp' (Scott and Wilkie 2001: 58).

Local councillors do find themselves in a difficult position. On the one hand, they are supposedly at the leading edge of a Scottish Executive-led drive for modernisation of local services, with the main emphasis on an enhanced scrutiny role for elected members, better management of council business and the promotion of change through community planning, partnerships and best value. On the other hand, councils are expected to engage with a reform agenda whose ultimate goals of increased local democracy and citizen 'inclusion' mean more activity in community involvement and tackling economic, social, cultural, environmental and community concerns. In the 1980s, in response to regeneration strategies in the inner cities, local councils realised their crucial role in community safety. This led to their developing initiatives in 'the regulation, surveillance and policing of civic space and the devising of social policies to tackle vagrancy, truancy, homelessness, drug dealing and disorder' (McLaughlin 1994: 118–119). Initiatives like these usually lie with committees and departments other than the joint police board. While the police continue to forge partnerships with local councils and citizen groups, the official local leg of the tripartite system lags far behind.

Constabulary independence and accountability

Responsibility for the delivery of policing within each force area is shared between the chief officer, the Joint Police Board and the Justice Department of the Scottish Executive. The traditionalist view of policing is that no one party should have control over the police and the police should be answerable only to the law, acting on behalf of the community rather than the government (Lustgarten, 1986). In the 1970s, Metropolitan Police Commissioner Sir Robert Mark wrote: 'We discharge the communal will, not that of any government minister, mayor or any other public official, or that of any political party, whilst remaining fully accountable to the community for what we do or fail to do' (Mark 1977: 12).

As a statement of principle that may be clear enough, but in practice there has always been considerable ambiguity and fuzziness surrounding police independence. Writing of the 1964 Police Act in England and Wales, Marshall states that '[it] gives to a chief constable no indication of which matters he should tell his police authority are outside its purview or not needed for the discharge of its functions. It in fact requires a chief constable to decide what the functions of a police authority are' (1973: 58–59). In the face of many current policies and trends, this doctrine of constabulary independence can be difficult to maintain and some commentators would argue that constabulary independence has 'outlived its usefulness for a police service in the 21st century' (Savage 2001: 20).

The balance between the central government and chief constables has altered in a number of ways. Under PMCA the Scottish Executive can direct chief constables to include specific topics in their statutory annual reports, and HMCICS may also be asked to carry out a force inspection or enquire into any matter concerning the operation of a force or of forces generally. Where a report suggests inefficiency or a need for remedial action, the police board may be directed to take particular measures. The Scottish Executive can also, following consultation with appropriate bodies, direct that common police services be provided and maintained, 'as is deemed necessary or expedient for promoting the efficiency of the police'. At the request of a member of the public, the manner in which a chief constable has dealt with a complaint against the police may be examined by HMCIC and as a result the chief constable may also be required to review the matter.

The complexity of the chief constable's position is well illustrated in a situation where a police board seeks to dismiss or discipline its chief constable. The only example in the Scottish experience of this scenario occurred in 1998, before devolution, in a dispute between the Chief Constable of Grampian Police, Dr Ian Oliver, and both his police authority and the Secretary of State for Scotland. The issue arose over the abduction of a young boy in Aberdeen, who was then found murdered near the spot where he had gone missing. In the face of an outcry from the local community about the police handling of the case and a subsequent report on it, members of the police board called for Dr Oliver's resignation and this appeared to be supported in public comments by the Scottish Secretary, Donald Dewar, and his Minister of State for home affairs, Henry McLeish. Under the traditional tripartite system, the police authority appoints a chief constable and can both discipline and dismiss him. However, the latter has to be carried out within regulations written by central government – the Police (Conduct) (Senior Officers) (Scotland) Regulations – which describe an exceedingly lengthy and complex process in serious cases involving a tribunal chaired by a person selected from a list nominated by Scotland's leading judge, the Lord President. More succinctly, 'while chief constables are not "directly" answerable to central government, it operates considerable "indirect" controls over them' (White 1998: 78). In this case, not only was the role of the police authority unclear and the precise procedure involved uncertain, but the validity of any charge against the chief constable was also debatable because the events could justifiably be argued to fall within the chief's sphere of operational independence, an argument very forcefully expressed by Dr Oliver.[2] The outcome, following several days of intense public and private discussion, was that the chief constable resigned from his post, but the constitutional position on constabulary independence from local and central government remained, officially at least, intact. In some respects, the more damaging aspect of it all was the inspection of Grampian Police carried out by HMIC in the wake of these events and the major criticisms of its operational effectiveness which this identified (HMCICS 1998).

The changing role of senior officers has been a matter of particular concern to their professional body, the Association of Chief Police Officers in Scotland (ACPOS). In a statement of common purpose and values published in 1998, ACPOS was quite clear on the police role in the accountability system: 'the conduct of operational policing in Scotland should be politically independent' (ACPOS, 1998 : 7). It was equally clear on its own role:

It is not only in the management, direction and staffing of these specific operational and support functions that members of ACPOS combine to overlay local policing with national coordination. The Association is also providing leadership by creating national strategies, which will help to shape developments in key areas of policing in the future.

(ibid.: 9)

The rise of ACPOS itself raises two issues of accountability. The first is the extent to which its corporate significance may compromise the independence of individual chief constables, who may find it difficult to break ranks with an agreement reached jointly by their representatives and another party, especially the government. The study of ACPO in England and Wales by Savage *et al.* (2000) not only argued that chief officers may have to relinquish some of their 'constabulary independence' to facilitate the progress of new public management, but their survey of ACPO members also revealed that the traditional view 'may even be identified very much with a "dying breed" of chief officer' (ibid.: 201). The second issue is the accountability of ACPOS itself. This organisation does not appear to have any statutory basis, although that may change in the future. Despite this, ACPOS maintains a very high profile and involvement in policy planning, both in the policing world and with respect to the criminal justice system. It is frequently consulted by the Scottish Executive and is represented on a wide range of national working groups. It is increasingly a key player in the promotion of central government strategies and initiatives, a role much to the benefit of the Executive.

Since devolution chief police officers have shown more of a willingness to work in partnership with both central and local government. More importantly, senior police management at the local area and divisional command level are doing so with good results. In some parts of Scotland local partnership projects are being funded directly by the local authority and the Executive with little or no chief officer involvement. This devolved decision-making and localised strategic planning, with funding direct from central government, would appear to be a way forward for both community planning and best value. However, for this type of joint venture to be a success, all partners have to be empowered and, paradoxically, it is often those from social work, education or housing who have to defer to decisions from headquarters. The advancement of community planning and problem-solving means more shared accountability and less 'police independence' when it comes to integrated policy-making because all partners expect to be equal. As one policing report from a very different context, that of Northern Ireland, clearly stated, in interdependent communities 'no public official, including a chief of police, can be said to be "independent"' (Patten 1999: 32). The future of constabulary independence in Scotland, as elsewhere, is therefore more problematic than before. As Savage (2001) succinctly put it: 'the question about the future of constabulary independence is this – is it a bottom line or is it the end of the line' (ibid.: 21).

'New' accountabilities

Target-setting

In England and Wales the Police and Magistrates' Court Act (PMCA) 1994 and Crime and Disorder Act 1998 empower the Home Secretary to establish national objectives and related performance indicators. This does not apply statutorily in Scotland, although it is becoming apparent that the Scottish Executive, through the Justice Minister, can and will allocate targets to chief constables and police authorities. This was made clear during the Executive's review of the implications of the recommendations of the Lawrence Inquiry which, although concerned entirely with matters in England, resulted in an 'action plan' for the Scottish police. The review commented that 'while there is no statutory mechanism for Scottish Ministers to set priorities or performance targets for the Scottish Police Service, chief constables are committed to supporting national priorities' (Scottish Executive, 2001a: 1). The idea seems to be that Scottish ministers will let chief constables know that they support particular recommendations and principles, and under the terms of the Police (Scotland) Act 1967 the Justice Minister can then direct HM Inspectorate of Constabulary for Scotland to inspect certain aspects of forces' performance. The Inspectorate can then include these recommendations in future inspection visits. In 2001 the Justice Department set national targets for all eight Scottish forces to be achieved by 2003–04. The minister explained that the targets were jointly agreed following detailed consultation with ACPOS and the conveners of police boards (Scottish Executive, 2001b). The Scottish Parliament was informed that 'the targets are intended to build on local plans and existing strategies and to provide a national dimension by highlighting areas of national concern'. The original ten targets are described in Table 4.4.

By the end of 2004 the performance of Scotland's police forces in relation to these targets was variable. The successes included a 44% decrease in housebreakings and a 22% reduction in vehicle crime. On the roads, the numbers killed or seriously injured was down by 39%, children killed or seriously injured by 32%, and slight injuries by 8%. The outcomes for drugs were complicated by the unreliability of some of the data, but, if those returns are included, the targets were met. Forces were less successful in clearing up racially aggravated crime, which fell 8% short of target,

Table 4.4   Scottish Police Service national targets for 2003–04

---

1   Housebreaking – 10% reduction on 1997–2000 average number of crimes recorded – to 25,133.

2   Drugs – 25% increase on number of drug seizures in 1998 – to 22,205.

3   Drugs – 25% increase on detections of supply and possession with Intent to supply in 1999 – to 10,642.

4   Road Traffic Casualties – 18% reduction on 1994–98 average total number killed or seriously injured – to 3,965.

5   Road Traffic Casualties – 25% reduction on 1994–98 average number of children killed or seriously injured – to 631.

6   Road Traffic Casualties – 4% reduction on 1994–98 average total number of slightly injured – to 16,776.

7   Racist Incidents – 10 percentage point increase in percentage of crime related incidents cleared up – to 80%.

8   Serious Violent Crime – 5% reduction on 1997–2000 average number of recorded incidents – to 14,640.

9   Serious Violent Crime – 4 percentage point increase on 1997–2000 average clear-up rate of incidents – to 62%.

10   Vehicle Crime – 17% reduction on 2000–01 number of recorded incidents – to 55,193.

Source: HMCICS Annual Report 2003–04.

and the most dramatic failure was in the number of recorded incidents of serious violent crimes which, instead of falling by 5%, was 12% higher than the target level. The clear-up rate for such crimes also missed target (Audit Scotland 2004).

Target-setting has emerged at a time when the rhetoric of government is to play down any kind of national organisation of policing in Scotland and to hold to local and community accountabilities. In other words, the drive towards national strategic policy and implementation so apparent in the legislation in England and Wales has become equally obligatory in Scotland by other means. Walker (2000) argues that the centralising reforms such as those contained in the Police and Magistrates' Court and Crime and Disorder Acts are being encouraged and facilitated in Scotland by non-legislative developments and reforms, for example, through the expanding role of HM Inspectorate of Constabulary. 'The Scottish Inspectorate has not been deterred by a lack of explicit legislative authority from developing, in conjunction with the Accounts Commission and ACPOS, a detailed and influential performance management framework' (Walker 2000: 164).

A stream of strategies, plans, objectives, initiatives, guidelines and directives from a variety of sources is testament to this 'minimalist' approach to policy development, which is tantamount to a set of 'new accountabilities' being placed on the shoulders of the police in Scotland. These include the changing role of HMCICS from the traditional inspection function to a more interventionist role on behalf of the Executive, the ubiquitous auditing network of the Accounts Commission and Audit Scotland, and the expansion of the best value finance regime in relation to public service delivery. In addition, a new set of national targets across the criminal justice system has been issued for the period 2005–08 (see Table 4.5).

Official auditing systems

Review and audit of the Scottish police is part of the remit of two bodies: the Accounts Commission and Audit Scotland. The Accounts Commission is responsible for securing the audit of the 32 unitary councils and 34 joint boards in local government. The Commission reports and makes recommendations to the Scottish ministers as well as to audited bodies. It also promotes value for money, assists audited organisations to achieve economic, efficient and effective use of their resources and publishes

Table 4.5   New targets for justice 2005–08

Target 1
To continue to increase the police clear-up rate for serious violent crime.

Target 2
An increase in the number of criminal networks disrupted.

Target 3
A 10% reduction in the number of persistent young offenders by March 2008.

Target 4
A 10% reduction in the number of drug misusers entering treatment by March 2008.

Target 5
A 2% reduction in reconviction rates in all types of sentence by March 2008.

Target 6
A 10% reduction in High Court trial adjournments by March 2008 in partnership with the Crown Office and Procurator Fiscal Service.

Target 7
60% of Sheriff Summary and District Court cases to be disposed of within 26 weeks of the date of caution and charge by March 2008 in partnership with the Crown Office and Procurator Fiscal Service.

Source: Scottish Executive (2004c) Building a Better Scotland: Spending Proposals 2005–2008: Enterprise, Opportunity, Fairness.

performance information. Audit Scotland is a statutory body which was set up in the year 2000 'to help to ensure that the Scottish Executive and public sector bodies are held to account for the proper, efficient and effective use of almost £200 billion of public funds' (www.audit-scotland. gov.uk). It achieves this by two main means: firstly, by carrying out audits to ensure the highest standards of financial management and governance; and secondly, by carrying out performance audits to ensure best possible value for money. All of Audit Scotland's work in connection with the police service is carried out for the Accounts Commission and is reported openly on its website.

Annual performance indicators (PIs) for the police are published by Audit Scotland, specifically to allow comparisons to be made across forces. There are six PIs that are used, some of which overlap with the national policing targets:

1 Crimes cleared up: As well as the overall clear-up rate, a number of areas of crime are chosen for their public interest; that is serious violent crime, car crimes and housebreaking.

2 Racially motivated incidents: The number of racist incidents recorded is reported under this indicator.

3 Drug offences: This includes the number of drug offences and the number of offences for supply and possession with intent to supply along with the percentage changes compared with previous years.

4 Road traffic casualties: This indicator covers the same ground as the national targets – people killed or seriously injured, children killed or seriously injured, and people with slight injuries.

5 Complaints against police officers and support staff: This information was reported for the first time in 2004. Previously it was only available for police officers. The indicator is calculated per 100 members of a force.

6 Sickness absence levels for police personnel: This indicates the proportion of working time lost due to sickness absence for both police officers and support staff.

The key concept which now underlies the use of PIs is best value. This has been defined as 'a duty to deliver services to clear standards – covering both cost and quality – by the most effective and efficient means available' (DETR 1998). The Scottish Executive's Best Value regime was introduced to the police service in 1999 and forces have been implementing it since then, primarily as a replacement for the strict guidelines that prevailed under compulsory competitive tendering (CCT) and it has been taken up with considerable enthusiasm in some Scottish police quarters.

The use of best value as a benchmark for police service delivery has led to a further addition to the performance management system. This is called the Business Benefits Unit, proposed by ACPOS and supported financially by the Scottish Executive to help forces improve their efficiency and cost-effectiveness across a wide range of functions and processes. The Unit is responsible for taking an overview of best value regimes and reviews within the eight Scottish police forces. The primary purpose is to identify good practice which could potentially be applied nationally and achieve positive outcomes. A pilot review of fleet management is being undertaken and may lead the way for other reviews into systems processes such as payroll, procurement, IT support and estates. This increasing network of monitoring, auditing and scrutiny in the Scottish police service is now a major part of its management. It is linked to the ultimate goal of improved delivery of frontline police services while stressing the benefits of increased financial and managerial accountability. Such accountabilities are a necessary result of recognising that the Scottish police is a large-scale public service organisation that is financed primarily from the public purse.

The new balance of accountability

In England and Wales the police reforms of the 1990s created a profound transformation in the relationships between the various parties in the accountability system, while retaining the traditional tripartite structure. In Scotland the balance of accountability remained overtly unscathed by the police legislation, but the structure was changed significantly by political and constitutional developments in the national environment. The real fear south of the border was the increasing roles of the Home Secretary and chief constables at the expense of the local police authorities, especially as a result of the increase in centrally appointed members. North of the border the direct changes appeared peripheral compared with the introduction of the Scottish Parliament and reorganisation of local government. Yet the unintended consequences of the changes have had quite opposing effects. In England and Wales, it has been argued, 'the clear centralisation apparent in the original version of the reforms has not materialised' (Reiner 1997: 1033). The combined impact of the broader and police-specific changes in Scotland is potentially much greater than expected (see Donnelly and Scott 2003).

The Scottish Executive and Parliament in Edinburgh are much closer, both geographically and politically, to policing than Westminster ever was. There is much greater potential for intervention from the Executive, through ministers, civil servants and the Inspectorate, and from Parliament's committees and individual constituency and list MSPs. To this must be added the weakened position of local police boards, which are now more diffuse in their composition and more limited in their capacity to fulfil their remits than before. Constabulary independence is constrained in a variety of ways by being opened up to wider legal requirements and by the growing corporate approach to consultation and policy-making. The centralising tendency predicted in England and Wales as the immediate consequences of the Police and Magistrates Court Act has become a gradual and almost unnoticed reality in Scotland. The three legs of Scotland's 'new' tripartite system have a very unbalanced look about them.

In addition, 'the police in Scotland are being pressured by several layers of politicians on the one hand and by ever-increasing bureaucracy and scrutiny on the other. Accountability now covers a great many more participants than the 1962 Royal Commission and the Police Acts ever considered' (Donnelly and Wilkie 2002: 53). The emergence of various performance audit groups, changes in the role of HMIC and increased accountability to other organisations within the community through multi-agency partnerships presents a formidable scrutiny machine for Scottish policing in the 21st century. The Scottish police service is well aware that it needs to demonstrate fairness and transparency in its dealing with the public. The dilemma is how to balance openness and dialogue with the effective provision of a law-enforcement service. Meeting the requirements of the 'new accountabilities' requires time, energy and resources and runs the risk of diverting attention away from the police's primary role. The big challenge for police managers is to find effective strategies for coping with the changing checks and balances that seem to appear continually on the landscape of police accountability.

Emerging issues in police accountability

Common services and multi-tiered policing

Common police services in Scotland exist to provide technical, scientific and training services to all forces on a national basis, such as the Scottish Police College, the Scottish Criminal Record Office (SCRO) and the Scottish Police Information Strategy (SPIS). The Scottish Executive funds these services directly, with some expenses being recouped from police authorities. Each service is managed by a centrally appointed director who is responsible to a board of management which represents in varying proportions the interests of chief constables, other police professional bodies and the Scottish Executive Justice Department. In only one case –

the College – does the board of governors contain independent members. Thus the traditional tripartite model of accountability does not apply here and the non-contentious nature of these services has tended to lead to the assumption that issues of accountability are of little importance. It makes both financial and organisational sense in a country the size of Scotland to organise provision of services designed to support operational policing rather than to carry it out on this basis. Oversight can then safely be left to those who make use of the service – the police forces – and those who allocate public funds to it – the civil servants.

Some recent developments have raised a number of serious questions about this cosy arrangement and have highlighted fundamental concerns about the adequacy of how these common police services are held to account. Three issues in particular are at the heart of these accountability concerns:

1 a miscarriage of justice involving the Scottish Fingerprint Service

2 the creation of the Scottish Drug Enforcement Agency (SDEA)

3 the growth in numbers of non-police support staff in such services, as well as in forces generally.

The first, and most public, of these areas of concern has been the McKie case (see www.shirleymckie.com). Shirley McKie was a detective constable in Strathclyde Police. Her fingerprint was identified at the crime scene of a murder in 1997, despite her claim that she had never been in the victim's home. Ms McKie vehemently insisted that the identification by the Scottish Fingerprint Service, part of SCRO, was wrong. Following evidence by a prominent American fingerprint expert, she was found not guilty of perjury at the High Court in Glasgow. Almost every fingerprint professional of any standing on both sides of the Atlantic has agreed that the fingerprint found at the crime scene did not belong to Shirley McKie, but the fingerprint service has continued to deny that it was wrong.

Initial responsibility for investigating this matter lay with SCRO's controlling committee, consisting of the eight chief constables and representatives of the Scottish Executive. The internal investigation found that, as fingerprint analysis was a matter of judgement, the procedures had been carried out properly and in good faith. Following continuing heated public interest, HMCICS was drafted in to carry out an inspection of the fingerprint service. Reporting two years after the McKie case had begun, the report concluded that there was no evidence to suggest that the misinterpretation of the print was other than a genuine mistake. Later representations directly to the Justice Minister led to no satisfactory explanations being forthcoming about Ms McKie's ordeal. The McKie case has become a *cause célèbre* in Scotland, and indeed beyond, as it has wound its way through criminal courts, investigations of various types, civil proceedings and into the chamber of the Scottish Parliament without succeeding in obtaining redress or finding an answer to the question: how can those in a common police service be held accountable for their actions?[3]

The second theme relates to the establishment in 2001 of the SDEA, the newest of the common police services, with the aim of disrupting the supply and availability of drugs in Scotland. However, the Agency differs from other common services in a number of ways. The director's post must be held by a police officer and the SDEA is conceived of, not so much as a support service, but as a frontline policing unit involved in the 'war against drugs'. The lines of accountability over the SDEA have certainly not been very transparent. The director reports to a standing committee of all eight chief constables on operational matters and to the Justice Department for financial resources. Police involvement is therefore at a generally higher level than for other common services and reflects the importance of drug enforcement in the overall crime situation. The SDEA is not only a potentially powerful organisation, it also has a very high profile in a key area of contemporary policing. Yet nowhere in its structures is there any public oversight.

The third theme arises from the fact that common police services are inhabited by substantial numbers of people who are not police officers. Virtually all the SPIS staff are civilians, as are 85% in SCRO. This runs ahead of the numbers of support staff in the eight forces, but even here the extent and rate of increase in civilianisation is considerable (see Table 2.1). Particularly in the common services, support staff with specialist skills are central to their operations. The intelligence-led approach associated, for example, with SDEA places considerable reliance on accurate recording of information and data processing by support staff in relation to the confiscation of drug dealers' assets under powers derived from the Proceeds of Crime Act 2002. This places considerable emphasis on the skills of crime analysts, accountants and information technology specialists, who in effect become an integral part of the activity called 'policing'. Procedures relating to complaints and discipline are an intrinsic part of the working lives of police officers. However, how civilian staff should be dealt with in relation to such matters is problematic. Yet it is important to remember that in the McKie case the people accused of misidentifying her print were not police officers, but scientific support staff.

One possible means of rectifying the democratic deficit which presently exists in relation to Scotland's national and central police services is the suggestion that that there should be a separate organisation given responsibility to oversee these services (Donnelly and Scott 2002b: 61–62).

There is a review being undertaken of the common services, but it has been a slow process with limited information coming forward into the public domain (see www.scotland.gov.uk /Topics/Justice/Police/17). It is highly likely that the end result will be another tier of policing in Scotland 'with the eight police forces at one level and an upper layer of national common services at a second level' (ibid.: 62). Such 'multi-tiered' policing will inevitably make control and accountability more complicated. There will be problems of hierarchy because there will be a tendency over time for the upper tier to take priority, especially in high-profile areas, such as serious and organised crime and drug enforcement. In a two-tier structure a single central authority will end up carrying greater influence than several local levels of authority and the accountability mechanisms may need to be equally mixed. Walker has highlighted this concern: 'a multi-tiered complex compounds the problems of transparency, co-ordination and accountability associated with the governance of any modern policing system' (Walker 2000: 169). Devising a system that will adequately reflect the interests of all stakeholders, especially the public, will not be easy and there is still much work to be done on how to hold multi-tiered policing to account.

Complaints against the police

A number of bodies have responsibilities in relation to complaints against the police in Scotland. Police authorities have statutory responsibility under the Police (Scotland) Act 1967 for monitoring the local complaints process and for handling complaints against chief officers. The responsibility for the investigation and prosecution of crime involving a police officer, as in all other cases, rests with the Crown Office and Procurator Fiscal Service. 'It is normally the role of the police to gather evidence and undertake enquiries on behalf of the procurator fiscal, but this should not obscure the fact that, whatever the degree of delegation, in practice the Fiscal retains primacy at all times' (HMICS 2000: 17). Complaints about misconduct are investigated by the officer's force either at local level or through a complaints and discipline branch or professional standards unit overseen by the depute chief constable. In both criminal and misconduct complaints officers from another force can be brought in to carry out the investigation, especially where the complaints are serious or sensitive. In cases of allegations of misconduct by senior officers, the police board must appoint an investigating officer of appropriate rank from another force.

The concern with this position has always been that too much of this process leaves investigation in the hands of the police themselves. This concern has become more urgent because in this respect Scotland is now lagging behind the rest of the UK. An Independent Police Complaints

Commission with its own investigating teams involving non-police personnel has now been established for England and Wales. In Northern Ireland there is now an independent Police Ombudsman for the Northern Ireland Police Service. In Scotland voices are being raised to suggest that some similar course for dealing with complaints against the police needs to be followed. 'Despite the fact that there has been no major crisis in police complaints in Scotland, the existing internal system is no longer seen as appropriate' (Seneviratne 2004: 343). In 2001 the Scottish Executive published proposals for change and put them out to consultation. A consultation paper in support of new legislation to be presented to the Parliament in 2005 has returned to the matter (Scottish Executive 2005). What is definite is that there appears to be significant support, not least in the Scottish Parliament, for a more independent approach to police complaints involving some element of public involvement.

Conclusion

This review of Scottish devolution and its impact on Scottish policing set out to consider three particular aspects of the topic. The first conclusion is that the new political context in which the police in Scotland now operate is much more political than it was under the previous constitutional arrangements. The amount of interaction between the police and politicians appears to have increased significantly. A whole range of elected members (MPs, MSPs, MEPs, local councillors) are now more likely to be seeking to meet with senior police officers; members of ACPOS and ASPS are to be seen in the committee rooms and major working parties of Holyrood; and even at the level of commanders of local sub-divisions and units, dealing with the Scottish Executive and its officials has become more commonplace. The corollary of this is that policing in Scotland has become more 'political' under devolution because of the significance of law, order and crime in electoral mandates and Executive programmes. Not everyone in police circles is comfortable with this situation, partly because political popularity potentially brings with it greater political control, and partly because it endangers that public political neutrality to which the Scottish police have traditionally and strenuously adhered.

The second conclusion, in relation to the tripartite system of police accountability, is that the balance between the three parties is changing profoundly. While the central government leg of the Justice Department and the Scottish Parliament is growing in the demands being made on the police to account for their activities, local government and the chief constables are arguably diminishing in influence. Local authorities find themselves in general under considerable pressure in establishing a clear role for themselves given the expanding control of Holyrood, and the police boards, especially where they are jointly constructed, have yet to demonstrate that they have the capacity to fulfil effectively the monitoring role demanded of them. Chief constables still legally and in principle retain considerable operational independence, but to some extent this is being continually undermined by both internal and external factors. The growth of corporate policy-making and strategy through organisations like ACPOS and the reciprocal accountability involved in multi-agency partnerships undoubtedly has a constraining effect on the traditional conception of constabulary independence. The growth of performance management as a form of accountability has a similar impact. The requirement to meet centrally set targets and performance indicators comes along with a range of auditing and monitoring mechanisms and reporting procedures within the public domain. While this has the potential benefit of increasing openness and transparency, it is likely to exert a disproportionate effect on the operational decisions which chief constables make.

The modern tripartite system of police accountability has now been in place for over 40 years, but the issues arising from it have never remained static. New variations on the traditional themes are continually emerging. In relation to the emerging issues reviewed here, the third conclusion is that the governance of Scottish policing appears to be moving inexorably in an ever more centralised direction. Unlike England and Wales, this new direction in accountability has come about without any statutory framework. The Police (Scotland) Act 1967 was the last piece of legislation to lay out comprehensively the responsibilities of the various parties involved in policing and since then the Scottish police has changed considerably. Issues arising from the growth in significance of common police services and the new police workforce were unthought of in the 1960s. Meanwhile, the self-investigation basis of dealing with complaints against the Scottish police has been overtaken by developments elsewhere in the UK which have demonstrated that non-police oversight is both possible and credible. In both of these areas, the direction in which developments are moving is that the institutions of central government will decide what is to happen. It is likely that an independent police complaints organisation will be established in the near future because this is an issue which has exercised the Scottish Parliament in recent times. It is also likely that there will be further moves towards increasing centralised organisation and co-operation between police forces in Scotland to an extent where their distinguishing features, policies and strategies become less pronounced.

There is still a public debate to be undertaken on whether or not the trends identified in this chapter leads Scotland towards a single national police force (Donnelly 2004: 25–26), and about the desirability or otherwise of that. What is clear, however, is that devolution for Scotland, through the establishment of a Scottish Parliament and Executive, proposed on the basis of power being given away by the centre, has led in reality for policing in Scotland to a greater concentration of power for government at a Scottish level.

Notes

1 Some of the material that appears in this chapter has been developed from papers by the authors which have appeared in *The Police Journal*, vol. 75, no. 1, March 2002, and *Policing Today*, vol. 8, no. 2, 2003, acknowledgement of which is duly given.

2 Ian Oliver has been chief constable of two Scottish forces, Central Scotland and Grampian, and obtained a PhD from the University of Strathclyde. Ironically in the light of these events, the subject of his thesis was police accountability, on which he is an acknowledged expert (see Oliver 1997).

3 There are two interesting asides arising from the case of Shirley McKie. One is that the man convicted of the murder in 1997 successfully appealed against his life sentence on the grounds that crucial fingerprint evidence was 'inaccurate'. The second is that at the March 2004 meeting of the Strathclyde Joint Police Board, four members voted against a recommendation that the Board should support legal measures to recover costs from Shirley McKie. This is the only occasion on which democratically elected representatives have had an opportunity to express a view on this highly publicised miscarriage of justice.

References

Association of Chief Police Officers in Scotland (1998) *Policing the Future – Statement of Common Purpose and Values*. Edinburgh: ACPOS.

Audit Scotland (2004) *Police and Fire: Performance Indicators 2003–04* (Prepared for the Accounts Commission) (accessed at www.audit-scotland.gov.uk).

DETR (Department of the Environment, Transport and the Regions) (1998) *Modernising Local Government – Improving Local Services through Best Value*. London: DETR.

Donnelly, D. (2004) 'A national service?', *Police Review*, December: 25–26.

Donnelly, D. and Scott, K. B. (2002a) 'Police accountability in Scotland – (1) The "new" tripartite system', *The Police Journal*, 75 (1): 1–12.

Donnelly, D. and Scott, K. B. (2002b) 'Police accountability in Scotland – (2) "New" accountabilities', *The Police Journal*, 75 (1): 56–66.

Donnelly, D. and Scott, K. B. (2003) 'Journey on a moving landscape', *Policing Today*, 8 (2): 25–26.

Donnelly, D. and Wilkie, R. (2002) 'States of Scotland: policing the police', *The Scottish Review*, 2 (6): 45–54.

Goldberg, R. (2004) 'Single issue campaigns for the Scottish Parliament', *Scottish Affairs*, 49, Autumn: 1.

Hassan, G. and Warhurst, C. (2001) 'New Scotland? Policy, parties and institutions', *The Political Quarterly*, 72 (2): 213–226.

The Herald (2005) 'Police fears on political neutrality', 20 January: 6.

HM Chief Inspector of Constabulary for Scotland (1998) *Grampian Police Primary Inspection*. Edinburgh: HMSO.

HM Chief Inspector of Constabulary for Scotland (2004) *Annual Report 2003–04*. Edinburgh: HMCICS.

HM Inspectorate of Constabulary for Scotland (2000) *A Fair Cop? The Investigation of Complaints against the Police in Scotland*. Edinburgh: HMSO.

Jones, T. and Newburn, T. (1997) *Policing After the Act – Police and Magistrates Court Act*. London: Policy Studies Unit.

Lustgarten, L. (1986) *The Governance of Policing*. London: Sweet and Maxwell.

Mark, Sir R. (1977) *Policing in a Perplexed Society*. London: Allen and Unwin.

Marshall, G. (1973) 'The government of the police since 1964', in J. Alderson and J. Stead (eds), *The Police We Deserve*. London: Wolf Publishing.

McConnell, J. (2003) *First Minister's Address to the Annual Conference of Chief Police Officers in Scotland*, 29 May.

McFadden, J. and Lazarowicz, M. (2002) *The Scottish Parliament: An Introduction*, 2nd edn. Edinburgh: T & T Clark.

McLaughlin, E. (1994) *Community, Policing and Accountability*. Aldershot: Avebury Gower.

Oliver, I. (1997) *Police, Government and Accountability*, 2nd edn. Basingstoke: Macmillan Press.

Patten, C. (1999) *A New Beginning for Policing in Northern Ireland: The Report of the Independent Commission on Policing in Northern Ireland*. Belfast: HMSO.

Peele, G. (2004) *Governing The UK* , 4th edn. Oxford: Blackwell Publishing.

Reid, G. (2002) 'The Scottish Parliament: how it works', in M. Spicer (ed.), *The Scotsman Guide to Scottish Politics*. Edinburgh: Scotsman Publications.

Reiner, R. (1997) 'Policing and the police', in M. Maguire, R. Morgan and R. Reiner (eds), *The Oxford Handbook of Criminology*, 2nd edn. Oxford: Clarendon Press, pp. 997–1049.

Savage, S. (2001) 'Forces of independence', *Police Review*: 20–21.

Savage, S., Charman, S. and Cope, S. (2000) *Policing and the Power of Persuasion*. London: Blackstone Press.

The Scotsman (1998) 'Police not a law unto themselves', 13 February.

Scott, K. (2003) 'Smash and grab', *Holyrood*, 100 (1), December: 24–25.

Scott, K. and Wilkie, R. (2001) 'Chief constables: a current "crisis" in Scottish policing?', *Scottish Affairs*, 35: 54–68.

Scottish Executive (2001a) *The Stephen Lawrence Inquiry – An Action Plan for Scotland* (accessed at www.scotland.gov.uk/library2/docoi/sli-02.htm).

Scottish Executive (2001b) *Wallace Announces New Targets for Police to Tackle Racist Incident* (accessed at www.scotland.gov.uk/news/2001/05/se1179.asp).

Scottish Executive (2004) *Building a Better Scotland – Spending Proposals 2005–2008: Enterprise, Opportunity, Fairness* (accessed at www.scotland.gov.uk/library5/finance/srtn04-01.asp).

Scottish Executive (2005) *Supporting Police, Protecting Communities: Proposals for Legislation*. Edinburgh: Scottish Executive.

Seneviratne, M. (2004) 'Policing the police in the United Kingdom', *Policing and Society*, 14 (4): 329–347.

Shirley McKie website: www.shirleymckie.com.

Sunday Herald (2001) 'Politics infecting police "like aids"', 10 June: 6.

Vestri, P. and Fitzpatrick, S. (2000) 'Scotland's councillors', *Scottish Affairs*, 33: 62–81.

Walker, N. (2000) *Policing in a Changing Constitutional Order*. London: Sweet & Maxwell.

White, R. M. (1998) 'Disciplining chief constables', *Scots Law Times*, 11: 77–80.

Chapter 5

Change and leadership in Scottish policing: a chief constable's view

John Vine

Introduction

During my police career the leadership of the service has been the subject of constant scrutiny and debate (Home Office 2001; Audit Commission Reports; HMCIC Reports; Leishman *et al.* 1995: 26–38; Reiner 1991). Throughout that time the police service has undergone tremendous change and demands upon the organisation have increased greatly. Many attempts have been made by successive governments to develop and improve the management of the police service, yet I would argue that in this area change has probably been least welcome and successful (Home Office 1993a, b). It was *The Guardian* newspaper that said of senior management of the police service, 'when fish start to rot, they rot from the head … most senior officers are technically competent [but] they tend to lack officer-like qualities' (*The Guardian*, 26 January 1990). Other derogatory comments appeared in the press around this time, which exerted additional pressure on a police service under siege. For example, in 1992 *The Economist* had this to say about police management: 'the police need an officer class to stiffen their fibre. The police are the last of the old style trade unions; over-manned; overpaid and riddled with restrictive practices. Clearly, police bashing is no longer a monopoly of the loony left' (*The Economist*, 8 February 1992).

The Conservative government was not to be outdone either, with the then Home Secretary, Kenneth Clarke, widely reported in the press as being on a crusade to 'sack' lazy police officers. At the Police Superintendents' Annual Conference in 1992, he gave a speech which covered many of the police reform issues at the time, but in particular was reported as saying, 'we have to accept, however, that it will not always be possible to bring everyone up to the required standard and that there will be people who are simply unable to achieve these standards. These people ought not, for their own sakes as well as those of their colleagues and the public, to remain as police officers (*The Guardian*, 23 September, 1992: 18).

I think we must recognise that the skill-set required for success as a police leader has changed. In the 1970s and early 1980s, chief constables like their counterparts in other public services were relatively anonymous individuals, rarely venturing into public view, with one or two notable exceptions. An annual report of the chief constable of my own force from that period hardly features police performance statistics in the report. Contrastingly, there are stories of human endeavour, bravery and one-off incidents that had occurred throughout the year. This was found to be typical during a review of chief constables' annual reports in one police force in England and Wales for the period of 1969 to 1998. In summary, the review concluded that the 'annual reports studied were poor, particularly in the early years – they contain no indicators of efficiency and only two measures which may be used as a proxy for efficiency ... [and] ... do not provide the information needed for police authorities to exercise indirect control' (Law 2001: 88).

It seems hard to imagine now but in that not so long ago era there was a great deal of consensus about policing across both the political divide and with the public, assisted by relatively low levels of crime and disorder. For some time now there has been a perception in government circles that the senior management of policing needs a shake-up with the injection of new thinking and a new customer focus to deliver tangible results in return for increased public spending upon the service. It is in this context that this contribution sets out to explore issues relating to the management of the Scottish police service. Particular emphasis will be placed upon the push for reform in the public sector generally and in the police service in particular, and on the Scottish police response to this in terms of a more strategic approach to management, the management of improved performance and the development of leadership capability.

Public-sector reform

As recorded crime rose dramatically in the 1980s and 1990s and new management techniques such as 'new public management' (NPM) came to replace traditional models of public administration with its attendant objectives, performance measures, devolved management structures and linking of resources to deployment (Jones and Newburn 1997). In addition, there was almost continuous major reform of the public sector with the injection of business management principles into all organisations. By the mid-1990s NPM encompassed many philosophies, approaches and doctrines, such as managerialism, market-led initiatives, entrepreneurialism and efficiency and effectiveness. A heavy emphasis on management style and less on policy and bureaucracy became dominant with the expansion of performance measurement techniques in many forms. Major examples of these included inputs against outputs, value for money, decentralisation and flexible management, setting of targets, objectives and goals, and performance-related pay.

It is true that government did not single out the police service for reform, indeed the police lay relatively untouched. It was other public-sector departments that were targeted much earlier and were experiencing critical change. The Civil Service, for example, experienced the transformation of a significant number of government departments into 'agencies' as a step towards privatisation and exposure to the market. By the early 1990s, 300,000 civil servants were reputed to have been transferred to 92 executive agencies (Painter 1995: 17–36). Furthermore, by the mid-1990s 'general management' was introduced into the National Health Service, with its 'customer ethos', quality assurance, performance audits and a performance inspectorate for community care (Spurgeon 1998). Lastly, but not least, education experienced the government's drive for quality, competition, performance measurement and efficiency. Throughout the 1980s and 1990s heated debates took place regarding proposals to link teachers' performance to pay, the introduction of an appraisal system for teachers, changes to working hours and to teachers' contracts. Five main areas of reform in education were focused upon: quality, diversity, increasing parental choice, greater autonomy for schools, and greater accountability (Sinclair et al. 1995).

Police reform

The police service experienced similar reforms during this period of public sector reform. Unlike other public servants the police had benefited from the favouritism of the Thatcher government during the 1980s. However, by the early 1990s questions were being asked and concerns shown in relation to the marked increase in recorded crime, as Loveday has noted:

In the 1990s, with the unions subdued [miners' strike over], the crime rate soaring, the government's popularity beginning to wane and its image of the party of law and order fast fading, the police service was to face a full frontal assault on its management and other practices in the name of efficiency, effectiveness and market forces in an attempt to reduce the crime rate.

(Loveday 1997: 216)

On a broad view, there had been little change in the crime rate from the beginning of the 20th century until the 1930s; then, as Pilkington highlighted, there was 'a gradual rise to the mid-1950s and a sharp and sustained increase since, except for the occasional slight fall as in 1993–94. Every decade since the mid-1950s has witnessed a doubling of the crime rate, a phenomenon paralleled in most other Western societies over the same period' (Pilkington 1995: 15–17). Nonetheless, the whole aspect of crime figures was critically viewed by the government of the day against a backdrop of ever-increasing expenditure on the police. For example, police expenditure rose significantly from £1,644 to £3,358 million between 1979 and 1984 (Newburn and Jones 1995: 131–132). Unfortunately, during this period crime continued to rise and there was little sign of its abatement or indeed any visible return from the police for this massive investment.

It is probably an oversimplification to suggest that the move towards police reform was solely the result of rising crime. It certainly suited the government during the 1980s to leave the police untouched, particularly at the time of the miners' strike for obvious political reasons. However once the industrial relations environment stabilised, the government focused its attention on what it perceived to be an inefficient and poorly managed police organisation. An incisive comment made in 1992 from Howard Davies, the ex-Controller of the Audit Commission (1987–92), is indicative of the mood at the time: 'in the police service, perhaps more than any other, inputs are confused with outputs. Both major [political] parties play a numbers game based on the headcount of men in blue helmets, with little close investigation of how these officers are deployed, or what they are achieving' (Davies 1992: 28). He believed that the 'inflexible management' and 'spanish practices' of the police had diminished appreciably 'police effectiveness' (ibid.).

The Conservative government announced an enquiry into Police Responsibilities and Rewards (Home Office 1993a), which formed part of the major thrust for change in the police service. Three other reviews and legislative change generated police reform in the early 1990s. These were the White Paper on Police Reform (Home Office 1993b), the Police and Magistrates' Courts Act (1994) and the Review of Police Core and Ancillary Tasks (Posen Inquiry) (Home Office 1995). However, it would be inaccurate to portray the police service of the time as being totally isolated from internal reform to such an extent that all change had to be imposed externally. '[T]here is no doubt contemporary police managers are now far more inclined to be sympathetic towards the new managerialism than their predecessors. They are likely to have been fully immersed in the philosophies of NPM through their professional training programmes' (Savage and Leishman 1996: 250). The Operational Policing Review (1990) was one example of a significant internal enquiry into policing undertaken by the three staff associations (ACPO, APS, Police Federation).

Strategic management

One major demonstration of change was the appearance of dedicated management training courses at police training establishments throughout the UK, with the topic of 'strategic management' high on the agenda. For example, the strategic management development programme at the Scottish Police College saw the introduction of a strategic management course for superintendents in 1994. The teaching of strategy became a vital component in the police reform movement and the management of change.

Strategy always begins with basic strategic choices, regardless of the type of organisation. Particularly, in the non-profit organisations such as the police which normally embark on a 'mission', the notion of strategy conjures up the idea that 'all multitudinous individuals who make up an organisation can be united around the effective pursuit of a coherent goal' (Oster 1995: 139). Bryson further defines strategy as the pursuit of missions, goals and objectives, 'a disciplined effort to produce fundamental decisions and actions that shape and guide what an organisation is, what it does and why it does it' (Bryson 1995: 4–5). Strategy also helps the organisation to relate to its environment and to acknowledge the interests of the sub-units, which normally differ from central headquarters and need continuous motivation and direction to ensure 'conformity with the general or shared interests of the organisation' (McKevitt 1992: 41). This strikes a chord with current thoughts on police management, structure and organisation. Some of the means of influencing the organisation's sub-units lie in the power to allocate resources, to create and restructure the organisation, to introduce performance measurement and reward systems, and to cascade policies and guidelines downwards. One interpretation of this assumption is that, although a key feature of the new public and police management is devolution of decision-making and power to the local level from the centre, it appears that the central government and police headquarters still retain substantial control of the organisation.

Strategy can also be innovative and generates the ability to rethink existing organisational models with a view to introducing 'new value' for customers and being a step ahead of competitors, while bringing quality improvement to organisational stakeholders. New themes in the world of strategy include: improved forecasting techniques and foresight; improved information and knowledge; better competencies; coalitions and networks; transformation and renewal systems. The key lies not only in having the knowledge and ability to implement change, but in having the freedom to utilise these strategic tools and techniques. Having the 'know-how' is insufficient in itself. One example of this was that many of those on the superintendents' course at the Scottish Police College in the 1990s, after having been introduced to the tools of strategic management, returned to their respective forces to be confronted by existing hierarchical structures and bureaucracies which made it virtually impossible for any meaningful, sustainable implementation of their new-found strategic knowledge. Since that time there have been significant improvements in strategic thinking and planning in the Scottish police service. However, there is still some way to go.

New police management

The leaders of the service are now public celebrities, keen to use the media when it suits them, and quickly judged by it when things go wrong. As with other public services, the public has become used to challenging our authority and our performance in the same way that they would hold accountable any other supplier of goods or services. Therefore the skills and qualities of leaders in the service has to change in order to address society's attitudes to what they want to see from *their* police service. Police managers can no longer afford to be isolated from the wider environment and to be 'internally focused on service delivery and organisational performance in the narrow sense' (Joyce 1999: xii). They are now expected to work in partnership with other public-sector groups, voluntary organisations and the private sector within a strategic management and planning framework. This strategic approach has as its ultimate goal improved performance and level of service to the customer, and the introduction of new problem-solving techniques and innovative solutions to existing difficulties.

Modernisation of police management, however, encompassed more than just a central thrust for improved efficiency and value for money. In order to combat the complexities of management in the public sector and, more importantly, to assist in the management of change, police managers, along with their colleagues in other parts of the public sector, were being directed and encouraged to 'think in managerial terms about resources and objectives' (Metcalfe and Richards 1987: 32). NPM had become associated with reform in public organisations, making them more businesslike and competitive, improving efficiency and adding value to service delivery. The developing 'new police management' has been no different and its main tenets are articulated in Table 5.1 by adapting a model compiled by Hood (1991) specifically to highlight seven precepts of doctrine that are referred to regularly by business analysts.

Table 5.1 Components of new public management within the police service

1 *Hands-on professional management*
   Emphasis on highly visible police managers with a sufficiency of discretionary power to enable them to manage unhindered. This relates to the new police managers who are expected to be more proactive and strategic in their everyday duties than ever before.

2 *Explicit standards and measures of performance*
   This is a prerequisite for clear goals and targets with associated performance indicators, which makes police managers more accountable for lucid objectives.

3 *Greater emphasis on output controls*
   There is a need to introduce reward systems and to make personnel more accountable through a system of measuring outputs. The new police manager is more concerned with measuring results and service quality than in the past.

4 *Disaggregation of public-sector units*
   New police management requires decentralisation and the break-up of traditional public-sector bureaucracy into more user-friendly, manageable and accountable units.

5 *Greater competition in the public sector*
   New police management has led to the introduction of contracts and best value with an increase in 'market' influences in the public sector.

6 *Private-sector style of management*
   An important theme of new police management is for public managers to emulate private-sector management. The new police managers have introduced fixed term contracts for senior management, flexible working conditions, performance-related appraisal, outsourcing and extensive use of consultants.

7 *Greater discipline and economy in resource use*
   New police management encourages financial cost-cutting and efficient use of human resources, which normally leads to 'doing more with less'. However, this position has changed somewhat with the advent of best value, which emphasises better value for money and improved service, rather than focusing on the cheapest service.

Source: Hood (1991: 4–5).

Hood's model is a useful tool which highlights many of the principles of new public management. It also indicates how the seven tenets have been accepted into the development of new police management. In Hood's own words, there is a universal applicability inherent in NPM, a 'public management for all seasons' (ibid.: 8).

Performance management

Increasingly in the delivery of public services the public wants results. Herein lies the dilemma for police chiefs. What does a 'good result' in policing look like? Is it something measurable, like reduced crime statistics or increases in detection rate, or is it something less tangible but equally important, such as the feeling of safety and security that individuals experience within their communities? Depending upon the stakeholder, the relative importance of one or other varies. If the Scottish Executive decides that figures matter more, then relative performance of forces represented by tangible measures is the only practical way in which to assess whether or not results are being achieved. Police management will be 'increasingly forced to deal with the politically-inspired and media-driven requirement to produce credible quantified evidence of police achievement in dealing with crime' (Edwards 1999: 269). In today's society performance indicators are a fact of life and I would argue that we need to learn to love them, not loathe them.

I am not, however, advocating a regime such as that which is beginning to appear south of the border, where accountability, whether in the form of a basic command unit or force league table, seems to have become an end in itself and an absolute judgement on the performance of the force and its leadership. There is also the assertion that there has been an increase in centralisation of services, a strengthening of core executive, increasing decentralisation of policy delivery while extending control over policy strategy and initially an increase in the privatisation of the traditional state sectors (Cope *et al*. 1997: 444–60). The results orientation seen in the police service is part of that overall trend and is removing the differences between the public and private sectors (Johnston 2000; Button 2002). If we compare police services with other forms of service, the dilemmas begin to become apparent. If you were to ring your bank you would expect them to know how much money you had in your account. If you contact your doctor or your local hospital about a medical complaint you expect them to know a little bit about your medical history. The story differs remarkably with policing, where we know a great deal more about our criminals than about our law-abiding customers. Our customers are treated as strangers every time they call. The service is designed with the criminal in mind. Indeed, we work from the premise that most normal law-abiding citizens spend their lives avoiding any contact with the police. We are simply not geared up to recognising the repeat call from the victim of housebreaking, or the despairing call from someone who is plagued by vandalism and nuisance in the community. Otherwise we would treat them with individual care and attention in the way that they have become accustomed to by their interaction with other services. Such sentiments embrace the concepts of community policing and problem-solving policing which forms the basis of how the police of today should work (see Tilley 2003: 311–339).

Police management is currently fond of the phrase 'what gets measured gets done'. As Hough reminds us, it was a recurring phrase in interviews with frontline officers in the study *Policing for London* (Hough 2002: 29). 'What can't be measured doesn't count and what doesn't count doesn't get done' (Fitzgerald and Hough 2002). This is not simply to make judgements about public services on the basis of performance figures alone. What I am saying is that a great deal more scrutiny could be paid to the performance of forces than is currently the case with the present oversight structure. We have become used to tables for school performance, and, despite attempts to decry them, they are a popular supplement to most of the newspapers when the figures are published. I doubt whether most parents who have studied the tables go to the lengths of removing their children from school on the basis of that information alone, but it is likely that they will be prompted to ask intelligent questions and demand answers from the head teacher or education authority.

Concern with quality at the individual level is nothing new to the police organisation, but pursuing a strategy of 'quality improvement' as an essential component of the success of the organisation's overall mission did not exist until recently. Indeed, in 1991 a National Audit Office report (NAO 1991) makes reference to the fact that most forces at that time had carried out 'efficiency scrutinies' and 'value-for-money' exercises and a number had even set up their own 'inspection units' to monitor performance. Equally, the report was fairly scathing in its criticism of a number of areas, for example, the need to develop reliable data on how police officers spend their working day and how resources are deployed. In referring to the NAO's report, Loveday reminds us that, due to a lack of accurate information, the comptroller of audit felt unable 'to make more than a broad assessment of police performance' (Loveday 1991: 318). A senior Home Office official, under cross-examination by the Public Accounts Committee of the House of Commons in relation to improving police efficiency, agreed that 'there was no means of measuring what police officers actually do' (*Police Review*, 10 May 1991: 945).

Quality can only be successfully achieved by establishing explicit standards sensibly arrived at which reflect the defined needs of the service users. This approach stresses the requirement for clear public indicators of standard. It also emphasises the central importance of the service users (consumer/customer) and their judgements of the appropriateness and effectiveness of services. Rogerson's view on performance measurement in the police in the mid-1990s highlights the delicate balance to be achieved, that 'performance measurement may threaten the operational independence of chief constables and alter the style of policing from that of service to enforcement' (Rogerson 1995: 25). This move towards a 'results-driven' service has important implications for police officers' appraisals and assessments. Bourne argues that if the police wish to 'attain a "performance culture", the service needs to emphasise results as the motivation behind operational excellence instead of what skills officers have been trained in' (Bourne 1999: 14).

The emphasis on performance measurement can have unintended consequences of focusing primarily on figures rather than the overall quality of service delivered. Hough (2002: 30) describes the police as an organisation that is particularly susceptible to this effect. However, this is not a reason to fail to embrace the concept of becoming accountable for our results; rather it is a cultural change that is required, which should be led from the top. Neither is it an either/or argument. The truth is that police forces have to do both. We have broad responsibilities around community safety and maintenance of order as well as maintaining a crime focus. The simplistic 'one or the other' argument displays a lack of sophistication of thinking. Indicators and targets are only a means to an end. If the workforce uses them otherwise and the broader responsibilities of policing are ignored as a result, then I believe that is a failing of police leadership.

Performance data

The service needs to become more comfortable with the ambiguity around police performance statistics. The public thrust for tangible results is not going to lessen and rather than being preoccupied with structural change and boundaries, there is a far more complex and difficult challenge ahead for the service if we are to satisfy this need. A new service culture is required, one that recognises that the provision of excellent service is essential to satisfying customer demand. A journey back in time reveals that such pleas have been made before. For example, in a perceptive speech in 1992, Sir John Woodcock, HMCIC for England and Wales, gave a perceptive speech in 1992 when he said:

the police are now listening, listening harder than they have ever done. They are picking up the sounds of a shift in society, they are understanding that the rights of the customers of police are now the great priority and that those customers include not only victims of crime, however important they are, but also suspects and the wider public.

(Woodcock 1992)

Any cultural shift of this nature will require the leaders of the service to be more open and to be prepared to be much more accountable for the comparative performance of their forces. I agree with Professor Richard Kerley when he stated that 'contextual data such as performance indicators, becomes an important part of the policy debate on how we organise public services and it is well worth keeping and using' (Kerley 2003: 27).

Local accountability is after all the bedrock of modern policing. I think the public have a right to know how well local forces are performing not just against a set of performance indicators, but also against each other. McKinnon (2004) points out that the release of baseline assessments south of the border has sparked a debate about police performance because the results show a wide variance in performance. The Association of Chief Police Officers in Scotland (ACPOS) has begun some work to identify ways in which this could be achieved without anomalies arising in respect of the size of forces. There are, however, real reservations about this work within ACPOS because of the potential for the media to make simplistic judgements on crime figures. The argument against goes something like this: we, the police, are the acknowledged experts in policing; in our view it would be wrong to disclose too much to the public because they do not understand the complexity of what we do nor the decisions we make and, in any case, if they knew the truth it would only increase their fear of crime beyond the known reported level. I believe that this traditional perspective of 'we know best' is no longer tenable. The open publication of comparative data is long overdue, and as the leaders of the service, we have to put our faith in the intelligent consumer to question why the detection rate in their force is particularly high or low, why offences of violence are rising or falling, and why sickness absence seems to be on the increase in one force compared with a neighbouring force. It is still rare in police mission statements or objectives to see words such as 'accountable', 'delivery', 'customer' or 'performance'. The Home Secretary's recent announcement that forces are to publish a charter of standards of service (Home Office 2004) was remarkable for its omission to date – in the objectives and plans of many forces.

Consensus and accountability

Officers in the Scottish police service value consensus over conflict and there has been a real willingness to come together to progress a number of key initiatives across force boundaries. The very timely adoption of the Scottish Intelligence Database is a case in point, where the overriding needs of the service have won out over local parochial interest. My own force was one that has invested heavily in homegrown information technology solutions and has had to compromise an excellent in-house product for the adoption of a Scottish-wide system. In the light of the Soham murder enquiry, it turned out to be an insightful decision, but typical today of some real co-operation within ACPOS on key issues across force boundaries.

The size of the Scottish service is often given as the reason for ease of co-operation, but my view is that there is far greater interest in and understanding of the service by the Scottish Executive, and ACPOS for its part has responded with constructive dialogue and a willingness to come up with ideas about improved service delivery. However, we need to do more. There is a pressure on the delivery of all public services to make effective use of resources. The best value regime is the latest incarnation of this trend. While policing is traditionally a local activity, the pressure on Scottish forces to collaborate in the development of common police services is considerable.

In addition, accountability of the police service in Scotland post-devolution has increased, as naturally the Scottish Executive are held directly accountable by the Scottish electorate for their feelings of safety and security. Although at present, probably because of the relative success of forces in reducing crime and improving detection rates, there is some measure of contentment with the service, the trend towards greater control by the Executive over policing services will continue. Scottish ministers will want to be satisfied that the large investment in policing is achieving results, to be reflected in the ballot box, and in an overall improvement in the perception of safety and security by ordinary members of the public. The way in which policing and other public services are delivered, including the existing structures, traditions and roles, are secondary to the outcome. We have seen this in a big way south of the border. Actions such as direct intervention in 'failing' forces by the Police Standards Unit, government funding going directly to basic command units, force structures being by-passed and league tables of local police performance being published on the Internet all demonstrate how little account is now being taken of the traditional forms of police governance.

Scottish communities have a vital role to play in this world of growing consensus and accountability and cannot be left out. Police management must also strive to create new and innovative communication links with the public and its communities. By this I do not mean the community officer or police supervisor meeting regularly with the community council, residents and tenants associations, however important these rendezvous are for police–community relations. A wider cross-section of the public needs to interface with the police in frequent and meaningful 'quality contact'; otherwise police attempts to articulate how the organisation and its members are changing and improving will be greatly hindered. Significant investment in seeking imaginative methods of outreach and marketing; strategic positioning of smaller police offices designed for the modern day; inventive use of communication technology; creative placement of police officers in places where the public frequents the most; and the stimulation of interest in policing within the wider public are crucial to a new interface between police and public. Failure to get the public 'on side' will hamper attitudinal and cultural change on both sides. This is critical to the successful reform of policing and the management of resources in the 21st century.

Leadership, professional development and competency

If transformational leadership is to be effective, the service also needs to change its attitude to personal responsibility. Leadership training throughout a person's career, where officers are expected to demonstrate a high degree of personal leadership, whether it be on patrol, as a shift manager, a basic command unit commander or a chief officer, needs to be far more part of the culture of the service. A more hard-nosed approach to the management of resources is needed if we are to satisfy this demand. For far too long, within my own experience, management somehow has felt undermined or disempowered in the police service. By this, I don't mean simple organisational restructuring to devolve budgetary responsibility. The power to challenge standards of delivery by our staff, to move resources around the organisation to where they are needed most, to challenge productivity of staff and demand excellent service delivery to the public is the approach required in the future.

At times it seems the police service is run like a social club, with consideration of the interests of its customers secondary to its members. A good example of this approach in practice has been the modern trend to address work–life balance issues of police officers by introducing variable shift patterns. Many have been introduced more with the aim of giving officers extra rest days than providing a greater police presence or a more effective policing service to the community. This has to change and the leaders of the service, in return for their relatively generous remuneration, need to be prepared to be unpopular with their staff in order to ensure that the public receives the best possible service.

Looking at the thrust of government policy, the trend to consumerism continues apace. In July 2004 the Westminster government revealed its five-year anti-crime plan entitled *Confident Communities in a Secure Britain*. Under this plan communities will be able to petition the local police commander and trigger a snap inspection of local policing. In launching the plan, the Prime Minister commented that the public wants a community 'where the decent law-abiding majority are in charge'. One of the dangers of the consumerist approach, however, is that the public may not see important crime as a priority. Squires (1997: 46–50), for instance, found that racial harassment and domestic violence incidents were not regarded as high on the community's list of priorities as they were for the police (ibid.: 47–48). Against this background the demand for a new management ethos is imperative. If we cherish local accountability in policing, together with the principles of operational independence, then chief officers need to confront this agenda and drive it rather than simply respond to it. While the Scottish police service has, with a new generation of chief constables, moved away from the command-and-control ethos, it is the intangible issues about how we embrace this new world that call for new forms of leadership, not just at the top of the service, but at all levels. Faced with consumer demand, all our staff will have to develop a higher level of personal leadership than has been traditional in the service.

I think there are two ways in which we can do this. Firstly, we have to move to develop a far more professional police service in terms of competency, professional development and skill acquisition. For far too long we have relied solely on experience within the ranks in order to qualify individuals for promotion or for lateral development into specialist departments such as the CID. However, competency to lead increasingly applies across all ranks of the service. As Jenny Deere, Director of the National Police Leadership Centre at Centrex, has said: 'developing high quality leadership skills at all levels in the organisation is a key element in the process to help improve morale, performance and ultimately the quality of service delivery to the public'. Accreditation of police officers by external institutions has been a relatively new feature of senior management training in the service. The link between the strategic command course at Bramshill and the University of Cambridge, to enable graduates of this course to obtain a postgraduate qualification in criminology, is probably the best-known example. In the future, however, accreditation of all police officers will help make the cultural shift. With the Scottish probationer training course having been validated by the University of Stirling, all probationer constables passing out from the Scottish Police College will now have credits that can be used towards a university degree. Chief police officers should take the lead and produce their own personal development plans to demonstrate that they are 'fit for purpose' to run a police force. Similarly, divisional commanders should do the same in order to qualify to continue in their role. For far too long we have used the uniqueness of policing in order to avoid applying good practice of this sort to the police service. Of themselves, these measures would not of course reduce crime or improve detection rates in the immediate term, but would enable the service to evidence modernisation and self-improvement, particularly around leadership as well as enhancing performance, morale, job satisfaction and productivity.

The emphasis on core leadership training by Centrex and their equivalents in Scotland, together with a refreshed High Potential Development Scheme and a Senior Leadership Development Programme, means that more direct emphasis than ever is being placed on leadership training and development. This emphasis on lifelong learning and personal professional development will in future avoid the situation we have now, where officers come to the end of a 30-year career with little to show for it despite thousands of pounds of training and development having been spent on them. The concepts of continuous professional development (CPD) and lifelong learning supported by accreditation will help to transform the service into a profession, leaving behind the 'blue-collar' mentality. These developments, which are well underway, underpin more radical change to the management and leadership of the service. There will be far more joint learning with other organisations under the banner of community safety than with other law-enforcement agencies.

Intriguingly, comment from Gordon Wasserman, ex-Home Office police advisor and present consultant and advisor on police affairs in the United States, sheds some light on the remaining uniqueness of police leadership in the UK: 'if one were to compare the 43 chief constables of England and Wales with the chiefs of the 43 largest US police departments, the British group would score significantly higher in terms of professional training, breadth of vision and variety of experience' (Wasserman 2004: 27). Despite this fact, he points out that the functioning environment is different for UK police leaders compared with their American counterparts. British police have 'far less managerial freedom', 'are subject to guidance and advice from civil servants who have no police training or experience', 'are controlled by Ministers who have national rather than local agendas', 'are inspected on a regular basis by former colleagues', and 'are expected to devote a certain amount of time away dealing with national issues [ACPO/ACPOS]' (ibid.: 27). Wasserman makes the point that policing in America is a genuine 'local service' while UK chief constables are given direction and instruction from the centre, through the bureaucracy of 'circulars, inspectorates, national targets and reviews' which tend to 'stifle innovation and enthusiasm' (ibid.: 27). These observations are just as pertinent to Scottish chief officers, particularly since devolution.

The prominence given to CPD and competency also supports the arguments for paths by which specialists can enter the police service and for an end to a single point of entry. This has recently been promoted in the White Paper on the next stage of police reform (Home Office 2004). The question is increasingly being raised as to whether or not it is necessary for ACPOS post-holders to have been in every case 'sworn' police officers. We have already seen the emergence of the senior 'civilian' police manager, appointed because of professional expertise in areas such as personnel management, finance and administration. Such appointments are challenging the traditional boundaries between 'officers' and 'civilians'. ACPOS as an organisation has recently recognised this with the creation of associate member status for certain senior non-police role-holders and current thinking would suggest that there is public support for such a move (Savage *et al.* 2000: 118).

The demand for excellent service is such that it is both unrealistic and unfair to expect a police officer to be a 'jack of all trades'. We need detectives trained to a high standard as investigators, we need specialists in fraud, computer and Internet crime, in firearms and less-than-lethal weapons, forensic analysis and DNA analysis in particular. The beat officer has to become a specialist, too, and the 'beat manager' concept is an attempt to define competence in the role, which the public acknowledge is very important to their feeling of safety and security. In Tayside the role of 'lead constable' has been created in an attempt to differentiate the 'specialist' beat officers, recognising their valuable role both in terms of reassurance policing but also in dealing with the bulk of recorded crime.

Lateral development needs to be encouraged given that the vertical promotion route will only satisfy a small proportion of the workforce. Although widely regarded in negative terms, the recent Police Negotiating Board pay settlement should be looked upon as an opportunity to consider levels of effort and expertise within the workforce. It enables managers, albeit imperfectly, to make the link between performance and individual effort and ability. One can argue whether or not, in a public service like the police, some form of performance-related pay will actually improve performance, but what it can enable us to do is to fulfil long-held aspirations such as the enhancement of the role of the Beat Constable and the greater holding to account of all individuals against their performance. In many forces the constable is no longer at the lower position in the service. With the advent of community support officers, community wardens and paid special constables, the regular officer is likely to find him/herself in a leadership position far more often in the future than has been the case in the past.

Conclusion

The Scottish police service has done well to produce a *People Strategy* supported by market analysis. This will allow for resource planning for the next five to seven years and has become the bedrock on which a number of policies have been developed. This gives us a tremendous opportunity to think creatively about how we are going to manage our workforce, and the different ways in which we may have to deploy our staff against a background of increasing demands on the police service. There are serious challenges here: is the service actually embracing part-time working and job share rather than regarding it as incompatible with the delivery of operational policing? Is there a genuine willingness to expand civilianisation in the police service?

Greater imagination around forms of working is essential for the service to move on. The Scottish Police Service needs to get into the difficult areas around organisational culture to ensure that frontline officers buy into the corporate objectives of the organisation. In order to overcome the feeling that performance reviews are merely a bureaucratic exercise done *to* them rather than *with* them, career development needs to become far more sophisticated, including the encouragement of more personal development to be undertaken by officers themselves within their own time rather than when on duty.

We need to overcome a cultural gap between chief officer/manager and the officers/staff on the frontline. A characteristic of successful organisations is the closure of this policy/practice gap, and within my service we have not realistically managed to address this point. Against a background of a single point of entry into the service, where those at the very top of the organisation have had to gain experience of front-line policing, this seems to be an issue which the public struggle to understand.

Above all, we need a new contract with the public on the delivery of policing services. This has to be based on a recognition of customer demand; on open, transparent and reliable data; and on a willingness to be held accountable for performance. The best way for the police service to regain the confidence of the public is to do its job within these new parameters. It is then up to the politicians, public and the media to act as intelligent consumers and to help foster the safer, stronger communities that are the goal of the Scottish Executive.

References

Association of Chief Police Officers in Scotland (2004) *People Strategy*. Edinburgh: ACPOS.

Bourne, D. (1999) 'Results driven', *Police Review*, 1 January: 14–16.

Bryson, J. M. (1995) *Strategic Planning for Public and Non Profit Organisations – A Guide to Strengthening and Sustaining Organisational Achievement*. San Francisco: Jossey Bass.

Button, M. (2002) *Private Policing*. Devon: Willan Publishing.

Cope, S., Leishman, F. and Starie, P. (1997) 'Globalisation, new public management and the enabling state: futures of police management', *International Journal of Public Sector Management*, 10 (6): 444–460.

Davies, H. (1992) *Fighting Leviathan – Building Social Markets That Work*. London: Social Market Foundation.

The Economist (1992) 'Embattled Bobbies', 8 February: 31–32.

Edwards, C. J. (1999) *Changing Policing Theories for the 21st Century Societies*. NSW: Federation Press.

Fitzgerald, M. and Hough, M. (2002) *Policing for London*. Devon: Willan Publishing.

The Guardian (1992) 'Clarke calls for sacking of lazy police', 23 September: 18.

Home Office (1993a) *Report of Enquiry into Police Responsibilities and Rewards*, Cmnd 2280. London: HMSO.

Home Office (1993b) *Police Reform – A Police Service for the Twenty-First Century*, White Paper, Cmnd 2281. London: HMSO.

Home Office (1995) *Review of Police Core and Ancillary Tasks*, Final Report. London: HMSO.

Home Office (2001) *Policing a New Century – A Blueprint for Police Reform*, White Paper, Cmnd. 5326. London: Home Office.

Home Office (2004) *Building Communities, Beating Crime – A Better Service for the 21st Century*, Police Reform Policy Paper. London: Home Office.

Hood, C. (1991) 'A public management for all seasons?', *Public Administration*, 69 (1): 3–19.

Hough, M. (2002) 'Missing the target: police performance measurement', *The Stakeholder*, May/June: 29–30.

Johnston, L. (2000) *Policing Britain – Risk, Security and Governance*. Harlow: Pearson Education.

Joint Consultative Committee (1990) *Operational Policing Review*. Surbiton: Joint Consultative Committee.

Jones, T. and Newburn, T. (1997) *Policing After the Act – Police and Magistrates Court Act*. London: Policy Studies Institute.

Jones, T. and Newburn, T. (2002) 'The transformation of policing?: Understanding current trends in policing systems', *British Journal of Criminology*, 42: 129–146.

Joyce, P. (1999) *Strategic Management for the Public Services*. Bucks: Open University Press.

Kerley, R. (2003) 'Public performance: targets can have a positive effect', *Holyrood*, 100, 1 December: 27.

Law, J. (2001) 'Accountability and annual reports: the case of policing', *Public Policy and Administration*, 16 (1): 75–90.

Leishman, A., Cope, S. and Starie, P. (1995) 'Reforming the police in Britain: new public management, policy networks and a "Tough Old Bill"', *International Journal of Public Sector Management*, 8 (4): 26–38.

Loveday, B. (1991) 'Police and government in the 1990s', *Social Policy and Administration*, 25 (4): 311–328.

Loveday, B. (1997) 'Management and accountability in public services: a police case study', in K. I. Henry, C. Painter and C. Barnes (eds), *Management in the Public Sector – Challenge and Change*, 2nd edn. London: International Thomson Business Press.

McKevitt, D. (1992) 'Strategic Management in Public Services', in L. Willcocks and J. Harrow (eds), *Rediscovering Public Services Management*. London: McGraw Hill.

McKinnon, G. (2004) 'Police performance in England and Wales', *Justice of the Peace*, 168.

Metcalfe, L. and Richards, S. (1987) 'The efficiency strategy in central government: an impoverished concept of management', *Public Money*, June: 32.

National Audit Office (1991) *Promoting Value For Money in Provincial Police Forces*. London: HMSO.

Newburn, T. and Jones, T. (1995) 'The future of traffic policing', *Policing*, 11 (2): 131–132.

Oster, S. (1995) *Strategic Management for Non-Profit Organisations*. New York: Oxford University Press.

Painter, C. (1995) 'The next steps reform and current orthodoxies', in B. J. O'Toole and G. Jordan (eds), *Next Steps – Improving Management in Government*. Aldershot: Dartmouth.

Pilkington, A. (1995) 'Measuring crime', *Sociology Review*, November: 15–17.

Reiner, R. (1991) *Chief Constables*. Oxford: Oxford University Press.

Rogerson, P. (1995) 'Performance measurement and policing: police service or law enforcement agency?', *Public Money and Management*, 15 (4): 25–30.

Savage, S. P., Charman, S. and Cope, S. (2000) *Policing and the Power of Persuasion*. London: Blackstone Press.

Savage, S. P. and Leishman, F. (1996) 'Managing the police – a force for change', in D. Farnham and S. Horton (eds), *Managing the New Public Services*, 2nd edn. London: Macmillan Press.

Sinclair, J. *et al.* (1995) 'Market driven reform in education: performance, quality and industrial relations in schools', in I. Kirkpatrick and M. Lucio-Martinez (eds), *The Politics of Quality in the Public Sector*. London: Routledge.

Spurgeon, P. (ed.) (1998) *The New Face of the NHS*, 2nd edn. London: The Royal Society of Medicine Press.

Squires, P. (1997) 'Consumer agenda', *Policing Today*, 3 (1): 46–50.

Tilley, N. (2003) 'Community policing, problem-oriented policing and intelligence-led policing', in T. Newburn (ed.), *Handbook of Policing*. Devon: Willan Publishing.

Wasserman, G. (2004) 'A lesson from America', *Policing Today*, 10 (3): 25–27.

Willcocks, L. and Harrow, J. (eds) (1992) *Rediscovering Public Services Management*. London: McGraw-Hill.

Woodcock, J., Sir (1992) *Speech given at IPEC Conference*. London: HMCIC.

Chapter 6

Policing crime and disorder in Scotland

Nicholas R. Fyfe

Introduction: a tale from Greenock

In a pioneering analysis of 'the state of crime in Scotland' published in 1964, Shields and Duncan paint a bleak picture of crime trends across the country. Drawing on police statistics, they reveal a 277% rise in crime between 1927 and 1962, the product, they contend, of increasing material possessions, rising aspirations and 'the diminution of formerly strongly held moral and religious scruples which in the past may have prevented those who could not obtain desired goods legitimately from helping themselves illegitimately' (Shields and Duncan, 1964: 19–20). Yet amidst this depressing picture of an unrelenting rise in crime they highlight a small but significant example of success in tackling crime. According to their analysis of police data in 1954–55, Greenock, a town on the Firth of Clyde to the west of Glasgow, was 'Scotland's top housebreaking area'. But over the next seven years, while Scotland's recorded housebreaking rates continued to rise steeply, Greenock was alone in showing 'a substantial decrease' and had 'fallen to seventh position in the housebreaking hierarchy'. What accounts for this remarkable change in Greenock's fortunes? Analysis at the time suggested 'certain special measures of crime prevention carried through from March 1955 by the Greenock police':

> These included special police patrolling of a criminal area in the town; attempts by the police in co-operation with other local

authority departments to improve physical and social conditions in this area; co-operation with the local gas and electricity authorities to replace pre-payment meters with credit meters; and the setting up of the Police Juvenile Liaison Office scheme (the first in Scotland). Along with these measures there is interesting evidence of civic enterprise and of high civic morale in the coming into being of the Greenock Arts Guild and the publication of the 'civic code', prepared in 1952 by the Corporation, assisted by clergy of the Protestant and Roman Catholic churches. This code ... affirms the obligation of all citizens in the home, in the community, at work and in spiritual matters.

(quoted in Shields and Duncan 1964: 61–62)

The extent to which each of these different measures actually contributed to Greenock's improving position in Scotland's housebreaking 'league table' is, of course, difficult to assess. What is intriguing, however, is that this description of crime prevention some 50 years ago clearly resonates with contemporary approaches to tackling crime and disorder. The importance of targeted police patrols and of co-operation between the police and local government to address environmental and social factors linked to crime; the emphasis on local businesses taking responsibility for reducing the opportunities for crime; the concern with youth offending; and the emphasis given to civic responsibility in tackling the underlying causes of crime, all feature prominently in the contemporary landscape of measures to tackle crime and disorder in Scotland.

In this chapter I examine this landscape by first tracing the contours of crime and disorder in contemporary Scotland, drawing on both police-recorded crime statistics and findings from the Scottish Crime Surveys. The second section then examines two key approaches to crime control which have dominated the 'law and order' political agenda in Scotland as elsewhere in the UK over the last 20 years: the so-called 'sovereign state' approach emphasising the importance of police powers in dealing with crime, and the 'adaptive' approach emphasising the role of partnership between the police, other agencies and individuals in preventing crime and disorder. In the third section, the idea of partnership is developed further to highlight the importance of 'policing beyond the police' (Crawford 2003: 136–168) in the fight against crime and disorder, focusing on the importance of 'active citizenry', municipal policing and the private security industry.

Tracing the contours of crime and disorder

Measuring crime and disorder

'Crime', as Smith and Young (1999: 15) remind us, 'is not an uncontested social fact'. Rather, crime arises from 'moral judgements, from a legal code, and from a multitude of decisions taken by officials and citizens about whether to invoke the legal process on a particular occasion'. Thus the measurement of crime and disorder is fraught with problems.

Police statistics of recorded crime clearly provide one source of information and have been published in Scotland since 1868, continuing to the present day in the form of an annual bulletin of *Recorded Crime in Scotland* produced by the Justice Statistics Department of the Scottish Executive. Based on returns made by each of Scotland's eight police forces, this bulletin presents information on crime and offences made known to the police for Scotland as a whole, by police force area and by local authority district. Yet the deficiencies of police-recorded statistics are well known. Such data largely reflect police practices and public propensity to report offences, yielding a partial and often distorted picture of the level and distribution of crime. As Smith and Young observe, police statistics not only leave out 'every kind of behaviour that citizens or officials decide to control by more informal means, or ignore' (Smith and Young 1999: 15), but for crimes such as the possession of illegal drugs or prostitution, recorded offences will largely reflect the priority given to dealing with these activities by individual police forces. Indeed, *The State of Crime in Scotland* recognised such difficulties over 40 years ago when reflecting on the impact of police priorities on recorded crime:

> If a police force is at full strength and each member is able for all or most of the time that he [sic] is on duty to be engaged in the prevention or detection of crime, it is likely that the incidence of recorded crime will be higher than if he were employed in directing traffic, controlling crowds which attend fashionable weddings or queue for tickets for football matches or theatrical performances by a 'pop' singer.
>
> (Shields and Duncan 1964: 6–7)

In an attempt to overcome some of these problems, there has been a proliferation of national and local crime surveys in Britain since the early 1980s, measuring the incidence and impact of victimisation among a random sample of the population. These surveys provide 'an alternative index of crime to set alongside the police recorded crime statistics' (MVA 2002: 1) and provide information about the nature and effects of crime. In terms of national crime surveys, the first sweep of the British Crime Survey (BCS) was in 1982 and comprised separate samples of 10,000 households in England and Wales and 5,000 in Scotland. Although regular surveys have been carried out in England and Wales since then, in Scotland 'national crime surveys have had a far more patchy history' (Anderson 1999: 48). Scotland did not participate in the 1984 BCS, and although it took part in the 1988 BCS, 'the experience was an unhappy one' (op. cit.) due to problems with both the fieldwork and data analysis. This resulted in the then Scottish Office launching its own survey, the Scottish Crime Survey (SCS) in 1993, followed by surveys in 1996, 2000 and 2003.

Like police-recorded statistics, however, crime surveys such as the SCS do have several important limitations. As the SCS only surveys adults in private households, it cannot provide estimates of crimes against businesses or other corporate bodies, nor of so-called 'victimless' crimes such as prostitution, traffic offences or drug misuse. Moreover, the SCS is dependent on the willingness of individuals to participate in the survey, which might lead to some response bias and, as Christie has observed, 'being a victim is not a thing, an objective phenomenon' and that therefore it is important to acknowledge that 'some sections of the population are more likely to see themselves as victims than others' (Christie 1986, quoted in Anderson 1999: 51).

National trends and local perceptions

Against this background, what do we know about changing levels of crime in Scotland? Smith and Young (1999) have traced recorded crime between 1950 and 1995, revealing substantial increases in violent crimes and sexual assault from 1950 to 1992 followed by a major drop in violent crimes (but not sexual assault) in 1993. The pattern of violent crime since then has been inconsistent. In terms of recorded thefts, these generally rose until the early 1990s, since when there have been steep falls. Recorded housebreaking has also dropped sharply since 1991. The most recent statistical bulletin of recorded crime for 2003 (Scottish Executive 2004) shows that the number of crimes recorded by the police continues to fall (by 5% in 2002–03). Almost 407,000 crimes were recorded, the lowest level for nearly 25 years and 29% lower than the peak 1991 figure. Nevertheless, there are significant variations across Scotland in terms of the levels of recorded crime. In 2003 the highest levels were in Fife (897 crimes per 10,000 population), followed by Lothian and Borders (878) and Strathclyde (840). The lowest levels of recorded crime per 10,000 population were found in Northern Constabulary and Central Scotland Police force areas, where the figures for 2003 were 524 and 693 respectively.

How do these trends in recorded crime compare with trends in crime measured by the Scottish Crime Surveys? Focusing on the period 1981 to

1995 and the 'comparable subset' of crimes that are covered by both the police-recorded crime statistics and the crime survey, Smith and Young have shown how recorded crime rose by 50% between 1981 and 1992 and then fell slightly between 1992 and 1995. Crime measured by the SCS, however, remained roughly level in this period and had started to fall by 1995. The most recent published Scottish Crime Survey for 2000 suggests that the overall crime levels continue to fall. It estimates that some 843,000 crimes were committed against individuals and households in 1999, a fall of 13% compared with 1995.

Although these temporal trends are clearly encouraging, it is important to place them within a wider UK perspective. In 1981 crime survey victimisation rates indicated that Scotland experienced similar levels of crime to that in England and Wales, but that, through the 1980s up until the mid-1990s, Scottish victimisation rates were lower for most categories of crime. However, the 2000 SCS indicates that by 1999 the gap between Scotland and England and Wales had narrowed due to decreasing crime rates for housebreaking and personal crime in England and Wales combined with rising rates of victimisation in Scotland. Moreover, within Scotland, there are significant spatial and social inequalities in the risks of victimisation. According to the 2000 SCS, those living on the poorest council estates are three times more likely to be victims of housebreaking than those living in agricultural communities, while in terms of violent crime, young males between the ages of 16 and 24 are more than nine times likely to be a victim than young females.

These unequal risks are important because they affect perceptions of crime and disorder, feelings of safety and anxieties about becoming a victim. Indeed, despite falls in overall levels of crime, the 2000 SCS reveals that over 40% of people felt that there was more crime in their locality than two years ago and only 7% felt it had decreased. Moreover, in terms of perceptions of disorder, 40% of people thought that people who had been drinking or taking drugs and youths hanging around the streets were a very big or fairly big problem. As with the risk of victimisation, there are also important local variations in the perceptions of crime and disorder. Less than 1% of the respondents living in the most affluent communities thought that people being assaulted or attacked was 'very common' in their areas, compared with nearly 8% of respondents living in the poorest council estates. Only 3% of respondents living in affluent areas felt very unsafe walking alone in their local areas after dark, compared with 18% of those living in the poorest council estates. In terms of anxieties about becoming a victim, only 6% of residents of affluent areas were very worried about having their home broken into, compared with 16% in the poorest council estates.

Policing and crime control: 'sovereign state' and 'adaptive' strategies

Against this background, what have been the main responses to crime and disorder over the last 20 years? In trying to make sense of this terrain, several commentators (Brake and Hale 1992; Fyfe 1995; Garland 1996) have drawn attention to the 'two-pronged strategy' (Johnstone 2004: 80) developed during the 1980s and 1990s by successive Conservative governments and which continues today in similar form under the 'new' Labour administrations in London and Edinburgh.

One element of this strategy has its roots in neo-conservatism and stresses the importance of a strong state to fight crime and maintain law and order. This is what David Garland refers to as the 'sovereign state' strategy of crime control of intensive policing and expressive punishment (1996: 445–471). The other element of the UK's law-and-order strategy has its roots in neo-liberalism and involves the state withdrawing its claim to be 'the chief provider of security' and instead attempting to remodel crime control on a partnership basis via 'the formation of hybrid organizations that traverse the old public/private boundaries; the activation of preventive action on the part of communities, commercial firms and citizens; and the re-defining of the organizational mission of agencies such as the police' (1996: 445–471). This is what Garland refers to as the 'adaptive' strategy of crime control based on prevention and partnership.

These observations about crime control provide a useful framework within which to consider the changing location of policing within the landscape of crime control in Scotland. The next section considers the traditional state-centred approach to crime control and the key role the police play in this, but, as the following section shows, this approach now exists alongside a strong emphasis on partnership in the delivery of crime prevention involving the police working with a range of other agencies.

The public police and the 'sovereign state' strategy of crime control

For Garland (1996) one of the central features of the sovereign state strategy of crime control is the introduction of more intensive modes of policing. In part this is achieved by using legislative changes to expand and enhance the range of police powers to tackle crime and disorder. Recent examples include the Proceeds of Crime Act 2002, which provides new investigatory and cash-seizing powers for the police to recover the proceeds of criminal activity and allows a more proactive approach to white-collar crimes such as money laundering; and the Criminal Justice (Scotland) Act 2003, which allows a police constable to take DNA samples without authorisation from a senior officer and permits the retention of DNA and fingerprints given voluntarily (HMCICS 2003). In relation to disorder, the Antisocial Behaviour (Scotland) Act 2004 contains controversial new powers for the police in relation to the dispersal of groups. Part 3 of the Act states that, where a senior police officer has reasonable grounds for believing 'that any members of the public have been alarmed or distressed as a result of the presence or behaviour of groups of two or more persons in public places' and 'that antisocial behaviour is a significant persistent and serious problem' in that area, the officer can require those people to disperse and that those that do not live locally to leave the area and not return for up to 24 hours. If someone refuses to comply, they can be fined or imprisoned for a period of up to three months.

The Scottish Parliament's concern to target anti-social behaviour by giving the police greater powers of dispersal nicely illustrates Garland's contention that at certain times and with respect to certain offences and offenders, governments are keen to invoke the notion of the 'sovereign state'. But not all 'sovereign state' strategies require legislative changes. The introduction of more intensive, so-called zero-tolerance style policing (ZTP) into the Strathclyde Police force area in the mid-1990s in the form of Operation Spotlight involved a strategic change in police priorities that specifically targeted 'quality of life' offences.

Operation Spotlight drew inspiration from the policing approach developed by William Bratton, Commissioner of the New York City Police Department in the 1990s, who introduced a strategy of targeting drunkenness, public urination, begging, vandalism and other anti-social behaviour. The rationale behind focusing on these quality-of-life offences was that 'strong and authoritative use of coercive police powers' in relation to these offences would reduce fear and prevent more serious types of disorder and crime from occurring (Innes 1999: 398). This approach to policing had been given academic credibility by the 'broken windows' thesis advanced by Wilson and Kelling (1982). This thesis contends that merely the signs of dilapidation, such as broken windows, can initiate a downward spiral of neighbourhood decline by generating a sense of fear among residents that then leads to the breakdown of informal mechanisms of surveillance and control, resulting in rising and more serious forms of crime. In New York City ZTP had, its supporters claimed, led to significant falls in recorded crime (Bratton 1997). In Strathclyde in the mid-1990s, the Chief Constable, John Orr, enthusiastically embraced zero-tolerance thinking. Echoing the 'broken windows' thesis, Orr argued: 'I hold the firm belief that minor and serious crime are not poles apart. Indeed, I believe that minor crime is often simply the breeding ground and nursery that spawns and nurtures more serious and violent crime' (Orr 1997: 113). Orr was also particularly concerned at the evidence emerging from the Scottish Crime Surveys about high levels of fear among the public. He cited the 1996 Scottish Crime Survey, which indicated that 92% of the public were concerned about crime and 52% were 'worried that they or someone they lived with would be the victim of crime' and that 'violent crime and disorder were also on the increase and proving difficult to combat' (ibid.: 109).

Following consultation with the public, the Operation Spotlight initiative was launched by Strathclyde Police in 1996 using high-visibility police patrols to focus on a range of specific crimes, for instance, vandalism, litter, drinking in public, carrying weapons, underage drinking, street robberies and truancy, and locations, such as parks, the transport network, licensed premises and sporting events. According to police statistics, over the first three months of the initiative detections for those crimes targeted by Operation Spotlight rose by 30%, while car crime fell by 22%, housebreaking by 13% and serious crime by nearly 10% (Orr 1997: 119). However, for Strathclyde's chief constable, it was reductions in the fear of crime which were the real test of this police initiative. 'If people now feel more confident in walking their dog at night, using the park, or travelling on public transport…then this is…the true evaluation of Spotlight' (Orr 1997: 122).

Critics of Operation Spotlight, however, have argued that it contained 'contradictory elements with particular problems emphasised one day only to be ignored the next' (Atkinson 2003: 18). More generally, it has been claimed that Strathclyde Police's approach to policing in the mid-1990s was one element of a 'revanchist' or vengeful approach to urban policy in Glasgow (Atkinson 2003; Macleod 2002) in which attempts to improve the economic fortunes of the city involved the targeting of vulnerable groups like the homeless and prostitutes, who were viewed as detracting from attempts to revitalise the city centre. In this respect, the policing of the homeless in Glasgow, it is claimed, stood in stark contrast with the approach taken in Edinburgh, where the local 'civic culture' encouraged a more compassionate approach to the policing of begging (Fitzpatrick and Kennedy 2000). There is a danger, however, that such contrasts can be overstated and, in the case of Glasgow, policing has moved from the zero-tolerance approach of the mid-1990s with the formation of Street Liaison Teams which aim to cultivate improved relations with street people and prostitutes rather than criminalising them (Macleod 2002).

The 'adaptive' strategy of crime control: pursuing policies of prevention and partnership

While 'sovereign state' approaches to crime control in Scotland are important, it is the 'adaptive strategy' of prevention and partnership which has come to particular prominence in the crime-reduction policy landscape over the last 20 years. The roots of this shift in emphasis can be traced back to the Conservative governments of the 1980s and 1990s which strongly promoted crime-prevention strategies focused on the responsibilities of civil society as much as the state. As a review of crime prevention in Scotland in the 1980s highlights, there was the development of a crime-control model premised on the view that all citizens, and not just the police, are responsible for fighting crime and for ensuring that individuals do not become victims of crime (Monaghan 1997).

In understanding this changing landscape, however, it is crucial to recognise the key role that central government in the form of the Scottish Office (and now the Scottish Executive) has played in encouraging the diffusion of responsibility for crime control beyond the police to individuals and communities. One early initiative that exemplifies this adaptive approach was the Safer Cities programme initiated by the Scottish Office in 1989 (Cairnie 1999). Four five-year funded projects were established: one in central Edinburgh, two on peripheral public housing schemes in Glasgow (Castlemilk and Greater Easterhouse), and one covering public housing schemes on the northeast fringes of Dundee. In 1992 a fifth project in Aberdeen was established. In most of the projects the main concern was crime prevention and particularly housebreaking, which was a serious problem for the residents of the local authority housing schemes who lived within the project areas. In Edinburgh, however, where the project covered the city centre, the focus was more on late-night alcohol-related violence and disorder, fear of crime and women's safety, and young people and crime. In each of the project areas, however, the emphasis was very much on prevention and partnership. Prevention was understood in both physical terms, particularly in relation to the provision of 'target-hardening' measures to reduce the risks of housebreaking, and social terms by working with schools and youth clubs to promote various initiatives to encourage children to participate in positive activities. Partnership meant involving a range of public, private and voluntary agencies in tackling issues relating to crime and the fear of crime. In Edinburgh, for example, the Committee of the Safer Edinburgh Project argued for more high-visibility police patrols at particular times and locations in order to curb late-night disorder, lobbied the city's Licensing Board to co-ordinate the closing of public houses in the central city, and put pressure on the local council to improve street lighting and public transport.

The impact of Scotland's Safer Cities projects on crime prevention is difficult to measure precisely 'since it is impossible to know what would have occurred had the Safer Cities Projects not existed' (Cairnie 1999: 89). At the very least, however, this initiative acted as a catalyst for other inter-agency activity to tackle local problems of crime and disorder. A recent and important example of this has been the introduction of public space closed-circuit television (CCTV) surveillance systems into Scotland's towns and cities. Like the Safer Cities programme, the development of public space CCTV systems has been driven by the twin concerns of prevention – the hope is that CCTV will be a 'magic bullet' by deterring potential offenders (Ditton *et al*. 1999: 57) – and partnership – the development, funding and operation of CCTV systems requires close co-operation between central government, local authorities, the police and local business communities (see Fyfe and Bannister 1996).

Scotland's first town-centre CCTV system was established in Airdrie in 1992, comprising fourteen cameras covering the main streets and car parks. By the beginning of 1996 there were a further eighteen schemes, ranging from quite small-scale systems, such as that in Glenrothes with just two cameras, to more extensive and intensive surveillance systems, like that in Stirling with 49 cameras, Falkirk with 33 and Glasgow with 32. Later in 1996 the Scottish Office introduced a CCTV challenge competition to contribute nearly £2 million of public money towards some of the capital costs of establishing public space CCTV surveillance systems, which led to a further eighteen schemes being approved. A similar amount was allocated in a second round of this competition in 1997–98, when 30 more schemes received funding. In all, between 1996 and 2002, the Scottish Executive awarded £10.3 million to 161 CCTV projects across Scotland, resulting in the installation of over 2,000 cameras (Scottish Executive 2002). The system launched in Fife in 2002 claims to be the largest in Europe. Costing £1.2 million, of which £250,000 was provided by the Scottish Executive, it covers eight towns in the region using 78 cameras, all of which are viewed from a single location in Fife Police headquarters in the town of Glenrothes.

Despite strong government support for CCTV surveillance, the research evidence in Scotland concerning its impact on crime is equivocal at best. In Airdrie the results were encouraging (Short and Ditton 1996). The police 'cleared up' 16% more crimes and offences in the CCTV area in the two years following the installation of cameras compared with the two years before installation and there was a 21% fall in the total number of recorded crimes and offences in the CCTV area in these time periods. The greatest reductions were in crimes of dishonesty, such as housebreaking, theft of and from motor vehicles and shoplifting, which fell by almost half in the study period. Concerns that such crimes might simply be displaced to areas not covered by CCTV in Airdrie appeared to be unfounded. According to the researchers, 'the crimes prevented in the CCTV area did not, as far as can be ascertained, re-emerge in adjacent or nearby areas' (Short and Ditton 1996: 1). In Glasgow, however, the evidence for crime reduction was less encouraging. Although in the year following the installation of CCTV cameras, the area covered by CCTV recorded just over 3,000 fewer crimes and offences than was the case for the average of the two years prior to installation (Ditton *et al*. 1999: 29–30), once these figures are adjusted for underlying trends, crimes and offences rose to 109% of previously recorded totals and there was also a slight fall in detections (from 64% cleared up to 60% cleared up). When overall levels of crime are disaggregated by types of crime, the pattern becomes more complex. Recorded crimes of violence, fire-raising and vandalism fell, but recorded crimes of indecency, dishonesty and 'other crimes' (which includes drug-related offences) increased. The report's authors therefore conclude that 'open-street CCTV has been a qualified success', but they go on to argue that it is foolish to view CCTV as some 'magic bullet' of crime prevention. Indeed, as the evaluations of Airdrie and Glasgow indicate, CCTV works in different ways in different situations:

> CCTV has had an impact very different in Glasgow than in Airdrie. In both, some occasional yet noteworthy success was obtained in capturing emerging incidents on camera. In Airdrie recorded crime declined as a whole, and no displacement effect could be discovered. In Glasgow, on the other hand, recorded crime as a whole rose slightly ... and thus no search for displacement could be undertaken. However, the use of the tape archive has been of great use in retrospectively investigating major crimes in Glasgow; but there has been little scope for this in Airdrie.
>
> (Ditton *et al.* 1999: 61)

While the Safer Cities programme and the diffusion of public space CCTV surveillance systems provide specific examples of what Garland calls 'adaptive strategies', the underlying political commitment to a more general diffusion of responsibility for crime prevention in Scotland has gathered momentum with the establishment of a Scottish Parliament and a 'new' Labour government in Scotland. In particular, the introduction of community planning under the Local Government in Scotland Act 2003 means there is now a statutory obligation on local authorities to ensure that communities are engaged in decisions made about public services, such as the police, and that public, private and voluntary-sector organisations work together. One of the clearest examples of the impact of community planning in relation to the work of the police is the development of community safety partnerships across Scotland. Such partnerships take different forms in different places. In Aberdeen, for example, there is one regional-level organisation, Aberdeenshire Community Safety Partnership, which includes the local authority, the police, the fire brigade, the coastguard and the health board, and seven local community safety groups who pursue their own initiatives to tackle issues like housebreaking and road safety. In Fife, there is also one regional group but rather than local organisations there are five 'task groups' which focus on specific issues: road safety, CCTV, youth justice, the safety of black and minority ethnic communities, and fire.

Tackling crime and disorder: the role of 'policing beyond the police'

The notion of adaptive strategies of crime control, based on prevention and partnership, also intersects with a broader set of issues that have emerged in recent years concerning 'a restructuring and proliferation of "policing beyond the police", as a result of which a more complex division of labour in the field of policing and security has emerged. A pluralized, fragmented and differentiated patchwork has replaced the idea of the police as the monopolistic guardians of public order' (Crawford 2003: 136). There are different forms of 'plural policing' but those which have emerged as particularly important in Scotland over the last 20 years include civilian policing (based around so-called 'active citizens'), municipal policing (involving local authorities acting in partnership with the public police and other agencies) and commercial policing (centred on the rise of the private security industry).

Active citizenry: Neighbourhood Watch and the Special Constabulary

Although there is a long tradition in Britain of 'policing by the public' (Shapland and Vagg 1988), it was really only in the 1980s and 1990s that the notion of civilian policing began to gain a higher profile in law-and-order policy debates as successive Conservative governments strongly promoted the idea of the active citizen and strategies of responsibilisation in relation to the provision of local services (Crawford 2003: 147). According to one Conservative Home Office minister, 'at the very centre of our ideas on how to control crime should be the energy and initiative of the active citizen' (Patten, 1998: v–vi), while the then Prime Minister, Margaret Thatcher, declared: 'Combating crime is everybody's business. It cannot be left solely to the police anymore than we can leave our health solely to doctors' (quoted in Brake and Hale 1992: 10). Under 'new' Labour the notion of the active citizen has been reworked in the form of the Active Communities Initiative, which promotes voluntary action and volunteering as a means of empowering communities to take responsibility for their social welfare (Scottish Executive 2000).

In the context of policing, the notion of active citizens and active communities helping address problems of crime and disorder is well established and exemplified by Neighbourhood Watch schemes and the Special Constabulary. Introduced into Scotland in 1986, Neighbourhood Watch grew rapidly in all force areas over the following ten years. In Strathclyde, for example, the number of schemes increased from just over 100 in 1987 to over 1,600 by 1995–96. Since then, however, the numbers of Neighbourhood Watch schemes in Strathclyde have fallen back slightly to 1,275 in 2001–02. This pattern appears repeated in several other forces.

The data presented in Tables 6.1 and 6.2 for the five years between 1997–98 and 2001–02 indicates that in five out of the eight forces the total number of schemes fell over this period and that in terms of the numbers of households in schemes, six forces reported falls over this period. There are incomplete data for the remaining two forces.

These temporal trends are important, perhaps suggesting that public enthusiasm for this type of civilian policing is diminishing as recognition

Table 6.1 Number of Neighbourhood Watch schemes by police force area

	1997–98	1998–99	1999–2000	2000–01	2001–02
Central	334	339	310	235	248
Dumfries and Galloway	484	461	422	424	350
Fife	194	197	203	121	201
Grampian	633	657	673	737	821
Lothian and Borders	906	826	827	848	887
Northern	28	27	25	23	23
Strathclyde	1,350	1,434	1,088	1,098	1,275
Tayside	604	625	622	602	619
Scotland	4,533	4,566	4,170	4,088	4,424

Source: HM Inspectorate of Constabulary for Scotland.

Table 6.2 Number of households in Neighbourhood Watch schemes by police force area

	1997–98	1998–99	1999–2000	2000–01	2001–02
Central	16,203	16,300	15,000	10,976	9,200
Dumfries and Galloway	17,900	17,990	No data	15,000	No data
Fife	67,000	67,00	67,000	54,000	74,000
Grampian	No data	No data	21,938	23,681	25,599
Lothian and Borders	55,677	47,208	50,568	49,900	54,025
Northern	1,146	1,090	897	2,730	452
Strathclyde	54,000	57,360	43,520	43,920	51,000
Tayside	24,363	24,580	24,282	22,409	23,897
Scotland	236,289	231,528	223,205	222,616	238,173

Source: HM Inspectorate of Constabulary for Scotland.

grows that Neighbourhood Watch has little impact on reducing levels of victimisation, a fact highlighted by government-funded research over a decade ago (see Bennett 1992). The fact that politicians have continued to promote Neighbourhood Watch as an important component in the fight against crime despite the lack of evidence as to its effectiveness suggests that it is the symbolism of such schemes in terms of emphasising the role and responsibilities of individuals and communities in tackling crime which has been of most political importance. As Garland observes, the importance of Neighbourhood Watch schemes 'as examples of the government's project of devolved crime control is demonstrated by the fact that political commitment to these schemes far outruns their level of success in preventing crime' (1996: 453).

A second form of active citizenship within the criminal justice system is membership of the Special Constabulary. Special constables are unpaid, part-time volunteers who on duty assume the powers of regular police officers and can therefore supplement frontline officers on routine patrols and at special events where there might be potential for public disorder. As a recent Inspectorate of Constabulary report observed, 'special constables represent the embodiment of active community participation and engagement. Citizens prepared to give a regular number of hours each month represent a true partnership of the police and the community working together to reduce local crime and anti-social behaviour' (HMICS 2004: 54). Significantly, despite a strong political commitment to this form of active citizenship at a UK and Scottish level, the numbers of special constables has been in steady decline since the late 1990s. Indeed, viewed in the longer term, the decline has been little short of catastrophic. In 1962 there were 7,312 special constables in Scotland; by 2003 there were just 991, a decline of over 86% in 40 years. There are also significant geographical variations in the numbers of 'specials'. The Strathclyde Police force area contains 44% of the Scottish population, but only has 24% of Scotland's specials, while Northern Constabulary, which covers only 6% of Scotland's population, has 20% of the country's specials (HMICS 2004).

In his 2002–03 Report, Her Majesty's Chief Inspector of Constabulary for Scotland expressed concern at the continuing decline in the numbers of Special Constables and sensed that this was not a priority area for many forces or the Scottish Police Service as a whole: 'Disappointingly, we found that in recent years there has been little corporacy attached to ... issues [of recruitment, retention and training of special constables] at either a national or local level' (2003: 45). There is now a commitment from ACPOS to make it a priority to increase the numbers of specials by 500 in 2006 and to ensure that this 'effective resource is properly valued, developed and deployed' (HMCICS 2004: 55). Indeed, in one of its strongest statements on the Special Constabulary, HMCICS 'strongly advises that ... the effective and efficient use of an active, well trained and properly motivated Special Constabulary remains a priority for all forces' (ibid.: 55)

It is clear that the problem is not just one of recruitment, but also of retention. A focus group held with specials as part of the 2003–04 inspection identified a range of areas of frustration, including: a lack of basic and ongoing training, poor management by and communication with regular officers, and a lack of recognition of the skills specials have. There is also an issue of the value placed by regular officers on specials. As the Inspectorate report acknowledges, the former often regard the latter 'simply as providers of corroboration'.

Municipal policing: community wardens and anti-social behaviour teams

The emphasis on partnership working and the criminalisation of anti-social behaviour means that local authorities are now much more closely involved in policing functions, whether in their own capacity or jointly with the police (Crawford 2003: 145). In Scotland the main drivers of this are the Criminal Justice (Scotland) Act 2003 and the consultation paper *Building Strong, Safe and Attractive Communities: a Consultation Document on Wardens and other Community Based Initiatives to Tackle Anti-Social Behaviour* (Scottish Executive, 2003).

The Criminal Justice (Scotland) Act 2003 places a new duty on police and local authorities to prepare and publish jointly an anti-social behaviour strategy. The Act requires that the strategy must set out how the local authority and the police are to co-ordinate their functions that relate to anti-social behaviour and the exchange of information between the authority and the police.

In *Building Strong, Safe and Attractive Communities* the Executive spells out other activities which it wishes to promote as part of a three-year, £30 million programme to tackle anti-social behaviour. One key area for development which has been allocated £20 million is the extension of community warden schemes across Scotland. Community wardens are defined as 'a uniformed, semi-official presence in a residential area with the aim of improving quality of life' (ibid.). Such residential areas are not confined to public housing, but can include housing association, privately rented and owner-occupied housing. The choice of the term 'community warden' is interesting in that it aims to distinguish what is happening in Scotland from what is happening in England, where there are both 'neighbourhood' wardens, focusing on crime prevention and anti-social behaviour, and 'street' wardens, focusing on environmental issues. As the Executive explains, 'In Scotland we are offering to support each of these roles and felt it would be helpful to use a different term.' The hope is that warden schemes will contribute to a reduction in crime, the fear of crime and anti-social behaviour.

Not all warden schemes will focus on crime. Some may be focused more on environmental issues; others might take the form of concierge or caretaker roles attached to housing developments. Where crime prevention is the focus of activities, the Scottish Executive envisages that this will involve wardens patrolling an area, but this needs to be done in consultation with the police 'to ensure a properly joined-up approach to policing and patrolling at a local level'. The consultation paper goes on: 'The role of wardens is to complement the work of the police, not to be a substitute for it. Wardens will not be given police powers to fulfil their functions and should not be trained in areas such as restraint techniques.' The Scottish Executive is also concerned about the legitimacy of crime-prevention warden schemes and 'would therefore expect these schemes to be run by and for wardens to be employed by either the local authority or the police. We will not provide support for private security firms or self-appointed "community" patrols to employ wardens and manage these types of schemes.'

Examples of pilot community warden schemes include that established by Renfrewshire Council, which has four teams working on estates in Paisley and West Johnstone. These were established in response to local concerns about anti-social behaviour and vandalism, and part of their role is to support the police, by observing and reporting incidents, providing information to support police investigations and acting as professional witnesses. However, they also play an environmental role, co-ordinating graffiti removal, and act as a link between the community and other agencies. In terms of the local impact of these wardens the first annual report on this scheme provides encouraging results. In the four pilot areas, vandalism costs in relation to housing stock fell by 43% in the year after the introduction of wardens (2002/03) compared with the preceding year and the costs in relation to school premises fell by 53% over the same period (Her Majesty's Inspectorate of Constabulary for Scotland 2004: 43). In another community warden scheme in Aberdeen, traffic wardens employed by Grampian Police are providing support to street policing, their presence on the streets in a uniform similar to the police providing a visible deterrent. In addition, Aberdeen City Council has handed control of its council wardens to Grampian Police. Although these wardens are funded by the local authority, they are effectively employed by the police, who will train, equip and deploy them according to local policing priorities. It is important to recognise, however, that community warden schemes are not without their critics. The Scottish Police Federation in particular has argued that 'community wardens are a cheap alternative to reassure the public' which while providing some short-term benefits do little to address the long-term problem of needing more police officers (*Evening Times* 2004).

In addition to community warden schemes, the Scottish Executive is also encouraging the development of dedicated anti-social behaviour teams to play a role in the identification of anti-social behaviour 'hot spots', the enforcement of anti-social behaviour orders and the intensive supervision of anti-social families. Such teams might include community wardens but also involve local housing managers, the police, social work staff and local authority legal services teams (Scottish Executive 2003).

The private security industry

For many who use Scotland's cities, the presence of private security is a routine and unremarkable part of the urban experience. Uniformed private security guards patrol shopping malls and hospitals; video-surveillance systems operated by private security firms observe people in shops and banks, on buses and trains, and at football matches and in bowling alleys. Part of the growth of the private security industry in Scotland as elsewhere undoubtedly reflects a favourable neo-liberal political climate created by successive Conservative governments in the 1980s and 1990s and which still continues to some extent under the 'new' Labour administrations. However, there are two broader structural conditions affecting late capitalist societies which have also encouraged the growth of the private security industry.

First, there is the impact of workload and fiscal pressures on the ability of the public police to meet the security needs of corporate capitalism. Over 25 years ago Spitzer and Scull (1977) drew attention to the way the growth of private policing reflected an increasing division between order maintenance (the concern of the public police) and profit protection (the focus of an expanding private security industry). In particular, they argued that growing workload pressures on the public police combined with increasing fiscal pressures helped create a perception of a 'security vacuum' in which the public police appeared to be losing the fight against crime. According to Spitzer and Scull, the growth of private policing was seen as a direct consequence of the inability of the public sector to provide sufficient resources to meet growing demands.

A second and related set of developments concerns the post-war expansion of mass private property, such as shopping malls, business parks, industrial complexes and university campuses. According to Shearing and Stenning (1987), the policing needs of these publicly accessible, but privately owned and managed spaces have not been met by the public police for two main reasons. First, the routine patrols of the public police are largely confined to publicly owned spaces given that officers only have limited legal powers to gain access to private property. Second, those who own and manage mass private property have wanted to maintain control over the policing of it. It is also important to recognise that private policing is guided by very different objectives to the public police. Much of it is focused on 'policing for profit' (South 1988) so that measures of success are not the apprehension of offenders or the detection of crime, but the ability to prevent financial losses.

Against this background, there is broad agreement that private security has become bigger in the UK over the last 20 to 30 years, although ambiguities surrounding the definition of private security mean there is less agreement as to precisely how big it is. One way of gauging its size is by using business entries to the Yellow Pages (see Jones and Newburn 1995). Of course, the number of entries will vary according to how broadly the private security sector is defined. It could include 'burglar alarms and security systems', 'car alarms and security', 'closed-circuit television (installers and manufacturers)', 'credit investigation services', and 'security services and equipment'. The last of these is the single largest sector and entries under this heading have been used to illustrate the expansion of private security services in Glasgow, which have grown from less than ten to over 80 in number from the mid-1960s to the late 1990s (Fyfe and Bannister 1999: 348). If this pattern of development has been repeated in other areas of Scotland it suggests there has been something of a 'quiet revolution' (Shearing and Stenning 1987) involving a massive expansion of private security activity and which may mean that, in some places, numbers of private police personnel may rival their counterparts in the public police.

This expansion of the private security industry has been viewed with some criticism and concern, however, not least by the public police themselves. There is evidence of poor standards, especially in guarding services, with very limited training and little or no professional development. Some police critics are particularly vocal about the opportunities for fraudulent practice and criminality which are provided (*Scotland on Sunday* 2004). Above all, there is still no regulatory framework for the private security industry in Scotland, although one is promised.

Conclusion

Despite strong evidence that overall levels of crime are currently declining, crime and disorder remain significant concerns for many people living in Scotland and continue to occupy a prominent position on the country's political agenda. As this chapter has shown, however, approaches to 'policing' these problems have developed in important ways over the last 20 years. So-called 'sovereign-state' strategies focused on the key role of the public police in fighting crime continue to be important, but now exist alongside 'adaptive' strategies based around ideas of prevention and partnership and a proliferation of other forms of policing involving, *inter alia*, active citizens, local authorities, voluntary organisations and the private sector. In Scotland as elsewhere in the UK then, 'the current policing terrain is complex and ambiguous' (Crawford 2003: 161) and any analysis of crime control needs to engage with this 'diverse totality' of policing (Johnston 1996: 54). Nowhere is this clearer than in relation to the Scottish Executive's current concern with anti-social and disorderly behaviour. Having accepted the 'broken windows' thesis that there is a direct link between anti-social activities and criminality, the 'new' Labour government in Scotland (like its counterpart in Westminster) has mounted a concerted effort to deal with the perpetrators of anti-social behaviour, partly by giving the public police more powers under the Anti-Social Behaviour (Scotland) Act 2004, but also by encouraging partnerships between police and local authorities and by developing 'policing beyond the police' in the form of support for community wardens and active citizens.

Against this background, it is interesting to consider how the public police has changed its own view of its role in tackling crime and disorder in Scotland. Over ten years ago, the 1993 Report of HM Chief Inspector of Constabulary for Scotland confidently declared that 'it is undoubtedly true to say that the [8%] reduction in crime is...tangible proof of the level of police effort over the past year. Crime pattern analysis, criminal intelligence and the pro-active targeting of persistent offenders...are now bearing fruit' (HMCICS 1994: 8). In the 2002–03 Report, however, HMCICS offers a much more cautious assessment both of trends in crime and of the ability to link falling crime levels just to police activities in some simple 'cause and effect' relationship. The Report notes that recorded crime figures 'can be misleading' and 'do not always reflect the real level of crime' and that changes in technology, legislation and demographic characteristics all impact on crime trends.

With the advent of community planning, the 2002–03 Report also emphasises that 'the strengthening of co-terminus links across services... has great potential for impacting upon crime and disorder' (HMCICS 2003: ix) and a year later in the thematic report, *Local Connections: Policing with the Community*, the Inspectorate talks of building a 'new model of policing' (2004: 2) based around active citizens and the role of the police in a 'civic renewal agenda' that includes community safety and community planning initiatives. Ironically, perhaps, this model takes us back to the case of Greenock in the 1950s with which this chapter began. There the fall in housebreaking was viewed in terms of a range of developments that involved the police, local authorities and the community working together to tackle rising crime. More than 50 years on it will be interesting to see whether this 'new' vision can deliver the kind of reductions in crime and disorder that it is claimed the citizens of Greenock enjoyed in the 1950s.

References

Anderson, S. (1999) 'Crime statistics and the "problem of crime" in Scotland', in P. Duff and N. Hutton (eds), *Criminal Justice in Scotland*. London: Ashgate, pp. 38–55.

Atkinson, R. (2003) 'Domestication by cappuccino or a revenge on urban space? Control and empowerment in the management of urban spaces', *Urban Studies*, 40: 18–43.

Bennett, T. (1992) 'Themes and Variations in Neighbourhood Watch', in D. Evans, N. Fyfe and D. Herbert (eds), *Crime, Policing and Place: Essays in Environmental Criminology*. London: Routledge, pp. 272–285.

Brake, M. and Hale, C. (1992) *Public Order and Private Lives: The Politics of Law and Order*. London: Routledge.

Bratton, W. (1997) 'Crime is down in New York City: blame the police', in N. Dennis (ed.), *Zero Tolerance: Policing a Free Society*. London: IEA, pp. 29–42.

Cairnie, J. (1999) 'The politics of crime prevention: the Safer Cities experiment in Scotland', in P. Duff and N. Hutton (eds), *Criminal Justice in Scotland*. London: Ashgate, pp. 74–93.

Crawford, A. (2003) 'The pattern of policing in the UK: policing beyond the police', in T. Newburn (ed.), *Handbook of Policing*. Devon: Willan Publishing, pp. 136–168.

Ditton, J. Short, E., Phillips, S., Norris, C. and Armstrong, G. (1999) *The Effect of Closed Circuit Television on Recorded Crime Rates and Public Concern about Crime in Glasgow*. Edinburgh: Scottish Office.

Evening Times (2004) 'Wardens will walk city streets in bid to beat anti-social behaviour' (accessed via www.eveningtimes.co.uk/print/news).

Fitzpatrick, S. and Kennedy, C. (2000) *Getting By: Begging, Rough Sleeping and the Big Issue in Glasgow and Edinburgh*. Bristol: Policy Press.

Fyfe, N. (1995) 'Law and order policy and the spaces of citizenship in contemporary Britain', *Political Geography*, 14: 177–189.

Fyfe, N. and Bannister, J. (1996) 'City watching: closed circuit television surveillance in public spaces', *Area*, 28: 37–46.

Fyfe, N. and Bannister J. (1999) 'Privatisation, policing and crime control: tracing the contours of the public-private divide', in P. Duff and N. Hutton (eds), *Criminal Justice in Scotland*. London: Ashgate, pp. 335–354.

Garland, D. (1996) 'The limits of the sovereign state: strategies of crime control in contemporary societies', *British Journal of Criminology*, 36: 445–471.

HM Chief Inspector of Constabulary for Scotland (1994) *Report for the Year ended 31 December 1993*. Edinburgh: HMSO.

HM Chief Inspector of Constabulary for Scotland (2003) *Annual Report 2002–03*. Edinburgh: The Stationery Office.

HM Inspectorate of Constabulary for Scotland (2004) *Local Connections: Policing with the Community*. Edinburgh: The Stationery Office.

Innes, M. (1999) 'An iron fist in an iron glove?" The zero-tolerance policing debate', *The Howard Journal*, 38: 397–410.

Johnston, L. (1996) 'Policing Diversity', in F. Leishman *et al.* (eds), *Core Issues in Policing*. Harlow: Longman, pp. 54–70.

Johnstone, C. (2004) 'Crime, disorder and the urban renaissance', in C. Johnstone and M. Whitehead (eds), *New Horizons in British Urban Policy: Perspectives on New Labour's Urban Renaissance*. London: Ashgate, pp. 75–94.

Jones, T. and Newburn, T. (1995) 'How big is the private security sector?', *Policing and Society*, 5: 221–232.

MVA (2002) *The 2000 Scottish Crime Survey Overview Report*. Edinburgh: Scottish Executive.

Macleod, G. (2002) 'From urban entrepreneurialism to a revanchist city? On the spatial injustices of Glasgow's renaissance', *Antipode*, 34: 602–624.

Monaghan, B. (1997) 'Crime prevention in Scotland', *International Journal of the Sociology of Law*, 25: 21–44.

Orr, J. (1997) 'Strathclyde's Spotlight Initiative', in N. Dennis (ed.), *Zero Tolerance: Policing a Free Society*. London: IEA, pp. 104–123.

Patten, J. (1998) 'Foreword' in T. Hope and M. Shaw (eds), *Communities and Crime Reduction*. London: HMSO, pp. v–vi.

Scotland on Sunday (2004) 'Security firms' ties to crime revealed by police', 24 October (accessed via www.scotlandonsunday.scotsman.com).

Scottish Executive (2000) *The Active Communities Initiative*. Edinburgh: Scottish Executive.

Scottish Executive (2002) 'New CCTV system launched in Fife' (accessed via www. scotland.gov.uk/pages/news).

Scottish Executive (2003) *Building Strong, Safe and Attractive Communities: a consultation document on other community based initiatives to tackle anti-social behaviour*. Edinburgh: Scottish Executive.

Scottish Executive (2004) *Recorded Crime in Scotland 2003*. Edinburgh: Scottish Executive Statistical Bulletin.

Shapland, J. and Vagg, J. (1988) *Policing by the Public*. London: Routledge.

Shearing, C. D. and Stenning, P. C. (1987) (eds) *Private Policing*. Thousand Oaks CA: Sage.

Shields, J. V. M. and Duncan J. A. (1964) *The State of Crime in Scotland*. London: Tavistock Publications.

Short, E. and Ditton, J. (1996) *Does Closed Circuit Television Prevent Crime? An Evaluation of the use of CCTV Surveillance Cameras in Airdrie*. Edinburgh: Scottish Office.

Smith, D. and Young, P. (1999) 'Crime trends in Scotland since 1950', in P. Duff and N. Hutton (eds), *Criminal Justice in Scotland*. London: Ashgate, pp. 14–37.

South, N. (1988) *Policing for Profit*. London: Sage.

Spitzer, S. and Scull A. (1977) 'Privatization and capitalist development: the case of the private police', *Social Problems*, 25: 18–29.

Wilson, J. Q. and Kelling, G. L. (1982) 'Broken windows', *Atlantic Monthly*, March: 29–38.

Chapter 7

Policing the Scottish community

Daniel Donnelly

Introduction

Police workloads have spiralled over the past 50 years, causing one police commentator to remark that 'there are twice as many police officers as there were in 1952, but they deal with ten times as many crimes' (Judge 2002: 29). If members of the public in Scotland were asked how they would invest in the police organisation in order to improve the service given, most would give the immediate and expected response of 'more bobbies on the beat'. It is highly improbable that the respondents would suggest spending money on expanding civilian support, or investment in technology or more research and development. Local and national politicians and police associations regularly express the opinion that the solution to rising crime and disorder problems lies with additional police resources. The Scottish community is no different. This chapter seeks to explain how the police in Scotland go about policing the Scottish community within the framework of community policing and how this form of policing is under continual pressure to survive in the modern day. It aims to demonstrate that the situation is more complex than merely putting extra 'bobbies on the beat' (Audit Commission 1996; Loveday 1998: 161–162). Comment is also made about new developments, such as the increasing importance of community partnerships in policing Scotland in the 21st century.

Community policing defined

The work of the police officer in the community is dependent on the economic and social environment and on the make-up of communities themselves. Whether in a rural or urban setting, a deteriorating sense of community associated with a breakdown in neighbourhood spirit and kinship, inadequate social support systems and networks, rising crime and public disorder, and a growing sense of individualism within society can hamper the successful implementation of policing in the community. As far back as the 1970s this was recognised by the then Secretary of State for Scotland, who, after advice from the Police Advisory Board for Scotland, issued a circular offering financial support to forces to encourage the establishment of 'community involvement departments' (SHHD Circular 6/1971). Such funding was to have a positive effect on the future development of community policing in Scotland.

Various community police initiatives existed in Scotland at the time. One in particular had been running from the mid-1950s, in Greenock (Schaffer 1980: 69–71). The Chief Constable, David Gray, appointed constables to each area with the remit of working closely with the local authority services and community groups, with a particular focus on juvenile crime. Gray believed joint partnerships with all interested agencies would improve the quality of life and the environment and eventually reduce crime. Gray's model could be judged to be the forerunner of modern community policing (Donnelly 2003: 25).

Scottish local authorities, particularly in the west of Scotland, had a long history of sharing Gray's views and had invested more in community involvement work and local participation than most other public authorities in the UK. In the 1970s there was an understanding of the need to strengthen local democracy, especially for underprivileged community members, and a system of community work, networking and outreach was seen as the way forward in order to give local communities more of a say in the running of local services (Barr 1996). By 1983 the concept of community policing had taken root across Scotland and an SHHD circular entitled 'The Community and the Police' was circulated, which underpinned the general philosophy of community policing and emphasised that 'it is part of the tradition of the Police Service in Scotland that the task of policing the community is undertaken in ways which have the consent of the community' (SHHD Circular 2/1983).

However, problems did exist, as a Scottish Office research paper entitled *Police Community Involvement in Scotland* revealed (Shanks 1980). It noted that the 'process' so far followed in Scotland seemed to have encouraged the belief that the development of relationships with the community was a matter for specialists, community involvement officers, rather than for general policing and that 'community involvement work is still seen by many officers as a soft option, as an activity inferior to "real" police work' (Shanks 1980: 25). In fact, in one force the branch was derogatively nicknamed the 'family planning department' (ibid.: 25). The research also noted a difference in attitude between rural officers and their counterparts in the cities, and put this down to community involvement being a normal part of the traditional police role in rural communities. On a more positive note, it was clear that the work of community involvement branches had become accepted into everyday policing and, from an individual officer's viewpoint, was a good place to work for career development purposes (ibid.: 26).

The prime duty of the police is the protection of life and property, the maintenance of order and prevention of crime. It is now well accepted that these goals cannot be achieved by the police alone, but require the assistance of the community, through community members accepting communal standards and values in partnership with the police and other public agencies. It follows that the police require the consent of the community in order to carry out their duties effectively. In addition, the police must understand the community's problems if they wish to be in a position to influence the community in the areas that prevent crime and maintain order. The idea that the police officer, through a regular presence on the beat, is working on behalf of the community, ever sensitive to its needs and concerns, is, in essence, 'community policing'. It is also 'a philosophy and an organisational strategy that allows the police and community residents to work closely together in new ways to solve the problems of crime, fear of crime, physical and social disorder and neighbourhood decay' (Trojanowicz and Bucqueroux 1990: xiii).

At the present time community policing plays a leading role in social partnerships, community planning and community safety initiatives, which are at the core of local and central politics. The difficulty lies in that the community police officer requires to achieve a balance between his/her role as a law enforcer accountable to the police organisation and, just as importantly, carrying out duties within the community to whom he/she is also accountable. In addition, community policing offers a variety of services to the public that do not fall within the ambit of enforcement and are of a non-criminal nature, leading the community to need the police and vice versa.

The above general description of the community police officer is sufficient for the purpose of this chapter, but community policing and, indeed, community itself, are open to numerous definitions by academics, practitioners and members of communities themselves (Willmott 1989: 11–14; Mawby 1990: 172; Mastrofski 1993: 65). It is not a clear concept because it does not merely involve a simple marginal change to policing;

it requires a major cultural shift in the way the police engage in their tasks. It involves a significant transformation in policing by placing the police officer at the centre of the community, even to the extent of being engaged at times in the community's inability to problem-solve and to manage its own relationships. Community policing is also the embodiment of the notion of customer, quality of service, adaptability, empathy, responsiveness, consensus and negotiation. The phrase 'community policing' has been accepted despite the fact that the component terms 'community' and 'policing' are open to many interpretations (Reiner 1995: 164). In Scotland, there is no 'ideal type' as Scottish police forces have adopted different styles, with different labels and designations being applied to community police officers; for example, community beat officer in Aberdeen and Edinburgh, community liaison officer in Tayside, community officer in Dumfries and Galloway and the Borders, to community police officers in the Strathclyde police area. However, all these officers have the same functions and job descriptions (HMCICS 2004a: 31).

Regardless of the difficulties with the definition, community policing represents a massive change in the way police officers think about their job and in the way the police organisation does its business. It is more than the iconic uniform beat officer patrolling the street. The community police officer is at the forefront of a new 'science of policing', where new skills and abilities pertaining to the specialist nature of the role are required, similar to other specialist posts such as a detective or traffic officer (Donnelly 2002a: 26–27). Indeed, a study of community policing in Strathclyde Police in 1996 revealed that 'senior police managers acknowledged that the calibre of officers selected to perform community policing duties had improved over the years, and a number explicitly stated that this reflected the recruitment policy within their own area of command' (Donnelly 2002b: 188). These local recruitment policies also address the perceptions identified in the Audit Commission's *Streetwise* report that 'patrol work can be complex and at times requires levels of expertise and interpersonal skills that can test the qualities of even the most experienced officers' (Audit Commission 1996: 42). It is clear that the status of the community police officer has risen over the years, despite the problems created by competing demands.

Future roles for the community police officer will include problem-solver, mediator, intelligence gatherer and community leader, and more importantly that of 'manager' in respect of working and liaising with restorative justice units, neighbourhood and anti-social behaviour teams and community wardens. Such a change will necessitate community police officers acquiring a new mindset for their expanding role (HMCICS 2004a: 33). However, in adopting a closer interface with the community the police are faced with the dilemma of how involved they should become in resolving community problems, especially those which may require local, or even national, political solutions. There is a great danger in overstepping the line of political neutrality which Scottish forces have traditionally taken.

Although community policing initiatives, projects and programmes vary from city to city and country to country, a review of the literature suggests there are a number of underlying assumptions common to the concept, that are generically widespread and pertinent to policing in Scotland (Donnelly 2002b: 30–65). Manning (1984: 205–227) listed a number of basic assumptions, which were added to and expanded upon by Riechers and Roberg (1990: 105–114) and others. These underlying assumptions provide a useful guide to a fuller understanding of community policing and are reproduced in Table 7.1.

Table 7.1 Community policing assumptions

1   The presence of the police through increased visibility reduces the public's fear of crime.

2   The public is of one mind, a homogeneous populace, whose satisfaction or dissatisfaction with the police can be readily measured.

3   The police should be responsible for helping to define and shape community norms.

4   Public fear stems more from disorder than from crime.

5   Signs of neglect and decay in neighbourhoods invite crime.

6   Community policing programmes are started at the initiative of the police with the aim of improving service, rather than to give influential citizens control over police services.

7   Community policing can be done without violating police political neutrality.

8   Police organisations, given their current mechanistic characteristics, can readily adapt to a more organic model required to effectively implement community policing.

9   Police organisations, given their current quality of personnel, can be responsive to the demands of community policing.

10   The police are the proper agency to attempt to fulfil the goals of community policing.

Sources: 1–3: Manning (1984: 205–227); 4: Kelling (1987: 90–102); 5: Wilson and Kelling (1982: 29–38); 6: Goldstein (1987: 6–30); 7: Short (1983); 8–10: Riechers and Roberg (1990: 105–114).

The community and community policing

In 1996 a survey was carried out in the Strathclyde Police area in order to identify how a cross-section of the community viewed community policing (Donnelly 2004). Out of 485 questionnaires circulated, 336 were completed and returned, giving a response rate of 69%, which was evenly spread throughout the Strathclyde area. The survey targeted a range of groups within communities, such as shop managers and staff (10), community councillors (34), residents' and tenants' associations (24), crime-prevention panels and Neighbourhood Watch (25), victim support (7), NHS workers (4), housing managers and staff (40), community workers (15), head teachers (15), teachers (48), local authority councillors (15), and members of the general public (73), including those in rural communities (26). The data provide a valuable insight into understanding community perceptions of community policing and the findings reflect two other studies carried out on behalf of the Scottish Police Service as a whole (HMCICS 2002, HMCICS 2004b).

Shop managers and staff

The group was generally very supportive of community policing and the need for the medium- to long-term continuity of officers in their posts. They also highlighted the difficulties caused by the regular abstraction of officers from their town/village areas.

Community councillors

Community police officers are an important constituent of community councils, and council members speak highly of the work carried out by them. However, members are critical of the quick turnover of officers and believe constant change weakens relationships and trust. Attendance of officers at community council meetings is crucial to community and police interaction, which is not helped by officers being taken from their posts to do duty elsewhere.

Residents' and tenants' associations

Members are of the opinion that not just any police officer can carry out the role of the community police officer; special qualities are required and the recruitment of the right calibre of officer is essential to good relationships. A major drawback to sound partnership working would appear to be the constant extraction of officers from their areas.

Crime-prevention panels and Neighbourhood Watch

Intriguingly, members showed concerns over officers working alone rather than in pairs. This may be due to the members' closer working knowledge of community policing and police practices. They also feel communities should have more involvement in choosing their community police officers and in deciding policing targets and objectives.

Victim support

Community policing provides a vital link between policing and the Victim Support Scotland organisation. Members appreciate the commitment shown by community police officers and believe the established liaison developed over the years is essential to continuing success.

NHS workers

Again, the focus is on the personality of individual officers being at the core of their success and hospital staff being grateful for the regular attendance of community police officers within hospital premises.

Housing managers and staff

Members believe the key to successful community policing is long-term relationships, trust and flexible partnership working. Housing and police liaison are viewed as an essential part of crime prevention and community safety, and a significant feature of each partner's everyday work. The joint arrangements improve communication between the public, housing and policing, which in turn enables local problem-solving to take place smoothly and amicably. Developing this joint relationship and seeking ways of improving the overall service to the public is seen as a positive step. Similar to good school liaison, the housing and police partnership is an important alliance within local community safety strategies.

Community workers

Members see partnership working with the community police as the way forward if resources permit. Improvements in the present system can also be made, by guaranteeing the continuity of officers in post. Respondents are very praiseworthy of the skills and commitment of community police officers and their genuine interest in the community. But community policing needs a higher profile, with a marketing strategy that makes certain the role receives wider publicity for the valuable work performed in the community. Recruitment is also crucial, as choosing the correct individual for the job is central to good community relationships. Due to the nature of their role, community workers regularly interface with community police officers. As a result they have a unique perspective on community policing and a better understanding of the problems officers experience, than most other community members.

Head teachers

Common cause of concern is community police officers being taken from their area on a routine basis. Head teachers view an individual officer's personality as crucial to successful community policing. They see officers providing an invaluable service to the school, pupils, parents and the wider community. A community police officer's ability to problem-solve in the confines of the school is singled out, particularly, with sensitive issues. Involvement in school projects and assisting with parents' problems is also highlighted as a key feature of community policing. It is a two-way process: positive relationships lead to both parties learning from each other. To foster good relationships officers should remain in post for longer periods.

Teachers

Teachers believe good police liaison is all about relationships and police/pupil contact is priceless. Such contact also develops a proactive role for the community police officer. Such school liaison has a knock-on effect, with officers gaining community information and local knowledge of their area of responsibility. Other police officers have different attitudes and teachers prefer to deal with their own community police. Community police officers' involvement with 'parent workshops' is seen to be productive and a positive move forward.

Local authority councillors

Elected members showed concern over the need for higher visibility and increased presence of community police officers. Additional finance is necessary to make sure community policing becomes an integral part of the community planning process. However, a word of caution is given that closer police involvement with issues such as 'anti-social behaviour' and 'matrimonial problems' could place community policing in a position where they are perceived to be taking sides within the community. Councillors have experienced a noticeable reduction in minor complaints from their constituents with the advent of community policing. They believe their constituents' first 'port of call' with minor complaints is the community police officers, whom they know personally. Therefore, logic would dictate that more community police officers would lead to a wider benefit in the community.

Members of the general public

The community should have more of a say in the appointment of community police officers and a wider input into policing policy. The public is not as aware as they should be of community policing and what they do; better communication and marketing are required. Community police develop an understanding of local culture and key issues of concern in the community, such as the problems experienced by ethnic groups. Community policing areas are too large for officers to be fully effective. Although officers regularly attend community meetings, there should also be local contact points in the community where officers can be found at particular times. Doubts were expressed as to the commitment of police management to community policing, referring to the high level of officers being extracted from their areas to police elsewhere and asking why this is allowed. There is common agreement that community policing in school liaison is fundamental to the early development of children and officers' involvement in wider social services education would be welcome. Many members of the public see community policing as more of a crime-prevention role than that of law enforcement, and achieving the balance between both is the key to success. Community policing needs to be developed and expanded, particularly at the grass-roots level, as this is where most problems originate.

Rural communities

Community policing areas are too large for the community police, in some instances covering two or three villages. Although, community policing is highly valued in the rural setting, there is a concern that in some rural parts it is nonexistent due to resources being stretched. The problems facing the police in rural communities are exacerbated by the perception of rising crime and public disorder in rural towns and villages.

Problems with community policing

The comments from the above survey reveal community policing playing a vital part in local social policy strategies as seen through the eyes of community members, and it would be reasonable to suggest the views are fairly representative throughout Scotland. Communities make ever-increasing demands on the police, which have an adverse impact on community policing. In particular, this causes an extraordinary level of abstractions of community officers from their regular place of duty, so much so that nearly all of the above groups of respondents disapprovingly commented on the issue of abstractions. In support of this, research carried out in the Strathclyde Police area in February 2001 revealed community police officers are not engaged in their normal duties for approximately 70% to 80% of the time (*The Herald* 2001: 4).

There is general agreement in Scottish policing that a critical success factor to sound police–community relations is community policing. It persuades the police to think of themselves as more than a reactive agency for calls from the public and promotes a more proactive, problem-solving role in tackling community problems. A broad spectrum of the Scottish community appears to believe that this is the case, judging community police officers to work hard and be committed to their communities when they are allowed to do so by the system.

There are, however, considerable problems, which have prevented the efficient and effective implementation of community policing for over half a century. These include insufficient change in police culture; the need for clarity of definition of community policing; problems with tenure, recruitment and training; more lucid goals and objectives; lack of monitoring, evaluation and measurement of effectiveness; failure to find a solution to the problem of abstracting officers from the community to other duties; and a policing system in overload with too much work and insufficient resources (Donnelly 2002b: 30–65; Loveday 1998: 177). The existence of these issues in the Scottish police forces has been shown conclusively in a number of studies (HMCICS 1995, 2002, 2004a, b). Whether the problem is deemed one of 'non-implementation' or 'unsuccessful implementation' is a moot point, as a review of the situation in Scotland reveals that no specific national strategy for community policing exists (Donnelly 2002b: 236; HMCICS 2004a: 33), although a national community policing strategy is being developed by ACPOS for 2005. The future strategy hopes to incorporate recent developments in community planning, the use of the National Intelligence Model, problem-solving, restorative justice and community wardens (ACPOS 2004).

Current emphasis on performance management dictates that the police focus on the attainment of goals and targets. Sometimes this is at the expense of how policing is to be achieved on the ground, with not enough emphasis on how police reform should be implemented locally. Ironically, this comes at a time when, more than ever before, there exists a consensus among the eight police forces and politicians as to the direction of Scottish policing. The agreement of a forthcoming strategy for community policing in the Scottish police service is one example of this.

Performance management is inextricably linked to the emerging professionalisation of the 'new' police officer, and both have led to increased specialisation and bureaucracy with an increase in police departments and specialist posts. As a consequence, the number of foot patrol or community police officers has remained static or, more commonly, has been reduced since the only source of recruitment for specialist posts in policing is from the pool of foot patrol officers. A review of community policing in the Strathclyde Police in 2001 revealed a reduction in the total number of community police officers to 587 from a figure of 700 in 1996 (Strathclyde Police 2001). Any increase in a force's complement of officers tends to lead to the additional recruits being subsumed into mainstream policing and helps to feed the police organisation's constant appetite for specialisation, which is gaining momentum rather than slowing down.

New thinking on policing communities

Strategic policing

The Scottish Police Service has undergone more change to its organisation in the course of the past 20 years than in the previous 120 years. The rate of change has also been prolific, driven on by a range of key reports, inquiries and legislation emanating from government over a short period of time. A number of independent inquiries has added to the debate and has contributed to an incremental but definite process of reform. Although only a small number of these have been aimed directly at policing in Scotland, there is no doubt that they have virtually all been influential in shaping Scottish policing in the past two decades. The key reform documents are listed in Table 7.2.

Table 7.2 Key documents in police reform

* Audit Commission Reports (1988–2002)
* Operational Policing Review (1990)
* ACPO Strategic Policy Document (1990)
* Promoting Value For Money in Provincial Police Forces (National Audit Office 1991)
* The Citizen's Charter (1991)
* The Justice Charter For Scotland (1991)
* The Police Authority Role – Strategic Issues (Association of Metropolitan Authorities 1991)
* A Police Service for the Twenty-First Century (White Paper 1993)
* Sheehy Inquiry into Police Responsibilities and Rewards (1993)
* The Role and Responsibilities of the Police (Cassells Inquiry 1993)
* The Police and Magistrates' Courts Act (1994)
* Review of Police Core and Ancillary Tasks (Home Office 1995)
* Crime and Disorder Act (1998)
* MacPherson Report into the Murder of Stephen Lawrence (1999)
* Policing a New Century – A Blueprint for Police Reform (White Paper 2002)
* Police Reform Act (2002)

Part of this change has been the arrival of performance management within the public sector, with its stricter rules of accountability, setting of goals and objectives, best value financial regimes, devolved budgeting and community planning. This has now impacted on the police organisation with significant results. The police may have been the last of the public-sector bureaucracies to be visited by government scrutinisers, but the repercussions for keeping this appointment have had a major impact on the management of Scottish policing. In particular, strategic planning and management have emerged in the Scottish police service with a resounding bang. Since the 1980s government pressure has been on police forces to change by both improving their efficiency and demonstrating their effectiveness. These have combined in the development of a more strategic approach to police duties and responsibilities (Allan 1989; Leishman *et al.* 1995: 26–38; Loveday 1997: 216–240).

Managers in the public sector are expected to be highly accountable for their actions, 'in light of their statutory obligations and fulfilment of expectations of the citizens they serve. The political, social, economic and cultural environment in which they operate is crucial to all forms of strategic and, increasingly, operational management' (Taylor and Popham 1989: 2). As a consequence, the idea of strategy and strategic planning has caught the imagination of Scottish police managers who, more than ever, face a dynamic, complex, and, at times, hostile environment. Strategy offers the opportunity to the Scottish police to set goals and objectives that aspire to meet the organisation's overall mission and purpose. It helps focus the efforts from all sections of the service, ensuring a sense of direction for police employees and also explains to those outside the purpose and aims of the police and what the service is trying to achieve.

Traditionally, the Scottish police service has worked in close co-operation with its communities and public and private agencies, adopting a joint approach to issues of mutual concern and ensuring local priorities are identified without the need for statutory legislation to facilitate the consultative relationships, as has happened in England and Wales. A positive side-effect of the Scottish position has been closer corporate working by the eight chief constables and elected members through ACPOS, the Scottish Executive and the Justice Department, and police authorities. This has facilitated the introduction of policing goals, objectives and initiatives at force level which focus on enhancing the safety of communities, reducing the fear of crime and influencing criminal behaviour. This 'core business' of the police is normally encapsulated by each force in the form of a 'mission statement', with each producing a 'business plan' that articulates how it intends to achieve its mission, including operational, financial and support strategies. Scottish police forces have also gone to great lengths to advertise these strategic plans to

Scottish communities, for example, in annual reports, newsletters, videos, force websites, press advertisements and at various media launches and public forums.

Whatever individual Scottish forces choose to do is set against a background of national strategic plans and policies. An example of this is ACPOS's *Policing Priorities for Scotland 2003–2006*, which sets out the Scottish Police Service's 'framework to determine and deliver its strategic priorities' (ACPOS 2003a: 1). The document focuses on the key business areas of the Scottish Police Service and articulates the police commitment to four main priorities over this time period: delivery of police performance targets, community engagement, intelligence-led policing, and improving police productivity. Action plans have been produced based on these four priorities and the relevant ACPOS business areas are tasked with monitoring and directing progress.

However, this high-order strategic approach gives rise to questions about whether or not such change significantly impacts on the way traditional policing is carried out at local level and whether it has a positive or negative effect on the pragmatic implementation of policing in Scotland (Cameron 1991; McLaughlin and Murji 1995: 110–127, Robertson 1996).

Local delivery of service

The Scottish Police Service is committed to delivering local policing plans with services that meet the community's requirements. These services are monitored and evaluated at the force level by regularly consulting internal and external customers, such as MPs, MSPs and local politicians, community members and the police themselves, to identify community needs, expectations and priorities and to measure police performance. Subsequent results update and improve policy, strategy and the allocation of resources to provide a balanced approach to meeting present and future needs. The pragmatic delivery of services is achieved through each force's chain of command from chief constable downwards to either area or basic command units, or divisions and sub-divisions, each with a chief superintendent or superintendent in charge. Management of local policing can be further devolved to smaller command units working out of local police offices.

The Scottish chief constables are responsible for all aspects of police operations and will set out the way their individual forces intend to meet statutory requirements. In addition, as a 24 hour a day, 365 days a year, open-ended emergency service, which can be called to a variety of incidents ranging from major disasters and firearms incidents to domestic disputes, the role of the Scottish Police Service is much wider than mere law enforcement. Even if the nature of the crisis is unclear, it is often the case that the police are summoned anyway (Stephens 1994: 237–251). A non-exhaustive list of services which the Scottish police forces offer both to meet their statutory responsibilities and to satisfy local policing plans is given in Table 7.3.

In delivering these services to the public, Scottish police forces have several difficulties to surmount over which they have little influence. These difficulties centre primarily on the limited resources available to each of the eight forces and the various constraints that restrict the flexibility with which they can utilise them. One example is the long-running debate on police time spent at court, which highlights the limited sway the police service has over such an issue. A survey in Lothian and Borders force revealed that out of a monthly average of 1,077 police witnesses attending court, only 152 (14%) were called to give evidence (Lothian and Borders Police 2004). The Scottish Executive, police and courts administration are continually searching for a solution to this perennial problem. A further example relates to the traditional administrative burden of fines recovery carried out by the police. HMCICS estimates that police involvement

Table 7.3   Scottish Police services

Crime Prevention	Architectural Liaison
Domestic Violence Unit	Female and Child Protection
Sex Offenders Unit	Serious Crime Unit
Road Policing	Drugs Awareness
School Liaison	Truancy Patrols
CCTV Unit	Speed Camera Unit
Community Wardens	Restorative Justice Team
Shoplifting Unit	Robbery Squad
Vehicle Crime Unit	Street Liaison/Prostitution Unit
Fraud/Cheque Squad	Warrants/Fines Unit
Armed Response Unit	Custody/Prisoner Centre
Traffic Wardens	Cadets/Special Constabulary
Crime Analysts	Fingerprint Identification
Citations/Process Unit	Enquiry Desk
Crime Management	Anti-Social Behaviour Unit
Crime Intelligence	Field Intelligence
Police Complaints	General Police Patrol
Criminal Investigation	Control/Call Centre
Scenes of Crime Unit	Forensic Services
Surveillance Unit	Media Unit
Criminal Records	Witness Protection Unit
Community Policing	Racist Crime/Asylum Liaison
Air Support	Road Crash Investigation
Underwater Search	Marine Policing
Mounted/Dog Support	Mountain Rescue

in fines recovery across Scotland equates to 'in excess of £5 million in opportunity costs' (HMCICS 2004b: 45) and recommends the freeing of police resources from such a task.

In achieving its goals and objectives, the Scottish police regularly face difficulties and challenges across a wide geographical area and the effective command and control of its limited staff are essential to the success of forces' operations. One way of ensuring smooth running is by strategic thinking, thorough planning and good supervision. However, things are not as easy as they seem, as, in police management terms, many decisions are made by the lower ranks, which means that 'those at the top find themselves managing constables on the beat or in the car, at the command centre or investigating a case, who have already taken vital decisions from which everything follows. It is a total inversion of the normal management problem' (Jones 1993: 154). This situation underlines the importance of accountability, professional standards and ethical guidance within the police organisation (Villiers and Adlam 2004; Kleinig 1996; Neyroud and Bleckley 2001; Council of Europe 2002) and the role of elected members and the general public in overseeing the performance of police managers. ACPOS is no stranger to this and has acknowledged that improved productivity in the police can be assured within an ethical environment with high professional standards, clearly articulated in the ACPOS statement of ethical principles and code of ethical practice (ACPOS 2003b). It is evident that senior police managers are increasingly taking cognizance of what communities believe should be the priorities of policing, and this includes what the politicians' perspectives of the police organisation's success factors are, and how well the police are achieving them.

Other 'stakeholders' in the process cannot be ignored either, in whatever guise they may be, for example, the general public, schools, neighbourhoods, colleges, universities, factories, business parks, industrial estates, hospitals, voluntary groups and football clubs. There is also self-interest on the part of senior police management in maintaining a close partnership with politicians, as political support in modern policing is not only crucial to the realisation of the organisation's goals, but also to an assurance of minimal intrusion and interference to the long-established and time-honoured 'traditional model' of policing. As Joyce (2000) succinctly puts it when speaking of the 'new' public-sector managers, 'wise top managers know that getting this support depends on managers fitting into the politicians' agenda, and not expecting the politicians to fit into the manager's agenda' (Joyce 2000: 42). The introduction of the new devolved constitutional settlement for Scotland suggests that strategic planning in the Scottish police is influenced more by elected politicians than by members of the public or other partners (Donnelly and Scott 2003: 26).

Alternatives to police patrol

Rhetoric still surrounds the subject of community policing and the wider issues of foot patrol. The dilemma for the police service in Scotland is that without a sustainable increase in the number of patrol officers, other methods will be introduced to fill the gap. There will always be arguments put forward for extra funding for policing, and patrol officers in particular, but funding is only part of the solution. The remarkable fall in crime and increase in detection rates achieved in the city of New York during the 1990s was accompanied by a rise in recruitment of over 6,000 officers (Harcourt 2001: 94). It is highly unlikely that an injection of funds of that magnitude will be witnessed in Scotland. In reality the demand for policing and general community security is such that it is unrealistic to believe public funding will ever reach the requisite level in the UK. The situation necessitates a serious look at alternatives or adjuncts to police patrol and the traditional patrol officer.

Auxiliary patrols

New models based on differing levels of patrol are increasingly being developed. One example is the community or neighbourhood warden who patrols with limited powers, but is funded from the public purse. Funding from the Scottish Executive has made provision for 400 wardens in a number of local authorities and the intention is to extend community warden schemes to all local authorities by 2005 (HMCICS 2004b: 41–42). Although the warden schemes have still to be fully evaluated in Scotland, preliminary assessment shows a reduction in vandalism and in new complaints of anti-social behaviour (Henry 2004). Feedback from communities in the wider UK has also been positive to date, with residents believing that wardens successfully tackle public nuisances, litter louts, and prevent graffiti on buildings (ODPM 2004). However, concerns exist with some senior police officers and the Scottish Police Federation as to the future role of wardens and how they will impact on the police service. Extending the role and remit of existing auxiliary patrols such as traffic wardens has also proved a success in one Scottish force. In 2002 Grampian Police extended the role of traffic wardens to deal with quality of life and community safety issues in a specific area of Aberdeen. In partnership with police and council workers and following 'high visibility reassurance patrols by a team of four wardens working nine to five, Monday to Friday, over a period of nine months, reported crime in the area fell by 25 per cent (HMCICS 2004a: 44).

Privately funded patrols

There has been a significant increase in private security provision in Britain in recent years, which is estimated to employ at least twice as many workers as the police service does (Button 2002: 98–99; Johnston 2000: 126). In some parts of England where the community, the local authority and elected members have not been satisfied with the levels of police patrol cover, private foot patrol wardens are being employed. Such provision is attractive to the community, as these resources are not subject to the vagaries of the abstractions experienced by their police colleagues, for example for court duty, public order detail, football duty, annual leave, sick leave, paperwork and training courses. In best-value terms, the patrol officers or wardens are there on patrol for the agreed expenditure of funds. The police cannot guarantee this. These initiatives are exceptionally attractive to a growing number of communities and could be viewed as an extension of a widening definition of community policing, i.e. policing organised by the community.

An alternative is the private funding of police patrols. For example, in some parts of the UK a number of privately financed police officers are on patrol at local business premises on crime prevention and staff protection duties. In other areas retailers pay for officers to patrol city centres and at least one NHS Trust is funding the salaries of police officers to patrol its hospitals. This is not an entirely new concept. Professional football clubs, the Open Golf Championship and major pop music festivals in Scotland, as elsewhere in Britain, are accustomed to meeting the bill for police attendance.

Civilianisation

In the past, the Scottish police service has successfully civilianised a number of police posts and released officers for street duty by replacing them with civilian support officers. Although this process of civilianisation continues, the Scottish forces are under pressure to go one stage further and hive off certain duties to the private sector. One example is the recent contract awarded by the Scottish Executive to the prisoner escort company Reliance in 2004, which is expected to release up to 200 police officers for street duty in the future. However, the concept of civilian personnel performing tasks hitherto carried out by 'sworn' police officers has only been investigated at a superficial level and deserves closer examination in the future. With some minor legislative changes, appropriately qualified civilian personnel could fill particular posts normally reserved for 'sworn' officers. For example, until the requisite legislation was introduced, civilian personnel were not allowed to fingerprint or take DNA samples from prisoners. The potential exists for civilianisation to be extended, specifically in the domains of crime investigation administration and support, crime and community intelligence and analysis, operational support, crime and prisoner processing, and support in case management. The only barriers to progress in these areas are the strength of police determination to maintain the status quo and the will to resist such change.

Partnership policing

Another alternative is to place less emphasis on traditional community policing and more on partnership policing; there is no requirement to give this partnership style of policing a label. This strategy of partnership working reflects many of the virtues of communitarianism and involves a more strategic approach to community safety, social inclusion, community development and community planning, and a more robust implementation of policy than at present. One example of such an approach is the recently launched problem-solving policing model being piloted in the South Lanarkshire Division of Strathclyde Police. The problem-solving unit acts as a link between communities, the police, local council, public and private agencies, and the voluntary sector. Protocols exist that facilitate close partnership working and information sharing, and the National Intelligence Model and the Scottish Intelligence Database play key roles within the joint problem-solving unit (HMCICS 2004a: 39–40). Strategic planning and decision-making in the unit are based on community information and intelligence, police tactical assessments, statistical analysis, area and person problem profiles, joint tactical assessments, and local liaison and local action plans (South Lanarkshire Council 2004: 8). The project has still to be fully evaluated, and in light of the new statutory responsibilities being placed on local authorities and the police for community planning, under the Local Government in Scotland Act (2003), it offers an interesting way forward for the future.

Community policing specialists

More and more Scottish police officers from various disciplines are working and specialising in areas that hitherto would have been the sole domain of the community police officer. Examples of this would include juvenile crime, domestic violence, prostitution, the elderly, mentally ill, business crime, drugs, schools, crime prevention, community involvement, anti-social behaviour and child protection. The resourcing of these specialist units normally comes from the pool of officers working on street patrol. Arguably, these specialist posts are as much a part of the broader definition of community policing and community safety as the community police officer with his/her immediate interface with the community. A large police division may have up to 800 police officers, of whom around 50 might be community officers. In addition there may be in excess of another 50 officers involved full-time on a daily basis carrying out the specialist work identified above. As these specialist officers are less likely to be abstracted from their work than their community police colleagues, a significant amount of specialised community police work continues undisturbed. Examples of this are drug and crime-prevention education in schools and community groups and a variety of work with juveniles.

Paradoxically, there are a number of police officers who do not wish to be involved in community policing, although supportive of the concept and philosophy (Donnelly 2002b: 281–283). These officers do not see a role for themselves in this style of policing and indeed for many officers community-style policing is not the main attraction of a career in the police service. A review of community policing in Strathclyde Police has highlighted the current difficulties of recruiting officers to work in community policing because the job's 'attractiveness has waned' (*The Herald* 2001: 4). This highlights one of the difficulties facing police management in the future if community-style policing is to be sustained or expanded.

Communitarianism and community participation

In terms of new thinking about the community, the idea of communitarianism is gaining momentum and support with its 'stress on communities taking responsibility for their own well-being' (Salmon 1995: 4), with some communitarians contending that there is a need to revisit the concept of community and to re-examine the role of the individual and public agencies, including elected members, within the local political structure (Etzioni 1993). However, there is a danger of placing too much reliance on the 'community' as a means of delivering public services on the cheap. For example, advocates of community safety could easily expand on and develop existing community support officers, neighbourhood wardens, Neighbourhood Watch schemes, special constabulary and voluntary community self-help groups to enhance policing and improve crime prevention in the locality. Responsibility for the provision and support of these services would then shift from the state to the local community, and with it the costs. But key questions have to be asked about who within the community would have legitimate authority and responsibility for the implementation of such policies and who would actually oversee and monitor the system (Crawford 1996: 250).

In Sir Robert Peel's original vision of communities being policed by their own members, the doctrine of 'policing by consent' takes on a broader meaning within the framework of communitarianism. Etzioni believes that 'the more viable communities are, the less need for policing' (1993: ix–x) and Crawford agrees that 'more community equals less crime'

(1996: 252). Abel states that '(crime) is the most emotionally compelling symbol of lost communities' (1995: 118) and gives the example of the doubling of crime figures in Britain between 1979 and 1990 based on the breakdown of traditional communities and the loss of social cohesion. Other examples put forward are increased marital and family breakdown, increased demand for individual privacy and increased political apathy. Communitarianism helps to clarify the idea of the local populace wishing more empowerment – and hence control – over public agencies which, in reality, exist to serve them. One example of the communitarian approach is seen in the situation where 'airline pilots, school bus drivers, and others who directly hold people's lives in their hands can be required to be tested for drug and alcohol abuse' (Crawford 1996: 2). Similarly, the Police Advisory Board has made representations to the Home Office for police officers to undergo drug tests and Merseyside, Greater Manchester, West Midlands and Grampian police forces have already tested officers. Warwickshire was the first police force to introduce random drug testing in 2004 (Daly 2004: 6). This is aimed at the random testing of individuals in security-sensitive posts or who could seriously affect their own health or that of others. A selection of posts that fall under these categories includes air support unit, dog handlers, firearms officers, police drivers, senior police officers, custody staff (including contracted staff) and tactical firearm advisors. Employees will be tested for alcohol and an assortment of drugs. Job applicants, whether internal or external, may also be screened where a medical is included as part of the recruitment process (Warwickshire Police 2004).

Achieving the correct balance between the rights of the individual and the needs of the community is the essence of success; for example, some groups may be against the compulsory wearing of car seat-belts, whereas communitarianism recognises that such enforcement is for the benefit and safety of all road users (Giddens 1997: 11). Salmon (1995) gives a further example in relation to the breakdown of the home environment, the failure of parents and links with delinquency. He contends that this can be translated 'into punitive legislation against one-parent families, and at the local level, self-policing activities in an inner city area can degenerate into physical and verbal abuse of prostitutes' (Salmon 1995: 7). The cessation of the Leith 'prostitution tolerance zone' in 2001 is one example of local residents pressurising the local authority into withdrawing support for an initiative which offered prostitutes a controlled space where soliciting was, in effect, 'decriminalised'. Although 'prostitutes live at the margins of society and are in need of help and protection ... for the wider community, prostitution presents a social problem impacting on quality of life' (Keogh 2004: 1350). The use of anti-social behaviour orders to exclude street prostitutes from designated areas and other enforcement measures has been described as a form of 'institutional intolerance' (Melrose 2003: 23; Muncie 1999: 147–176).

Any expansion of communitarian policies within Scottish communities would almost certainly impact on policing, and the police will have to learn how to use engagement with the community to achieve its own objectives. A prime example waiting to be addressed in this way is the 'knife culture' which afflicts so many urban areas and which contributes significantly to the unacceptable levels of violent crime in Scotland. 'A strong community sounds like the recipe required to fight knife culture' (Donnelly 2002c: 14). Unfortunately, the dilemma facing the police and communities is that people in high-crime neighbourhoods usually 'withdraw from any form of integration in community life and take no part in the broader policing of the area' (ibid.: 14).

As a means of engaging with and empowering local communities, Scottish local and central government has developed since the 1970s a strategic approach to community development which has attempted to find a conduit for transferring local issues onto the national agenda and into the electoral process (Craig and Mayo 1995). However, this approach tends to come up against the barrier of the fragmented nature of modern communities and scepticism about how significant the voice of the individual citizen really is. For example, a report for the Council on Local Democracy in 1994 focused on trying to identify who the active citizens in the community really were. The evidence was 'that the better educated, upper socio-economic groups in a local community are more knowledgeable about the functions and structures of local government' (Rallings *et al.* 1994: 30) and it was apparent that such groups were more active and participated far more in voluntary work as well. Consequently, 'local problems can be articulated in a way that means the decision makers have to listen to the community' (ibid.: 35). However, the lack of participation and under-involvement of ethnic groups, the unemployed, women and the working class in community decision-making was noted as a major deficit to the community being fully represented.

As with other parts of the UK, Scotland is a very different place from the pre-war era, with significant changes taking place in many local neighbourhoods. The composition of communities has been greatly altered, for example 'multi-ethnicity and multi-culturalism are no longer confined to the back-streets of a few city ports of entry' (Finer 1998: 155–156). May (1997), in discussing the future direction of Scottish local government in terms of partnership and empowerment, expressed the need for extending empowerment beyond existing boundaries and groups, of those who 'are, in the main, representative of the more articulate and militant elements of our communities' (May 1997: 5), to the many disadvantaged groups who are still excluded from active community involvement. These non-participant groups are very relevant in the wider world of citizens' democracy and a future challenge for local government in Scotland 'will be to lift these groups to the same level on the ladder as their more articulate or politically active counterparts' (ibid.: 5).

The Scottish Executive has shown commitment to the development of robust communities, as evidenced in the policy document *A Partnership for a Better Scotland* (Scottish Executive 2003), with its focus on community safety partnership agreements. The eight Scottish police forces have given a high priority to the issue with at least one chief constable holding the chair of the community planning task force. However, to maximise the success from the sound work being done, there has to be a wider representation from the community into the community decision-making forums than at present.

The dilemma for the police and for society in general is that police resources are at full capacity and any additional personnel in the future will be of a minimum number. Therefore, it is essential to encourage community members and voluntary groups to become more involved in self-help initiatives, designed to improve the safety and well-being of the community. Banton (1964) recognised this issue over 40 years ago when he commented that 'a close investigation is required with a view to identifying what prevents communities from being more participative in their own community safety and how other social organisations can assist more' (Banton 1964: 267–268).

Conclusion

Policing the Scottish community in the 21st century is an intricate business and involves a critical mass of strategy, planning, performance and resource management, local service delivery, and community liaison and partnership. This requires new skills, abilities, specialisms and changing roles for the community police and patrol officer. A significant section of the Scottish community is satisfied with community policing and is keen for it to continue in its traditional forms. Yet in reality a considerable amount of good will on the part of community police officers makes the present system work against all odds. The problem is that this good will is shrinking, placing community policing as it has been known in the past under threat.

Policing the community in Scotland is at an historic crossroads. There is a growing ambiguity about the nature of policing, what it consists of and who is responsible for it, which arises from the conflicting requirements of different sections of the Scottish public and the competing demands of community safety and global security. HMCICS (2004) has raised similar concerns: 'the nature and complexity of the demands society places on its police service [are such that] it is vital that recognition be given to the distance that now exists between the 1967 legislative baseline (Police (Scotland) Act 1967) and the reality of the modern police requirement' (HMCICS 2004: 39).

Sadly, there has been little research in the field of policing the Scottish community and how both policing and community should develop and interface over time. Part of innovative police reform in Scotland must include the funding of meaningful research into operational policing at community level, and specifically to critically examine what is meant by the terms 'policing' and 'community' in the post-modern age.

For the police to play their part in any substantial reform of the present system, new and innovative approaches to community safety partnerships at the local level have to be adopted. The policy of the Westminster government on the issue was made clear during a speech given by the Prime Minister, Tony Blair, in Edinburgh in December 2004. Clearly coming from a communitarian context, the Prime Minister stated, 'what we can do is give the power to the people in those communities, the police and local authorities and ordinary representatives … and make sure they create the law-abiding community they want to live in … they [the people] no longer want or expect government to solve all their problems.'

The Scottish Executive is in agreement with its Westminster counterparts on this core theme of community empowerment. However, senior police managers, police staff associations and some elected members are concerned that further expansion of private security, auxiliary support and civilianisation risks going too far and should not be at the expense of police tradition, customs, routines, habits, practices and culture. Therein lies the dilemma, as modern policing and indeed, community policing are much more than a small cadre of dedicated officers ensuring a regular interface with the community. Policing is part of a wider movement towards a 'new community' where community safety is king and not solely the statutory responsibility of the police. The contention here is that any sustainable reform in the delivery of police services can only happen if communities as well as the police organisation show a willingness to change their traditions, customs, routines, habits, practices and culture. Changing how the Scottish community is policed is not a one-way street.

References

Abel, R. (1995) 'Contested communities', *Journal of Law and Society*, 22: 118.

Allan, D. L. (1989) *How Do the Police Measure Up? – A Study of Efficiency and Effectiveness in the Police Service*. University of Strathclyde, Glasgow: Unpublished MPhil thesis.

Association of Chief Police Officers in Scotland (2003a) *Policing Priorities for Scotland 2003–2006*. Edinburgh: ACPOS.

Association of Chief Police Officers Scotland (2003b) *Statement of Ethical Principles and Code of Ethical Practice*. Edinburgh: ACPOS.

Association of Chief Police Officers Scotland (2004) *Annual Report 2003–2004*. Edinburgh: ACPOS.

Audit Commission (1996) *Streetwise – Effective Street Patrol*. London: HMSO.

Banton, M. (1964) *The Policeman in the Community*. London: Tavistock.

Barr, A. (1996) *Practising Community Development – Experience in Strathclyde*. London: Community Development Foundation.

Bennett, T. (ed.) (1983) *The Future of Policing*. Cambridge: Institute of Criminology.

Blair, A. (2004) *Speech on Public Service and Welfare State Reform*, 3 December. Edinburgh: Napier University.

Brodeur, J. P. (ed.) (1995) *Comparisons in Policing – An International Perspective*. Aldershot: Avebury.

Button, M. (2002) *Private Policing*. Devon: Willan Publishing.

Cameron, H. R. G. (1991) *The Management of Change in Police Organisation*. University of Strathclyde, Glasgow: Unpublished MPhil thesis.

Council of Europe (2002) *The European Code of Police Ethics*. Strasbourg: Council of Europe.

Craig, G. and Mayo, M. (eds) (1995) *Community Empowerment – A reader in participation and development*. London: Zed Books.

Crawford, A. (1996) 'The spirit of community – Rights, responsibilities and the communitarian agenda', *Journal of Law and Society*, 23 (2): 250.

Daly, M. (2004) 'Passing out parade', *Druglink*, January/February: 6–7.

Donnelly, D. (2002a) 'New community', *Police Review*, 3 May: 26–27.

Donnelly, D. (2002b) *New Police Management – The Strategic Management of Community Policing in the Strathclyde Police*. Glasgow Caledonian University: Unpublished PhD thesis.

Donnelly, D. (2002c) 'A communal approach to crime', *Police Review*, 20 September: 14.

Donnelly, D. (2003) 'Pioneering Scots', *Police Review*, 3 January: 25.

Donnelly, D. (2004) *Local Perspectives on Community Policing in the West of Scotland*, Occasional Paper 1. Hamilton: Scottish Centre For Police Studies.

Donnelly, D. (2005) 'Community policing', in G. Kurian (ed.), *World Encyclopedia of Police Forces and Correctional Systems*. New York: Gale.

Donnelly, D. and Scott, K. (2003) 'Journey on a moving landscape: the effects of Scottish devolution on policing', *Policing Today*, 8 (2): 25–26.

Etzioni, A. (1993) *The Spirit of Community*. London: Fontana Press.

Finer, C. J. (1998) 'The new social policy in Britain', in C. J. Finer and M. Nellis (eds), *Crime and Social Exclusion*. Oxford: Blackwell, pp. 154–170.

Finer, C. J. and Nellis, M. (eds) (1998) *Crime and Social Exclusion*. Oxford: Blackwell.

Giddens, A. (1997) 'Anomie of the people', review of Etzioni, A. 'The New Golden Rule – Community and Morality in a Democratic Society', *The Guardian* (G2), 31 July: 11.

Goldstein, H. (1987) 'Toward community-oriented policing – Potential, basic requirements and threshold questions', *Crime and Delinquency*, 33: 6–30.

Harcourt, B. E. (2001) *Illusion of Order – the False Promise of Broken Windows.* Cambridge, MA: Harvard University Press.

Henry, H. (2004) *Speech by the Deputy Justice Minister Hugh Henry MSP*, 3 December. Glasgow: National Conference of Community Wardens.

The Herald (2001) 'Role of bobbies on the beat reviewed'. Review of Community Policing (2001) in the Strathclyde Police. *The Herald*, 5 May: 4.

HM Inspectorate of Constabulary for Scotland (1995) *Thematic Inspection on Community Policing*. Edinburgh: HMSO.

HM Inspectorate of Constabulary for Scotland (2002) *Narrowing the Gap – Police Visibility and Public Reassurance: Managing public expectation and demand.* Edinburgh: HMICS.

HM Inspectorate of Constabulary for Scotland (2004a) *Local Connections – Policing with the Community. Thematic Inspection of Community Engagement.* Edinburgh: HMCICS.

HM Chief Inspector of Constabulary for Scotland (2004b) *Annual Report 2003–2004.* Edinburgh: HMCICS.

Johnston, L. (2000) *Policing Britain – Risk, Security and Governance*. Harlow: Pearson Education.

Jones, J. H., Sir (1993) *Trouble Shooter 2*. London: Penguin.

Joyce, P. (2000) *Strategy in the Public Sector – A Guide to Effective Change Management.* Chichester: John Wiley & Sons.

Judge, T. (2002) 'Change Mr Blunkett – We've been changing for years!', *Police,* September: 28–29.

Kelling, G. L. (1987) 'Acquiring a taste for order – The community and the police', *Crime and Delinquency*, 33 (1): 90–102.

Keogh, A. (2004) 'The oldest profession or an age-old injustice?', *New Law Journal*, 17 September: 1350–1351.

Kleinig, J. (1996) *The Ethics of Policing*. Cambridge: Cambridge University Press.

Leishman, A., Cope, S. and Starie, P. (1995) 'Reforming the police in Britain – New public management, policy networks and a "Tough Old Bill"', *The International Journal of Public Sector Management*, 8 (4): 26–38.

Leishman, F., Loveday, B. and Savage, S. P. (eds) (2000) *Core Issues In Policing*, 2nd edn. Harlow: Pearson Education.

Lothian and Borders Police (2003) *Silent Witnesses*. Edinburgh: Lothian and Borders Police.

Loveday, B. (1998) 'Improving the status of police patrol', *International Journal of the Sociology of Law*, 26: 161–196.

Manning, P. K. (1984) 'Community policing', *American Journal of Police*, 3 (2): 205–27.

Mawby, R. I. (1990) *Comparative Policing Issues*. London: Unwin Hyman.

May, C. (1997) *Citizens' Democracy – Theory and Practice*. Glasgow: Scottish Local Government Information Unit, Discussion Paper 5.

Mastrofski, S. D. (1993) 'Varieties of community policing', *American Journal of Police*, 12 (3): 65–77.

McLaughlin, E. and Murji, K. (1995) 'The end of public policing? Police reform and "the new managerialism"', in L. Noaks *et al.* (eds), *Contemporary Issues in Criminology*. Cardiff: University of Wales Press, pp. 110–127.

Melrose, M. (2003) 'Street prostitution and community safety: a case of contested meanings', *Community Safety Journal*, 2 (1): 21–31.

Muncie, J. (1999) 'Institutionalised intolerance: youth justice and the 1998 Crime and Disorder Act', *Critical Social Policy*, 19 (2): 147–76.

Neyroud, P. W. and Bleckley, A. (2001) *Policing, Ethics and Human Rights*. Devon: Willan Publishing.

Noaks, L., Levi, M. and Maguire, M. (eds) (1995) *Contemporary Issues in Criminology*. Cardiff: University of Wales Press.

ODPM (2004) *Neighbourhood Wardens Scheme Evaluation*. London: Office of the Deputy Prime Minister.

Popham, G. (1989) 'The management of law and order', in I. Taylor and G. Popham (eds), *An Introduction to Public Sector Management*. London: Unwin Hyman, pp. 150–175.

Rallings, C., Temple, M. and Thrasher, M. (1994) *Community Identity and Participation in Local Democracy*, Research Report No 1. London: Commission for Local Democracy.

Reiner, R. (1995) 'Community policing in England and Wales', in J. P. Brodeur (ed.), *Comparisons in Policing – An International Perspective*. Aldershot: Avebury, pp. 161–165.

Riechers, L. M. and Roberg, R. R. (1990) 'Community policing: a critical review of underlying assumptions', *Journal of Police Science and Administration*, 17 (2): 105–114.

Robertson, W. A. (1996) *Creating an Excellent Police Force – A Guide for Chief Police Officers*. University of Strathclyde, Glasgow: Unpublished MPhil thesis.

Royal Commission on the Police (1962) *Final Report*, Cmnd 1728. London: HMSO.

Salmon, H. (1995) 'Community, communitarianism and local government', *Local Government Policy Making*, 22 (3): 4.

Schaffer, E. (1980) *Community Policing*. London: Croom Helm.

Scottish Executive (2003) *A Partnership for a Better Scotland*. Edinburgh: HMSO.

Scottish Home and Health Department (1971) *Community Involvement Departments*. Edinburgh: SHHD Police Circular: No 6/71.

Scottish Home and Health Department (1983) *Consultation between the Community and the Police*. Edinburgh: SHHD Police Circular: No 2/83.

Shanks, N. J. (1980) *Police Community Involvement in Scotland*, Scottish Office Central Research Unit Paper. Edinburgh: HMSO.

Short, C. (1983) 'Community Policing beyond Slogans', in T. Bennett (ed.), *The Future of Policing*. Cambridge: Institute of Criminology.

South Lanarkshire Council (2004) *South Lanarkshire – Joint Problem Solving Model*. Hamilton: South Lanarkshire Council.

Stephens, M. (1994) 'Care and control: the future of British policing', *Policing and Society*, 4: 237–251.

Strathclyde Police (2001) *Review of Community Policing.* Strathclyde Police: Unpublished report.

Taylor, I. and Popham, G. (eds) (1989) *An Introduction to Public Sector Management.* London: Unwin Hyman.

Trojanowicz, R. and Bucqueroux, B. (1990) *Community Policing – A Contemporary Perspective.* Cincinnati: Anderson. Villiers, P. and Adlam, R. (eds) (2004) *Policing a Safe, Just and Tolerant Society – An International Model.* Winchester: Waterside Press.

Warwickshire Police, (2004) *Policy on Drug Testing – Alcohol, Drugs and Substance Abuse.* Warwickshire Police.

Willmott, P. (1989) *Community Initiatives – Patterns and Prospects.* London: Policy Studies Institute.

Wilson, J. Q. and Kelling, G. (1982) 'Broken windows: the police and neighborhood safety', *The Atlantic Monthly*, March: 29–38.

Chapter 8

Policing drugs in Scotland

Joseph McGallagly

Introduction

Although this chapter examines the policing of drugs from a Scottish perspective it is not wholly contained within a Scottish context. Any examination of the drug trade has to expand beyond Scotland's borders and consider the influences exerted from within the United Kingdom, and indeed globally, in terms of production, trafficking and distribution of illicit drugs. From a legislative perspective, it is important to note that, while most police powers and functions are devolved to the Scottish Parliament, drugs remain the legislative responsibility of Westminster, albeit that Scottish ministers retain overall responsibility for policing policy.

In terms of empirical research surrounding the policing of illicit drugs, there is a distinct lack of Scottish studies, although this gap has been addressed by the Scottish Executive in an examination of low-level drug markets (Bland and Coope 2003). We have to look south of the border to gain any meaningful insight into how drug markets operate within the United Kingdom. Any discussion surrounding the policing of drugs has to be set in the context of the legislation, strategies and policies that have been developed by government to control the use of illicit drugs. As a consequence of the spiralling increase in use of illicit drugs, a myriad of strategies and policies to address the problem has developed within the UK.

This chapter briefly examines the development of UK drugs legislation; highlights drug policies in the UK and Scotland in particular; and describes some of the key organisations, committees and policing strategies that have emerged as a consequence of the increasing use of illicit drugs within Scotland and the UK. It also describes the prevalence of drug misuse and drug seizures, and explores what the future may hold for Scotland as Westminster embarks upon a process to strengthen cross-border co-operation on the investigation of serious and organised crime, which is so closely related to drugs trafficking.

Legislation

United Nations conventions

Although it is almost 35 years since its introduction, the Misuse Of Drugs Act (MDA) 1971 remains the main legislative instrument relating to the control of drugs in the United Kingdom. The MDA, however, cannot be viewed in isolation as it developed as a consequence of other relevant Acts of Parliament and influences exerted by the United Nations. Indeed, to a large extent, legislation enacted to curtail drug consumption and trafficking is firmly rooted within international obligations and treaties. For example, United Nations conventions require the states that are party to them to meet certain broad obligations, including the creation of criminal offences. However, the conventions leave considerable latitude with respect to how those obligations are to be met in the domestic law of the country concerned. In terms of drug control, the MDA is the legislation by which the UK seeks to meet its international obligations as a signatory to those conventions.

The relationship between domestic law and international agreements can be traced back to 1920, when the Dangerous Drugs Act was passed to enable the United Kingdom to ratify the Hague Convention of 1912 (preceded by the Shanghai Commission of 1909). The signing of the International Opium Convention at The Hague established the principles of international co-operation against the trafficking of narcotics as a matter of international law. This set the blueprint for international agreements to influence United Kingdom legislation. Notwithstanding this, the United Kingdom and other signatories can take action in advance of, or separately from, international conventions.

There are three United Nations conventions on international co-operation concerning drugs. First, the Single Convention on Narcotic Drugs 1961 consolidated and replaced earlier multilateral treaties and conventions with respect to narcotics control and reduced the number of international agencies tasked with controlling the distribution of narcotic drugs. Second, the Convention on Psychotropic Drugs 1971 was directed at 'psychotropic' substances and, although the term psychotropic is not defined, the substances listed include hallucinogens, stimulants and sedatives. Third, the United Nations Convention against the Illicit Traffic in Narcotic Drugs and Psychotropic Substances (The Vienna Convention) 1988 supplements and reinforces the earlier conventions. New precursor chemical controls were introduced and signatories were required to create new offences of money laundering and develop mechanisms to remove the proceeds and profits from drug traffickers. Trafficking was defined to include all possible forms of organisation, management and financing of illicit drug activity. All three conventions were concerned with punishment, prevention and treatment.

The Misuse Of Drugs Act 1971

The Misuse of Drugs Act 1971, replaced the Drugs (Prevention of Misuse) Act 1964 and the Dangerous Drugs Acts of 1965 and 1967. It brought all controlled drugs under one statutory framework with six main objectives:

* to control the use, distribution and production of all drugs identified as medically or socially harmful
* to establish an advisory council comprising of experts to advise the government
* to increase the understanding of drug misuse issues by undertaking research
* to reinforce the law by criminal sanctions where required
* to facilitate the treatment of drug dependants
* to educate members of the public.

The Act introduced a system of classification where drugs were placed in three classes, listed in Schedule 2 to the Act as 'Class A', 'Class B' or 'Class C'. The significance of the classes is that, where a criminal offence is committed, the class of drug involved in the offence determines the maximum penalties. The offence of unlawful possession was split between possession and possession with intent to supply. A new defence was provided for people claiming lack of knowledge of the essential elements of certain drugs offences. Section 23 of the Act gave the police powers to search premises and to stop and search persons on suspicion that they are in possession of a controlled drug. Powers of arrest (section 24) remain valid in Scotland; however, in England and Wales sections 24 and 25 of the Police and Criminal Evidence Act 1984 have since replaced this power.

Drugs are sometimes described as being Schedule 1, 2, 3, 4 or 5 drugs. This refers to the schedules contained in the Misuse of Drugs Regulations 1985. In addition, the definition of 'cannabis' in section 37 of the MDA was extended by section 52 of the Criminal Law Act 1977 to include practically the whole plant. In January 2004 cannabis was reclassified from a class B to a class C drug across the UK. As a controlled drug its production, supply and possession remained illegal. With regard to supply, dealing, production and trafficking the maximum penalty remained at 14 years for cannabis with the maximum penalty for 'dealing' in all class C substances increasing from 5 to 14 years. In terms of the possession of cannabis the maximum penalty was reduced from 5 to 2 years' imprisonment.

In the United Kingdom, those arrested for drug offences may be dealt with in a variety of ways. In England, Wales and Northern Ireland they may be prosecuted or, depending on the circumstances, the police may formally caution. In Scotland, all offences are reported to the Procurator Fiscal (PF) and cautioning is not an option. The PF has two options for dealing with offenders in lieu of prosecution: issue written warnings or make a conditional offer of a fixed penalty known as a 'fiscal fine'.

As a consequence of cannabis reclassification, ACPO in England and Wales has issued guidance to police officers with a presumption against arrest for adults found in possession of cannabis unless certain aggravating circumstances apply. In Scotland the possession of cannabis remains an arrestable offence with all persons found in possession of cannabis reported to the PF.

Under the Customs and Excise Management Act (CEMA) 1997, HM Customs and Excise may offer compounding (the payment of a monetary sum in lieu of prosecution) to people attempting to import small quantities (10 grams or less) of cannabis. Under the Crime (Sentences) Act 1997 a third consecutive trafficking offence involving a Class A drug attracts a mandatory minimum sentence of seven years' imprisonment.

Advisory Council on the Misuse of Drugs

The MDA established the first UK statutory advisory body, the Advisory Council on the Misuse of Drugs (ACMD). The ACMD is tasked with advising ministers on 'measures (whether or not involving alteration of the law) which ... ought to be taken for preventing the misuse ... of drugs or dealing with social problems connected with their misuse' (MDA 1971). Interestingly, the 1994 report by the Advisory Council intimated that the elimination of drug misuse is regarded as an unobtainable goal and that containment rather than elimination of drug misuse is a more realistic objective. The Council recommended the acceptance of harm-reduction principles in developing enforcement strategies: 'Enforcement should support the efforts of other agencies working to reduce the harm caused by drug misuse', and 'A recognition that harm reduction has a part to play in returning areas to normality through improvements to the environment, such as better street lighting, public buildings and amenities' (ACMD 1994).

A White Paper on *Tackling Drugs Together* was published in May 1995 and set out the government's plans for tackling drug misuse over a three-year period. At its core was a statement of purpose outlining effective action by vigorous law enforcement, accessible treatment and a new emphasis on education and prevention. Its main objectives were to increase the safety of communities from drug-related crime; reduce the acceptability and availability of drugs to young people; and to reduce the health risks and other damage related to drug misuse (HM Government 1995).

While police anti-drugs strategies have traditionally been enforcement-oriented, the underlying principle of *Tackling Drugs Together* expanded the approach taken by the police. Consequently, emphasis was placed on the significance of education and harm-reduction measures. Indeed, the UK White Paper required all forces in England and Wales to develop and publish drugs strategies. Chief constables were asked to establish formal drugs strategies and forces were required to report to the Home Secretary by September 1995. However, this was not the case in Scotland, where the Scottish forces continued to work towards local drug targets.

Prevalence of drug use

The total number of drug users in the world is estimated at some 185 million people, equivalent to 4.7% of the global population aged 15 to 64. Broken down into drug types, estimates confirm that cannabis is the most widely used substance (150 million) followed by amphetamine-type stimulants (38 million). More than 13 million of the world's population are reported to use cocaine, with 15 million using opiates, including some 9 million people who take heroin (UNODC 2004a).

United Kingdom position

The British Crime Survey for 2001–02 estimated that 34% of 16- to 59-year-olds have used an illicit drug at some time and 12% have used a class A drug. Of all 16- to 59-year-olds, 12% reported having taken an illicit drug and 3% reported using a class A drug in the last year. This equates to around four million users of any illicit drug and around one million users of class A drugs.

Notwithstanding the problems of establishing a robust and reliable estimated measure of drug misuse, the annual supply of class A drugs to the UK has to be measured in tens of tonnes. The National Criminal Intelligence Service (NCIS) estimates that the amount of class A drugs smuggled annually into the UK to be 25 to 35 tonnes for heroin and 35 to 45 tonnes for cocaine. There are no reliable estimates for the ecstasy market (NCIS 2003). The Home Office's commissioned research on *Sizing the UK Market for Illicit Drugs* (Bramley-Harker 2001) estimated that 'ecstasy' consumption in the UK was 26 million tablets and the annual UK market for heroin was about 31 tonnes. In recent years the UK has accounted for the greatest proportion of heroin seized in western Europe. Indeed, heroin has been the most frequently seized class A drug in each of the last ten years, with the number of western European seizures rising steadily, reaching a peak of 18,260 kg in 2001 and reducing by 15% to 15,370 kg by 2002.

The Scottish position

The results of the Scottish Crime Survey (SCS) 2000 suggest that a previous upward trend in drug misuse observed during the first half of the 1990s may be tailing off. In particular, the 2002 survey found a smaller percentage than in the 1996 SCS of people aged 16 to 25 reporting drug use in the last year.

The first UK study (McKeganey *et al.* 2000), which examined national and local estimates of the prevalence of problematic drug misuse, took place within Scotland. The study identified that problematic drug misuse (defined as the misuse of opiates and/or benzodiazepines) was occurring in all areas of Scotland and that, on average during the year 2000, 2% of the population aged between 15 and 54 used these drugs.

> In simple number terms this means that we estimate that there are approximately 56,000 problematic drug misusers within Scotland. Over the last few years the figure of 30,000 has generally been taken to be our best guess as to the extent of problematic drug users. Clearly on the basis of the estimate we have produced that figure is likely to have been a substantial underestimate.
>
> (McKeganey *et al.* 2000)

The second national study to provide estimates of problem drug misuse in Scotland examined data for the calendar year 2003. The main results estimated that there were 51,582 problem drug users (1.84% of the population aged 15 to 54) in Scotland in 2003 and the prevalence of problem drug use had decreased by 1.96% compared with 2000. The study also estimated that there were 18,737 drug injectors in Scotland (Hay *et al.* 2005).

In a 1999 Scottish pilot of the Arrestee Drug Abuse Monitoring (ADAM) methodology, 89% of arrestees stated that they had used at least one illegal drug in the past and 63% stated that they had used an illegal drug within the last three days (McKeganey *et al.* 2000). The extent of opiate misuse among arrestees in the Scottish ADAM pilot was substantially higher than that identified in a previous English ADAM study (Bennett 1998). This level was also higher than that identified in any of the 35 ADAM sites in the US in 1998 (ADAM 2000). Despite the ADAM pilot being a success in Scotland, it was never repeated. However, ADAM continues to operate successfully in England and Wales.

The Scottish Drug Misuse Database (SDMD) offers a profile of drug misuse based on problem drug misusers attending services for their drug problems. In 2003–04, 12,657 'new' individuals were reported to the SDMD, an increase of nearly 1,000 individuals (8%) from 2002–03. Of those reporting illicit drug use in 2003–04, 71% used heroin, 32% used diazepam, 7% used cocaine and 3% used crack cocaine (SDEA 2004). For those individuals who reported heroin as their main drug of use, 33% reported illicit diazepam use, 7% cocaine and 4% crack cocaine. There are a number of reasons for engaging in polydrug misuse. Some combinations either enhance or extend the effects of the main drug (diazepam and ecstasy) or reduce its after-effects (crack used by heroin users). Alternatives may also be used to replicate the effects of the drug of choice if the latter is not available.

Heroin seizures

The United Nations Office on Drugs and Crime has conducted the Afghanistan Opium Survey annually since 1994. In 2000 the total area under opium poppy cultivation in Afghanistan was 82,000 hectares. The following year (2001) witnessed a steep decline to 8,000 hectares following the ban imposed by the former Taliban regime. However, in 2002 there was a sharp rise to 74,000 hectares, which continued to the level of 80,000 hectares in 2003.

Shortly before the start of the 2004 opium season, the United Nations Office on Drugs and Crime (UNODC) and the Afghan Counter Narcotics Directorate (ACND) launched a Farmers' Intentions Survey. Amongst other issues, the survey investigated the potential cultivation trend for 2004. The results of the survey indicated that over two-thirds of the opium farmers interviewed intended to increase their level of opium poppy cultivation in 2004 (see Figure 8.1).

Until 1999, HM Customs and Excise (HMCE) seized a greater portion of heroin than police forces. The weight of heroin seized by the police in Scotland increased almost fivefold from 360 kg in 1998 to about 1,500 kg in 1999. Since then the police have continued to seize larger quantities of heroin than HMCE. In 2001 the police seized 71% of the total weight and 62% of the total weight in 2002 (see Figure 8. 2).

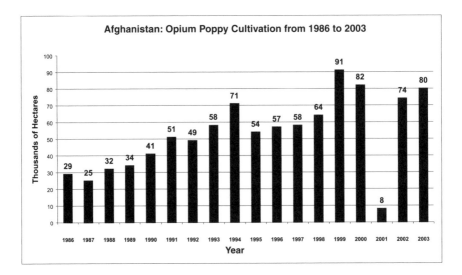

Figure 8.1 Afghanistan: opium poppy cultivation from 1986 to 2003
Source: ONODC (2004b).

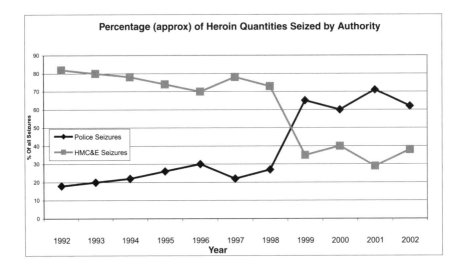

Figure 8.2 Quantity of heroin seizures in Scotland, 1985 to 2000
Source: Home Office (2004a).

When examining the number of seizures it is important to note that seizure numbers do not necessarily reflect the quantity of drugs recovered. An examination of Scotland-specific data demonstrates this quite clearly. Seizures of heroin steadily increased from 1990 through to 2000 (see Figure 8.3), whereas the quantities of heroin seized peaked in 1999, and fell back in 2000 (see Figure 8.4).

Drug markets and distribution systems

Following the outline set by the National Intelligence Model (NIM), drug markets can be described as operating at three levels:

- Level 1 covering local issues (primarily at divisional level)
- Level 2 covering cross-border issues (at force and inter-force level)
- Level 3 covering serious and organised crime (on a national or international scale).

The Scottish policing response to tackling drugs operates at these three levels. The Scottish Drug Enforcement Agency (SDEA) tackles the highest level of serious and organised crime at level 3. Police force drug squads and to a certain extent the SDEA deal with level 2 middle markets, while local police areas (basic command units or divisions) police the lower level 1 dealers/users (NCIS 2003). The profitability of different criminal ventures is difficult to gauge and will fluctuate, but it is clear that drugs trafficking, whatever the commodity, offers sufficient profit at each stage of

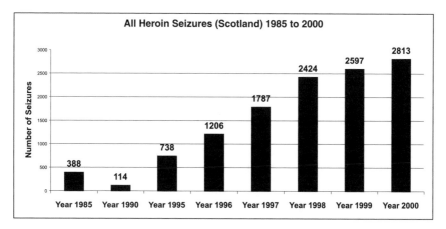

Figure 8.3 Number of heroin seizures in Scotland, 1985 to 2000
Source: Home Office (2004a).

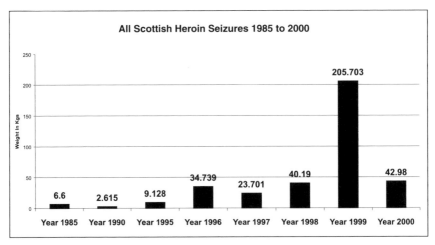

Figure 8.4   Heroin seizures by weight in kg in Scotland, 1985 to 2000
Source: Home Office (2004a).

the trade, from cultivation or manufacture through to street-level dealing, to encourage the involvement of criminals at all levels. At the local level empirical research evidence from within the UK describes three distinct retail drug market types.

Open markets

These are specific markets, usually street-based, in which drugs are sold to any credible buyer (Edmunds *et al.* 1996; Lee 1996). The main advantage of an illicit open street market is the ease of locating buyers and sellers, but it does present major disadvantage for participants, as it renders them vulnerable to policing. In response to the risks of enforcement, open markets tend to be transformed into closed markets.

Closed markets

This is where dealers only do business with known buyers, or other persons for whom another trusted person will vouch. The degree to which markets are closed will depend largely on the level of threat posed by the police. Intensive policing can quickly transform open markets into closed ones (Edmunds *et al.* 1996; May *et al.* 1999).

Semi-open markets

This describes liquor-licensed venues such as pubs or clubs providing retail markets, in particular for ecstasy and other drugs used by 'clubbers'. These should be considered as 'semi-open' in that dealers will generally sell drugs in the absence of any prior introduction. Ruggiero and South (1995) considered that most illicit drug buying operates in private or semi-public places such as pubs and clubs.

Understandably, given the increased use of mobile phones and changing technology, contact between dealer and buyer is increasingly facilitated by mobile phone (Edmunds *et al*. 1996; Chatterton *et al*. 1995). Mobile phones reduce the risks associated with illicit transactions by increasing the difficulty for the police of carrying out surveillance. In response the police have become increasingly sophisticated, with a variety of techniques employed when targeting dealers. The significance of these observations becomes evident when considered alongside the statistics for property interference and intrusive surveillance authorisations, which reveal that drugs offences are the major target of authorisations (Office Surveillance Commissioner 2003/04). In terms of enforcement, three categories of covert activity are authorised:

- *Intrusive surveillance* – This is covert and carried out in relation to anything taking place on any residential premises or in any private vehicle. It involves a person on the premises or in the vehicle, or is carried out by a surveillance device.

- *Directed surveillance* – This is covert but not intrusive, undertaken for a specific investigation or operation in a way likely to obtain private information about a person.

- *Covert human intelligence source (CHIS)* – The use or conduct of someone who establishes or maintains a personal or other relationship with a person for the covert purpose of obtaining information.

Traditionally, drug distribution systems are seen as pyramidical, with importers and traffickers operating at the apex, cascading drugs downwards to street-level dealers who operate on the lowest layer. Until recently no systematic research had been carried out in Scotland in terms of how drug markets operated. However, Bland and Coope (2003) examined low-level dealing in a series of interviews with police officers.

Low-level distribution networks are the crucial means by which drugs become available within a neighbourhood – these networks operate both by sustaining existing drug-using subcultures, and also by recruiting new users ... The police in all the areas we visited reported heroin dealing as the primary problem they were facing. Dealing of crack was identified as a developing problem in a couple of areas, cocaine in another. Diazepam was also identified in an inner city market. The most commonly dealt quantity of drug was for heroin, for example, the 'tenner bag', under a tenth of a gram of heroin sold for about ten pounds. Such a quantity would usually provide only one or two 'hits' for the user.

This research also identified that the majority of low-level drug dealers were users operating in a chaotic and unpredictable way. Small amounts sufficient for one or two 'hits' were the common dealing quantity. Least common were the organised low-level dealers operating for profit. Similarly, Dorn *et al.* (1992) describe disjointed and fluid systems operating in Britain in the late 1980s. Far from being neat and organised top-down hierarchies controlled by a 'Mr Big', the reality was a panorama of small groups of opportunistic entrepreneurs.

Based on interviews with convicted drug traffickers and law enforcement representatives, Pearson *et al.* (2001) described how illicit drugs are moved from importation to street level in the UK. This study represented the first attempt to map out the middle levels of the UK's drug markets. Criminal networks at the middle level are described as being small, with a small number of dealers and users. There was no support for the complex and tightly run mafia-style organisation operating at an international level. The reality was one of networks of independent traders or brokers.

The middle-market, multi-commodity drug dealer is identified as occupying a strategic position linking upper (importation and wholesale) and lower (retail) levels of the market. The middle-market dealer sphere of operation involves considerable horizontal complexity in terms of linking wholesale suppliers to multiple retail-level customers. Pearson describes a series of loosely interlinked local and regional markets as opposed to a national drugs market.

There is a distinct lack of empirical research on drug dealing at the mid to higher serious and organised crime level. Research within the upper echelons of serious organised drug dealing is far from extensive, with the overwhelming majority of research concentrated at the lower retail level and mainly undertaken in the US.

UK and Scottish drugs policies

Government ten-year drug strategy

In April 1998, the UK government published a ten-year strategy for tackling drug misuse called *Tackling Drugs to Build a Better Britain* (Home Office 1998). The strategy was based on the work by the then UK Anti-Drugs Co-ordinator, Keith Hellawell, the so-called 'drugs czar' who was also responsible for monitoring progress made under the strategy. The strategy set out four broad aims:

- preventing young people misusing drugs
- protecting communities from drug-related anti-social/criminal behaviour
- treating people to overcome their drug problems
- stifling availability of illegal drugs.

Each of these aims related to a key objective, a programme of action and performance indicators to assess progress. Through the Co-ordinator's annual report and plan of action against drugs, it was hoped to track progress objectively to ensure that resource input, performance measurement and achievements are accurately known and quantified.

Concerted Inter-Agency Drugs Action

In 1999, the Concerted Inter-Agency Drugs Action (CIDA) group was formed under the chairmanship of HM Customs and Excise, bringing together the agencies and departments most concerned with tackling class A drugs' availability in the UK. This group is composed of all of the agencies responsible for enforcement activity from the point of production to local supply. CIDA has responsibility for action at national and international level to reduce the availability of class A drugs to the UK under the government's updated drugs strategy. CIDA membership consists of NCIS, security and intelligence agencies, Home Office, Cabinet Office, Metropolitan Police Service, National Crime Squad, Scottish Drugs Enforcement Agency, Association of Chief Police Officers, HM Customs and Excise, Foreign Office and Ministry of Defence. Multi-agency 'end-to-end' strategies devised for tackling the trades in heroin and cocaine have led to closer working between law-enforcement agencies.

CIDA has developed comprehensive action plans to tackle heroin and cocaine which co-ordinate action in the following areas:

- intelligence and interdiction operations in key heroin and cocaine source and transit regions

- diplomatic initiatives, including programmes to develop law enforcement capabilities in source and transit regions and support for illicit crop monitoring

- activity to improve knowledge of cocaine and heroin distribution and identify and address gaps in current knowledge

- targeting of major heroin and cocaine traffickers who impact on the UK

- distribution activity targeted at middle market and local level dealers and distributors

- depriving criminals of the proceeds of their crimes and disrupting the movement of drug-related money flows
- activity against precursor chemicals.

It is not entirely clear to what extent CIDA influences the enforcement response within Scotland. However, given SDEA membership, the group's influence is likely to be significant.

The Scottish Drugs Task Force

In Scotland the 'Drugs Task Force' consisting of experts from the statutory and voluntary sectors led by the then Minister of State at the Scottish Office, Lord Fraser, conducted a review of the efforts to tackle drug misuse in Scotland. Reporting in October 1994, Lord Fraser and his task force reached a number of conclusions:

- An increased emphasis should be placed on efforts to reduce the demand for drugs.
- In schools new drug prevention packages should be developed.
- A review should be undertaken of drugs services.
- Specific guidance on the prescribing of substitute drugs should be drawn up.
- Community drug problem services in Scotland should be developed to increase referrals from and to social work services.
- In dealing with drug misuse offenders, a range of options should be available to prosecuting authorities and the courts.
- The Scottish Prison Service should develop existing initiatives from reduction through to abstinence and piloting of throughcare schemes.
- Drug action teams should be established.
- A Scottish Committee on the Misuse of Drugs, reporting to the Scottish Executive, should be set up to advise on policy, priorities and strategic planning.

Scottish Advisory Committee on Drug Misuse

As a consequence of the 1994 Fraser Report the Scottish Advisory Council on the Misuse of Drugs (SACDM) was established to advise on policy, priorities and strategic planning. Within the Scottish Executive, the Minister with overall responsibility for co-ordinating drug policy is the Deputy Minister for Justice and he/she chairs the SACDM, which is responsible for Scotland's co-ordination and monitoring of drug misuse issues. Membership includes a number of representatives of relevant organisations, the voluntary sector and a number of other experts. SACDM aims to assess progress on the implementation of Scotland's drugs strategy set out in the document *Tackling Drugs in Scotland: Action in Partnership* (Scottish Office 1999). In addition, the group oversees the monitoring arrangements; develops policy; watches over information and research requirements; and makes adjustments to the strategy as necessary.

Scotland's drugs strategy

Tackling Drugs in Scotland: Action in Partnership set out a Scottish approach based on the four national priority areas identified in the aims of the UK strategy: treatment, young people, availability, communities. The strategy drew together themes that emerged from the 1994 Drugs Task Force Report (Lord Fraser Report), experiences of drug issues within Scotland and areas for further action described in the UK White Paper. The strategy is described as Scotland's contribution to further development of the UK drug strategy. For each of the four areas, specific Scottish objectives and action priorities were outlined. Subsequently, the Scottish Executive's Drug Action Plan published in May 2000 reported on the action taken or planned by the Executive to implement the national strategy. However, it was not until December 2000 that measurable targets first appeared. 'For the first time ever, Scotland is to have measurable targets to aim at in the fight to cut both the supply and the demand for drugs … what Scotland has never had before are clear and measurable objectives for us all to work to' (Scottish Executive news release [SE3101/2000] 1 December 2000). The targets set included:

- To reverse the upward trend in drug related deaths and reduce the total number, by at least 25% by 2005 (1999 figure 340).

- To reduce the proportion of drug misusers who inject by one-fifth by 2005 (1999 figure 39%).

- To increase the number of drug seizures by 25% by 2004 (1999 figure 17,764).

- To increase the number of offences recorded by Scottish police forces for 'supply or possession with intent to supply drugs' by 25% by 2004 (1999 figure 8,514).

- To reduce the proportion of people under 25 reporting use of illegal drugs in the last month and previous year substantially, and heroin use by 25% by 2005.

- To reduce the proportion of young people under 25 who are offered illegal drugs significantly, and heroin by 25%, by 2005.

These are the official government measures which determine the success or failure of Scotland's approach to drug misuse. Despite the Scottish Executive producing annual reports on drug misuse from 2000 onwards, which track progress towards achieving these targets, no annual report has been published to date for the main target year 2004. The foreword to the 2003 *Annual Report* by the Deputy Justice Minister sheds some light on this omission:

> As this *Report* confirms, we are making steady and encouraging progress towards attainment of many of our published targets and standards. We have to acknowledge, however, that not all developments over the last twelve months or so have been positive. Particularly worrying is the current level of drug-related deaths … No-one has ever claimed that turning around Scotland's drugs problem was going to be easy or quick. There are, after all, estimated to be nearly 56,000 opiate and benzodiazepine misusers alone. We are in a long game …
>
> (Scottish Executive 2003)

Harm reduction

The evolution of harm reduction in the UK drug policy has been in the main a response to the HIV epidemic among injecting drug users. Faced with a potential HIV/AIDS epidemic in the late 1980s, the Conservative government established a series of harm-reduction initiatives such as needle exchanges. In Scotland this policy continued with Scotland's drug strategy *Tackling Drugs in Scotland* (Scottish Office 1999) and the subsequent Scottish Executive Drug Action Plan (2000).

On 27 October 2004, in a Scottish Executive press release, the Justice Minister announced the expansion of drug treatment and rehabilitation services in Scotland: 'more help for addicts would be matched by a stronger partnership between the criminal justice and health services to get a firm grip on drug related offending and loosen the dealers' grip on our communities' (Scottish Executive 2004).

ACPOS drug strategy

The ACPOS Drugs Strategy (ACPOS 2003b) highlights the primary role that the police continue to play in supply reduction. The strategy emphasises the importance of demand and harm reduction approaches and set three high-level objectives to reduce supply, demand and harm.

However, despite describing in detail the Scottish police service's response to drug misuse, the strategy fails to identify specific and measurable targets against which to measure success. The first coherent national targets were not set by ACPOS until 2003 in their *Policing Priorities for Scotland 2003–2006*. There it was stated that 'the service is committed to tackling the levels of violent crime and acquisitive crime related to drug misuse and distribution' (ACPOS 2003a). ACPOS set the following targets for the Scottish Police Service. They proposed, firstly, to increase the weight of class A drug seizures by 10% by 2005–06; and secondly, to increase the number of offences for possession and possession with intent to supply drugs by 10% by 2005–06. Against a background of record seizures of illegal drugs, the eight police forces in Scotland, working with and supported by the SDEA, will continue to develop their established track record of joint working with other involved agencies at both local and national levels.

Drug enforcement

The National Criminal Intelligence Service

The National Criminal Intelligence Service (NCIS) first emerged as the National Drugs Intelligence Unit in the Home Office, subsequently developing into a separate organisation in 1992. Following the Police and Criminal Justice Act 2001, NCIS returned to direct funding by the Home Office in 2002. Section 2 of the Police Act 1997 describes the functions of NCIS:

- To gather, store and analyse information in order to provide criminal intelligence.

- To provide criminal intelligence to police forces in Great Britian, the Police Service of Northern Ireland (PSNI), the National Crime Squad and other law enforcement agencies.

- To act in support of the above in carrying out their criminal intelligence activities.

United Kingdom Threat Assessment

The United Kingdom Threat Assessment (UKTA) describes and assesses the threats to the UK from serious and organised crime. It is produced by the NCIS using intelligence and information provided by UK law-enforcement agencies and other sources. In producing the UKTA, NCIS examines the range of serious and organised criminal activity and provides a window into it based on intelligence assessments. The UKTA is used to inform UK law-enforcement priorities for tackling serious and organised crime. Class A drug trafficking (heroin, cocaine powder, crack cocaine and ecstasy) is considered to be the most significant threat facing the UK.

For organised criminal groups to survive and prosper, their activities require organisation and support from criminal or quasi-legitimate infrastructure. Serious and organised criminals are involved in a wide range of criminal activity. They are readily adaptive to opportunities and challenges and actively protect their businesses and enterprises by whatever means. Throughout the United Kingdom there are distributors and dealers whose participation is critical to the criminal business of organised trafficking groups. Although they may associate with, buy from and even pay a percentage of profits to an organised crime group, they operate independently of the group.

Class A drugs trafficking remains highly profitable at all stages from production through to street-level dealing, thus attracting serious and organised criminals and street-level dealers. The profit accrued by serious and organised crime is reinvested to fund other forms of criminal activity and lavish lifestyles. Patterns of poly-drug use provide an incentive for traffickers to engage in multi-drug trafficking rather than limiting to one commodity. The key elements are opportunity, capability and profit. Class A drug traffickers will readily smuggle other drugs such as cannabis, amphetamine or pharmaceuticals, and adequately cope with the logistics of importation and trade at a profit.

The National Crime Squad (NCS) works at the heart of tackling serious and organised crime. It is dedicated to dismantling and interrupting criminal enterprises, which in effect means tackling serious drug trafficking, illegal arms dealing, money laundering, contract killings, counterfeit currency, kidnap and extortion. The NCS supports domestic UK police forces and works closely with NCIS, HM Customs and Excise (HMCE), Immigration (IND) and the Home Office. HM Customs and Excise is a government department that plays a vital frontline role in the detection of illegal imports of drugs, alcohol and tobacco. Tackling class A drug smuggling is identified as one of the main priorities, with specialist investigators and dedicated anti-smuggling teams established at ports and airports throughout the UK. In addition, HMCE operates four sea-going cutters that operate around Britain's coastline.

Scottish Drugs Enforcement Forum

The Scottish Drugs Enforcement Forum (SDEF) was originally established by the Scottish Office Home Department to bring together the agencies which have enforcement functions in Scotland. It was established primarily to ensure that enforcement was applied in a concerted way to improve the overall effort against drug misuse. In organisational terms, ministerial interest in drug enforcement policy, its strategic direction and effective outcomes, rests with the Deputy Minister for Justice, who (in addition to chairing SACDM), chairs the SDEF. This dual functionality ensures that SDEF activity is directly linked with the work of SACDM.

Scottish Drug Enforcement Agency

The SDEA is an organisation established and maintained by the Scottish ministers under section 36(1) of the Police (Scotland) Act 1967. The organisation is under the direction of a director, first appointed by Scottish ministers on 25 February 2000. The operations co-ordinated by the SDEA involving the discharge of police functions are carried out in accordance with a collaborative agreement among the chief constables of the eight Scottish police forces, and the convenors of the police authorities and joint police boards made under section 12(1) of the 1967 Act. The joint operation established by the agreement is known as the operational and intelligence groups of the SDEA.

The director reports annually to the SDEF, and seeks the Forum's agreement on the Agency's enforcement priorities. This places the traditional tripartite structure and in particular, the operational independence of the SDEA and ultimately the Scottish Police Service in jeopardy. As a consequence of this arrangement, the Deputy Justice Minister (as Chair of the SDEF) has a direct involvement in setting the SDEA's operational priorities and therefore the tripartite structure and political independence of the police are somewhat blurred.

As a result of the collaborative agreement, the director of the Agency cannot operate independently and consequently the director is required to report, through the Standing Committee of Chief Constables (SCCC), to Scottish ministers. The director is responsible to the SCCC for operational matters relating to the SDEA and is accountable to Scottish ministers and the Scottish Parliament for the financial resources granted by them to the Agency. The SCCC oversees all aspects of the operation: financing, personnel management, development and general administration of the Agency.

The SDEA is physically co-located with NCIS and HM Customs and Excise at premises situated in Paisley on the outskirts of Glasgow. The structure of the SDEA comprises three distinct business areas: crime co-ordination, strategy co-ordination and corporate services. Crime co-ordination, as the name suggests, reflects the Agency's 'co-ordinated' response to serious and organised crime. Within this specific business area an Intelligence Group and an Operations Group perform a separate but complementary role. The Intelligence Group is made up of the Scottish money-laundering unit, intelligence development, special projects, and a source management unit. In gathering, assessing and disseminating intelligence the group supports the operational wing of the Agency. The Operations Group comprises operational syndicates located in the east, west and north of Scotland. The function of this group is to carry out operational activity and convert intelligence received from the intelligence group into covert policing operations with the ultimate aim of securing the conviction of individuals involved in serious and organised crime.

The strategic aims of the Agency articulated in the 2003–04 annual report identified that the objectives of the SDEA include the prevention and detection of serious and organised crime, 'including drug trafficking ...' This indicates that drug trafficking is only an additional task among a host of others and not a primary function. This theme is further developed in the director's foreword to the Annual Report, which identifies that the SDEA will extend activity across all aspects of serious and organised crime to meet the threats posed by increasingly diverse criminal networks. 'The SDEA approach to serious organised crime is increasingly founded on the Proceeds of Crime Act 2002 ... the seizure of criminal assets will become central to all the Agency's activities ...'. One of the SDEA targets for the year 2004–05 is 'to identify and report £21m of realisable assets to the Crown for restraint' (SDEA 2004).

While the SDEA is primarily engaged in intelligence-led enforcement activity concentrated on the 'availability' pillar of the Scottish Executive's national drug strategy, it also acknowledges the significance of demand and harm reduction. This is reflected in the role of the SDEA National Drugs Co-coordinator, who leads the Scottish Police Service's response to drug prevention and education.

It is difficult to reconcile the obvious necessity to respond to the operational requirements of the SDEA in tackling serious organised crime and the 'collaborative agreement' when viewed in terms of, for example, the Regulation of Investigatory Powers (Scotland) Act 2000 (RIP(S)A). Passed by the Scottish Parliament in September 2000, RIP(S)A provides a statutory basis for the authorisation and use by public authorities of covert surveillance, both intrusive and directed, within Scotland and the use of covert human intelligence sources.

The *Annual Report of the Chief Surveillance Commissioner* to the Prime Minister and to Scottish ministers for 2003–2004 makes direct reference to this arrangement relating to RIP(S)A. 'I referred to the obvious importance of the Director of the SDEA being entitled to authorise the agency's covert operations. This recommendation has been ignored. I accordingly repeat it, with no less respect but with more force. I am satisfied that, unless the Director has this right, covert operations that have to be conducted by SDEA as agents for other forces are liable to be compromised' (Chief Surveillance Commissioner, 2004).

Association of Chief Police Officers in Scotland

The ACPOS Crime Business Area meets bi-monthly with drug misuse among the standing items discussed. The Crime Business Area is informed of current drug-related issues by a Drugs Sub Committee and is chaired by the director of the SDEA. Membership of the Drug Sub Committee is made up of representatives of all Scottish forces. Force drug co-ordinators from each of the eight Scottish forces make up a force drug co-ordinators' forum (FDCF), which considers local and national drug misuse issues. As the chair of FDCF, the SDEA National Drugs Co-ordinator carries out a secretariat function for the Drug Sub Committee, thereby ensuring members are kept aware of current and emerging issues.

The Scottish tasking and co-ordination process

In keeping with the principles of the National Intelligence Model, ACPOS established a formal Scottish tasking and co-ordination process to identify threats posed by crime groups to Scottish communities, set priorities, pool together knowledge and prepare a collective response. The tasking and co-ordination process in Scotland differs somewhat from the English model. In Scotland, a single national tasking and co-ordination group is supported by the NCIS Scottish and Northern Ireland Branch Office. The SDEA performs a role similar to that of the National Crime Squad (NCS) in the English model. However, there are no regional crime squads or regional intelligence group equivalents in Scotland.

Scottish Strategic Tasking and Co-ordination Group

The role of the Scottish strategic tasking and co-ordination group (Scottish Strategic Group, SSG)) is to direct resources according to priorities identified as impacting upon Scottish communities, including serious and organised crime that transcends force and national boundaries, ensuring effective investigation, intelligence gathering, crime prevention and disruption techniques. Effort and resources are focused on areas where they would have most impact and expectations are defined in terms of the NCIS Scottish Strategic Assessment (SSA). The SSA examines the principal threats to Scotland from serious, organised and cross-border crime and examines how these threats are likely to develop. This Strategic Assessment is undertaken to inform the law-enforcement community of the current situation regarding serious and organised crime in Scotland and offer a starting point for the Scottish tasking and co-ordination process.

The SSA informs the National Intelligence Model (NIM) control strategy (set by the SSG) for law-enforcement activity aimed at the arrest and disruption of the most serious organised crime groups whose activities impact upon Scotland. The NIM control strategy could be defined as a process for choosing an appropriate action when there are many alternative steps, thereby controlling the response. It identifies priorities, resources and determines policy. Membership of the SSG consists of chief officer rank or equivalent from Scottish forces and law-enforcement agencies. The chair of the ACPOS Crime Business Area chairs the SSG and it meets bi-annually. The group aims to assess threats posed to Scottish communities by 'serious organised crime' and to identify priorities in formulating a response to these threats.

Scottish Tactical Tasking and Co-ordination Group

The Scottish Tactical Tasking and Co-ordination Group (STG) meets bi-monthly and has three main functions. First, it has to apply the NIM tactical menu to the Control Strategy set by the SSG. The tactical menu comprises four main elements:

- targeting offenders in line with the control strategy
- management of crime and disorder hotspots
- crime series and incident investigation
- preventative measures.

Second, the STG has to respond to new and emerging trends, and third, it has to check that agreed plans and enforcement work are on course to meet set objectives. Together with the tactical menu, the STG controls the selection and management of targets. This ensures that the targeting regime is consistent with priorities set within the control strategy. The SDEA crime co-ordinator is the chair of the STG and is a full member of SSG. This safeguards accountability and provides the best possible communication between both groups. This arrangement is reinforced and formalised in the cross-circulation of minutes between the strategic and tactical groups. The co-ordinator's primary role is to oversee the SDEA Intelligence, Operations and Operational Support Groups.

Policing drugs in Scotland – the future

The Serious Organised Crime and Police Bill introduced in the House of Commons in November 2004 is designed to strengthen cross-border co-operation on organised crime and regulate the private security industry. It provides for the establishment and functions of a Serious and Organised

Crime Agency (SOCA), but extends beyond the creation of SOCA and reflects the full range of issues covered in the SOCA White Paper 2004. The following proposals within the Bill represent significant changes to existing law enforcement:

- abolition of NCIS and NCS
- conferring the powers of constables, immigration officers and customs officers on certain SOCA employees
- providing for persons to be compelled to give evidence for use against others
- providing for a reduction in sentence for those who plead guilty and provide evidence against others
- making provision for the protection of witnesses.

In addition, the Bill contains provisions, which, following consultation, will enable the Scottish ministers to determine 'strategic priorities' for SOCA. The consultation exercise includes consultation with Scottish ministers and ACPOS. Thereafter, SOCA will be responsible for the subsequent production of performance targets relating to strategic priorities. SOCA represents a significant shift from the traditional police model and represents one of the most significant changes in UK law enforcement since the 1962 Royal Commission into the Police.

Exactly what impact SOCA will have on policing in Scotland remains to be seen. However, in October 2004, the Director of the SDEA announced the proposed establishment of the first anti-organised crime campus in the UK based at Gartcosh, in Lanarkshire (BBC News release, Sunday 17 October 2004). The proposed campus should be operational sometime in 2006 to coincide with the establishment of SOCA.

It would appear, therefore, that while the Serious Organised Crime and Police Bill does not legislate for the establishment of a Scottish equivalent of SOCA, a campus housing all national law-enforcement agencies involved in the investigation of serious and organised crime in Scotland (including SOCA agents) would in effect be a Scottish equivalent. An article appearing in *The Scotsman* newspaper reinforces this view: 'Jack McConnell, the First Minster, believes the English proposals for SOCA mirror the Scottish plans for Gartcosh. He strongly believes the two can work together without any question of subordination. He is now urging the Home Secretary to sign up to his Gartcosh scheme, by having the Scottish staff of SOCA based there' (*The Scotsman*, November 2004).

Conclusion

It was never the intention that this chapter should examine the rhetoric or debate that divides opinion on issues surrounding drug misuse. The emergence of harm reduction within a framework of prohibition and a rigorously enforced 'war on drugs' within the United Kingdom has created what could be described as a contradiction, where the interest in the health of drug misusers collides directly with law enforcement. The dilemma for the policing agencies is that both enforcement and treatment are central to the UK, and indeed Scotland's drug strategy. The 'war on drugs' is an example of a policy that engages 'drug experts' and 'opinion makers' with opposing views, engendering debate surrounding cause and effect where it is argued that enforcement relates causally to harm inducing prohibition.

With regard to trafficking and supply of drugs by serious and organised crime, there are probably significant changes ahead in terms of the policing of such crime. Indeed, the introduction of a new Drugs Bill in 2004, which has recently received its second reading in the House of Commons, will add to the pace of change. However, despite the continual focus on the 'war on drugs', it is important to remember that the three United Nations conventions on international co-operation concerning drugs, discussed at the beginning of the chapter, are concerned not only with punishment but also with treatment and prevention.

The 1961 convention requires the parties to 'give special attention to and take all practicable measures for the prevention of abuse of drugs and for the early identification, treatment, education, after-care, rehabilitation and social reintegration of the persons involved ...' (Single Convention on Narcotic Drugs 1961). It also provides that, 'when abusers of drugs have committed offences, the parties may provide, either as an alternative to conviction or punishment or in addition to conviction or punishment, measures of treatment, education, after-care, rehabilitation and social reintegration ...' (ibid.). To a great extent the same wording appears in the 1971 convention and a similar approach is further refined in the 1988 convention.

It is important, therefore, not to lose sight of the non-enforcement contribution to tackling drug misuse when considering the future of policing illicit drugs in Scotland. To date the Scottish police have a sound track record of involvement in strategies dealing with the treatment of drug dependants and education, as well as enforcement of drugs legislation.

References

Advisory Council on the Misuse of Drugs (1994) *Drug Misusers and the Criminal Justice System Part II: Police, Drug Misusers and the Community*. London: HMSO.

Arrestee Drug Abuse Monitoring (2000) *1999 Annual Report on Drug Use Among Adult and Juvenile Arrestees*. Washington, DC: National Institute of Justice.

Association of Chief Police Officers in Scotland (2003a) *Policing Priorities for Scotland 2003–2006*. Edinburgh: ACPOS.

Association of Chief Police Officers in Scotland (2003b) *Drug Strategy*. Edinburgh: ACPOS.

BBC News Release (17 October 2004) *Agencies to Get Organised Over Crime*.

Bennet, T. (1998) *Drug Testing Arrestees*. London: Home Office.

Bland, N. and Coope, S. (2003) *Reducing the Impact of Local Drug Markets: A Research Review*. Scottish Executive Drug Misuse Research Programme. Edinburgh: Stationery Office.

Bramley-Harker, E. (2001) *Sizing the UK Market for Illicit Drugs*. RDS Occasional Paper No 74. London: Home Office Research, Development and Statistics Directorate.

Chief Surveillance Commissioner (2004) *Annual Report to the Prime Minister and Scottish Ministers for 2003–2004*. London: Stationary Office.

Dorn, N., Murji, K. and South, N. (1992) *Traffickers: Drug Markets and Law Enforcement*. London: Routledge.

Dorn, N., Oette, L. and White, S. (1998) 'Drugs importation and the bifurcation of risk: capitalisation, cuts out and organised crime', *British Journal of Criminology*, 38 (4): 537–60.

Edmunds, M., Hough, H. and Urqua, N. (1996) *Tackling Local Drug Markets in London*. Home Office Police Research Group Paper 80. London: Stationery Office.

Hay, G., Gannon, M., McKeganey, N., Hutchinson, S. and Goldberg, D. (2005) *Estimating the National and Local Prevalence of Problem Drug Misuse In Scotland*. University of Glasgow: Centre for Drug Misuse Research.

Hay, G., McKeganey, N. and Hutchison, S. (2001) *Estimating the National and Local Prevalence of Problem Drug Use in Scotland*. Edinburgh: ISD.

HM Government (1995) *Tackling Drugs Together: A Strategy for England 1995–1998*. London: HMSO.

Home Office (1998) *Tackling Drugs To Build A Better Britain*. London: HMSO.

Home Office (2002) *British Crime Survey 2001–2002*. London: Home Office.

Home Office (2004a) *Drug Seizure and Offender Statistics 2001 and 2002*. Home Office Statistical Bulletin 08/04. London: Stationery Office.

Home Office (2004b) *Serious and Organised Crime*. Government White Paper. London: Stationery Office.

Lee, M. (1996) 'London: community damage limitation through policing' in N. Dorn, J. Jepsen and E. Savona (eds), *European Drug Policy and Enforcement*. Basingstoke: Macmillan.

May, T., Edmunds, M. and Hough, M. (1999) *Street Business: Links between Sex and Drug Markets*. Crime Prevention and Detection Series Paper. London: Home Office Policing and Reducing Crime Unit.

McKeganey, N., Connelly, C., Knepl, J., Norrie, J. and Reid, L. (2000) *Interviewing and Drug Testing of Arrestees in Scotland: A Pilot of the ADAM Methodology*. Crime and Criminal Justice Research Findings No 48. Edinburgh: Central Research Unit.

National Criminal Intelligence Service (2004) *United Kingdom Threat Assessment*. London: Home Office.

Pearson, G. (2001) 'Normal drug use: ethnographic fieldwork among an adult network of recreational drug users in Inner London', *Substance Use and Misuse*, 36 (1): 167–200.

Ruggiero, V. and South, N. (1995) *Eurodrugs, Drug Use Markets and Trafficking in Europe*. London: UCL Press.

The Scotsman (2004) 'Scotland and England go their separate ways', 25 November 2004.

Scottish Drug Enforcement Agency (2003) *Annual Report for 2002–2003*. Edinburgh: Stationery Office.

Scottish Drug Enforcement Agency (2004) *Annual Report for 2003–2004*. Edinburgh: Stationery Office.

Scottish Executive (2000) *Iain Gray Targets Scotland's Drug Misery*. News Release SE3101/2000, 1 December 2000. Edinburgh: Scottish Executive.

Scottish Executive (2000) *Drug Action Plan*. Edinburgh: HMSO.

Scottish Executive (2002) *Scottish Crime Survey 2000*. Edinburgh: HMSO.

Scottish Executive (2003) *Annual Report on Drug Misuse*. Edinburgh: HMSO.

Scottish Executive (2004) *More Help For Drug Addicts. Press Release 27 October 2004*. Edinburgh: Scottish Executive.

Scottish Office (1994) *Drugs in Scotland – Meeting the Challenge*. Drugs Task Force Report. Edinburgh: HMSO.

Scottish Office (2000) *Tackling Drugs in Scotland: Action in Partnership*. Edinburgh: HMSO.

United Nations Office on Drugs and Crime (2004a) *World Drug Report by the United Nations Office on Drugs and Crime*. United Nations: UNODC.

United Nations Office on Drugs and Crime (2004b) *Afghanistan Opium Survey*. United Nations: UNODC.

United Nations Office on Drugs and Crime (2004c) *Farmers' Intention Survey*. United Nations: UNODC.

Chapter 9

Policing youth in Scotland: a police perspective

David Strang

Introduction

Juvenile-related crime is an emotive issue in the United Kingdom. There is a widespread belief that since the Second World War offending by children and young people has risen alarmingly. Several high-profile cases, such as the killing of Jamie Bulger, together with the increase in offending related to substance misuse – alcohol, glue and illegal drugs – have provided grounds for increased concern.

Throughout the last 50 years, repeated attempts have been made to prevent children from drifting into delinquency by providing guidance and support to ensure they were diverted away from crime. In the 1950s police involvement in social crime prevention was limited in scope and imagination. By the 1960s the police service in Scotland had discovered a more appropriate role in dealing with juvenile offending, in proportion to the extent of juvenile crime and delinquency at the time. A broader understanding of the causes of crime was emerging, which recognised that not only was the individual blameworthy, but families, environmental factors and the wider community also had to bear some element of responsibility. In the police service, community involvement branches (CIBs) sought to increase close co-operation between the police, communities and local authority agencies (SHHD Circular 6 1971). Public concern about young people and delinquency inevitably meant that much of the work of CIBs was focused on youth.

More recently the Scottish Executive has updated its policies on juvenile crime and re-offending by young persons, based partly on the relative success of the Children's Hearings and police warning systems, but also to address a growing public concern at the rising levels of juvenile crime and disorder. Latest estimates reveal that young people commit 30% of recorded crime in Scotland (Scottish Executive 2004). In Glasgow alone, from January to June 2003, 1,755 children were reported to the children's hearings, showing the city's 'uniquely high rate of youth crime' (*Sunday Herald* 2003: 6). The majority of these offenders were aged between 12 and 15 years. In addition, the need to deal quickly and effectively with the perpetrators of minor crimes is being given priority by the Executive in the form of action plans and significant funding in the short to medium terms. It is with these issues that this chapter deals, the long-standing and significant interaction between the Scottish police and Scottish youth; that is, young people in the age range up to eighteen.

Young people

Age and youth are very much matters of perception. 'You are as young as you feel,' we are often told. Even within the age range being considered here, there is a large variation in abilities and experiences. Generalisations are inevitably inaccurate; each individual is different. In the field of youth justice it is too easy to try to categorise young people into particular groups, but this can lead to stereotyping, often polarising views and descriptions. For example, some hold the view that children and young people are intrinsically vulnerable and therefore should be seen as potential victims. Others would rather see the young as potential offenders and thereby a threat to order and security. The reality is that neither stereotype is accurate. Within each person is the potential for good and evil; each is a potential victim and offender.

How adults view young people depends on their own life experiences. Perceptions are shaped from faulty memories from their own childhood and by their adult experiences of interacting with children and young people, whether with their own children and grandchildren, or encounters through work or in other settings. Although we cannot generalise about young people, it is possible to make some observations about how society portrays being young. Youth is seen as an asset in marketing, with many products and services being advertised and presented positively by young, and usually glamorous, people. Tony Blair was perceived positively as a young Prime Minister and for a time it was 'cool' to be young.

There is general recognition that society depends for its future survival on investing in the next generation, that our future is in their hands. A positive view of young people produces an optimistic expectation of the future and what it holds. But what of young people's own perceptions of themselves? How does it feel to be young in Scotland today? Teenage years are a time of change as they grow up from childhood to adulthood. With that change comes a range of emotions from excitement at opportunities ahead to fear and anxieties which uncertainty brings. Young people today feel under pressure from a great many angles. The transition from child to adult is for many a difficult time. Most significantly, young people go through a process of forming their own values and want to experience life for themselves. This involves questioning and challenging the values of their parents and others in authority over them, and deciding for themselves whether to adopt them or not. For many, pushing back boundaries and experimenting with different experiences are important facets of growing up. Rebelling against those in authority, whether parents, teachers or police officers, is a natural process as young people seek to find answers to questions about their own identity: Who am I? What do I want to become?

Many young people feel under pressure from the world around them, bombarded with messages about becoming consumers and the importance of image. Peer pressure to conform to an acceptable lifestyle and the desire for belonging are also strong influences on young lives. These pressures and the need to rebel lead to high levels of teenage smoking and drinking and unsafe sexual activity. We should not underestimate the role that alcohol plays in shaping the lives of many young people, increasing the risk and vulnerability through loss of control and judgement. On top of this are the pressures for achievement, for success at school and college and the need to find employment.

A less comfortable generalised view of young people sees them as a threat, especially to older people. In employment, there is a perception that once past a certain age it is harder to compete with younger applicants. In the area of personal security, many older people see the young as threatening, unsettling and an intrusion on their sense of well-being. 'Youth' is linked too readily with youth crime, youth disorder and anti-social behaviour. Crime statistics show that young people commit a disproportionate number of crimes (Scottish Executive 2004).

Older people's negative perceptions are reinforced through the media, whether in news reports or real events or dramatisation. Their own experiences and those of their friends all shape their perception of young people. In many cases this has developed to the extent that the mere presence of young people in numbers is seen as a threat. The Antisocial Behaviour etc. (Scotland) Act 2004 contains provisions which give a power to police officers to disperse groups of people where their presence may cause fear or alarm. In every village, town and city across the country, young people do gather in groups without any intention to do anything – but simply to 'be'. For young people it is a social activity, which provides a sense of identity and a secure place to be.

A balanced view has to be achieved; for example, a recent study of thousands of young people by Edinburgh University revealed a fifth of 13-year-olds are members of gangs (Smith *et al.* 2004). Members were mainly boys from broken homes and difficult backgrounds, and the study found that being associated with the group gave them moral support, that on occasions encouraged and excused criminal acts. The reality is that young people commit crime across the whole range of offending behaviour from petty offences to the most serious of crimes. And many communities are adversely affected by the damage done by young people in their midst. That said, juvenile offending rates have remained relatively static in the last ten years; 92% of young people never offend and less than 1% are persistent offenders (Scottish Executive 2004). 'In 1991, 2.7% of all eight to 15-year olds had been reported to the children's panel – amounting to 13,462 cases. In 2003 it was 2.8%' (*Scotland on Sunday* 2003a: 15). One senior Scottish police officer pointed out, in the same newspaper report, that 'the facts are that young people are no worse or better today than they have been. And there is no more youth crime than there ever has been, at least not in the last 10 years' (ibid). There is an obvious need to question and clarify the extent to which people's perceptions, particularly those of older people, are shaped by the reality of the threat or by a disproportionate and irrational fear. Because feelings of well-being are intrinsically emotional, it is notoriously difficult to alter these, despite positive experiences and reasoned argument.

In relation to young people's exposure to crime, their most likely experience is as victims of crime, ranging from minor assault, bullying and theft at school to the potential for more serious offences on the streets or at home. Despite years of advances in child protection arrangements, there are still unacceptably high levels of child abuse – physical, emotional and sexual – at all levels in society. The Internet has added a new level of threat and danger to children. In what are considered to be the best interests of children and young people, the safety messages they are given reinforce the view that the world is a dangerous place and they are right to feel afraid. We want our young people to grow up feeling confident and positive about the world in which they live. We know that it is an exciting, challenging and difficult time in their life, and a time when many are misunderstood, stereotyped, blamed and criticised.

Policing

To understand what we expect from the police in relation to young people, we need to have an understanding of what it is we want the police service to do in our communities. In Scotland there is a long tradition of policing as a public service. Police officers are civilians, largely unarmed, who act on behalf of society to maintain order, prevent and detect crime and to deal with incidents and emergencies. A fundamental function of the police is to provide reassurance and confidence, which build a strong sense of safety and security for all Scotland's citizens.

At the heart of policing in Scotland lies the principle of policing by consent. The police is not an army of occupation, controlling the people on behalf of a hostile government, but rather it is delivering a service with the co-operation and approval of the vast majority of the people. In a liberal democracy where the law-makers are subject to re-election every four or five years, there should be a reasonable level of support for legislation enacted. Society in the main remains civilised because the majority of the population live within the constraints of the law. A major part of policing is dealing with the minority who do not.

While the police act on behalf of society in general, they have a particular duty to act on behalf of those who are the most vulnerable in society. There is a special responsibility to protect the weak and the disadvantaged who would otherwise be at the mercy of the bully, the strong, the unscrupulous and the criminal. Others would place a different and less benign interpretation on the function of the police, arguing that the police service is an instrument of social control, protecting those in power from those who would seek to remove them. They would argue that the original purpose of policing was to protect the wealthy property-owning classes against the riots of the masses, and would point to the role of policing during the miners' dispute in 1984 and the poll tax riots in 1990 as evidence of such a continuing role in modern times. Notwithstanding these arguments, a primary responsibility of policing in Scotland is to protect those who are most weak and vulnerable.

Policing is a daily activity rooted in every community, where the police are viewed as the agency of first and last resort: first resort, because people call the police in the event of an emergency when they need help urgently; and last resort because when faced with problems and having tried all else, people turn to the police for help and assistance. The range of events to which the police respond is endless, from the catastrophic to the mundane and unexceptional. However, their core role of preserving life, protecting property, maintaining order and preventing and detecting crime has remained largely unaltered over the last two centuries. Community policing best describes the approach of the police service in Scotland.

In addition, the police provide, in most cases, the gateway into the criminal justice system in Scotland, primarily because they have a duty to report crimes and offences to the procurator fiscal. It is popularly believed that dealing with crime is the main activity of the police. In reality, activity analysis in the police service has shown that less than 50% of operational officers' time is spent on crime investigation and detection (HMICS 2003). More time is spent on dealing with other incidents, road crashes, missing persons, crime prevention, targeted patrolling and road policing.

A great deal of police work is a consequence of broken relationships. In the most obvious sense, cases of domestic violence, assault, neighbour disputes and theft are the result of, and certainly exacerbate, a collapse in a relationship between two people. It is also possible to see that other, perhaps less personal crimes, are the product of failed relationships: drug dealing, traffic offences, vandalism and disorder all indicate a lack of respect for other people and a disregard for the impact of their behaviour on the wider community. So much of policing is dealing with the consequences and picking up the pieces of wider social problems. Many police interventions are aimed at re-establishing broken relationships, and restoring peace where this has been breached. Inevitably many of these activities bring the police into contact with young people.

Successful police interventions should be designed to contribute to addressing more than just the consequences of problems elsewhere in society, whether caused by substance misuse, inequalities or family breakdown. The police service in Scotland is committed to a more proactive problem-solving approach.

Problem-solving has three underpinning principles. First of all, it seeks to address the causes of problems and not merely deal with the consequences. Traditionally, police officers get called repeatedly to deal with a recurring incident or crime, and normally deal with the immediate circumstances or consequences of the problem. Rarely do they have the time or mindset to get to the root of the problem. As a result, the police are called back again and again. What is needed is some careful analysis of the cause of the problem in the first place, with a view to resolving it and thereby reducing the need for further police intervention.

Secondly, a long-term view is required for successful problem-solving. In general, the police have tended to take a short-term approach, resolving immediately the presenting problem. This can be successful and produce a beneficial impact in the short term, but may result simply in displacement or delay if the problem is not solved at root. There are no simplistic solutions or quick fixes to deep-rooted social problems. Lasting improvements in community well-being need to be grounded in a long-term problem-solving approach.

The third principle behind problem-solving is a recognition that progress can only be made through partnership working. Neither the police alone, nor any single agency, can solve these deep-rooted problems. Only by sharing information, data, ideas, resources and solutions can real impact be made. There are good examples across the country of successful partnerships producing real results. Examples such as alcohol and drug action teams and youth justice strategy groups provide platforms for joint problem-solving including the police service, local authorities, the health service, housing, social work, procurator fiscal service, voluntary sector, business community, prison service and fire service. Community Planning is the statutory framework laid down in the Local Government in Scotland Act 2003 to support partnership working at a local level. Across the 32 local authority areas in Scotland, partner organisations share responsibility for leadership and the identification and analysis of problems, which, following public consultation, lead to the production of joint strategies and action plans.

Within a problem-sharing framework, community policing is the chosen vehicle to deliver the service locally. Community policing recognises that successful policing depends on the quality of the relationship between the police and the communities they serve (see Alderson 1979; Brown and Iles 1985; Fielding 1995; Friedmann 1992; Goldstein 1990; Trojanowicz and Bucqueroux 1990; Weatheritt 1987). Levels of confidence felt by the public and their sense of well-being will be dependent to a large extent on the view they have of their local police service, both in a general sense and specifically their local community officer, area inspector, divisional commander or chief constable.

There are three features of a successful community–police relationship. Firstly, the police need to be accessible. The public need to be able to contact the police and to communicate effectively with them, either through a personal encounter with an officer or at a police office, or by telephone, or increasingly by e-mail and via the Internet. Secondly, the police service must be responsive. The public need to know that the police are committed to taking their problems seriously and to acting in a professional and effective way. Thirdly, they must be accountable for their actions, especially answerable locally for the decisions they have made. A successful relationship between a local community and the police will contain all three of these elements to a high degree.

In the context of young people, there is no exception to the principles set out in this section. The police service exists to protect the weakest in society. They must do this through a problem-solving approach, delivered through community policing which rests on a good relationship between the police and young people.

Policing and young people

In December 2004 the Association of Chief Police Officers in Scotland (ACPOS) launched its Youth Strategy, which set out what young people could expect from the police service in Scotland. Its guiding principle is this: 'Young people are citizens in their own right and each is entitled to fair and equitable treatment and service from the Scottish Police Service' (ACPOS 2004).

The development of the ACPOS Youth Strategy has been informed by the understanding articulated in this chapter of the critical nature of relationships in successful policing and a commitment to problem-solving partnerships. There is no doubt that encounters between police officers and young people can be strained at times. There is a natural suspicion on both sides, fuelled by a lack of understanding of intentions and motives. However, improvements can be made in the effectiveness of policing as it relates to young people.

From a very early age many young children are taught that the police are there to help them. If they are lost, in fear or in danger, they are told to 'ask a policeman'. It is not uncommon for a police officer to be smiled at and waved to: 'Hello Mr Policeman'. A great many children consequently grow up with a positive view of the police. There is, of course, another side, when parents use the threat of the police to seek to instil a sense of discipline and order, usually to unruly children: 'I'll get a policeman to take you away if you don't behave'. This message can come to reasonably well-behaved children in a light-hearted manner. So from their earliest days some children develop an ambivalent attitude to the police: part protector to be welcomed, part threat to be feared. This is true of many adults' attitudes to the police too. They are happy to call on the police in time of need of assistance, but are most unwilling to see a police officer when they are driving badly, have drunk too much or are offending in some other way.

As children grow up, they may encounter police officers for themselves in what may be a confrontational intervention. The police uniform represents the authority that many young people are seeking to test and rebel against. Police officers themselves sometimes feel caught between young people's desire for freedom, expressed through unconventional individuality, and society's desire for order, conventional behaviour, and the need for all citizens (including the young) to live within the constraints of the criminal law.

The potential conflict can be at a low level of misbehaviour: noise, aggressive car driving, gathering in groups which others may find threatening, drinking in public places and minor infringements of the law. When complaints are made, it is the police who are called on to deal with them, and the potential for confrontation and conflict is immediately apparent. There is a risk of negative stereotyping occurring on both sides, with trouble expected in every encounter. This leads to a downward spiral of mistrust and a rising level of hostility, which we have seen spill over into violent confrontation in a number of English cities over the last 20 years.

Successful policing requires that the stereotypes are broken on both sides. Clearly, where young people are committing serious offences, the police response inevitably needs to be robust, firm and effective, but more generally the police need to develop strategies for engaging positively with young people. The route to this lies in the two approaches described earlier, community policing and problem-solving partnerships.

Police officers in every community must make themselves accessible and responsive to the needs of young people. There is a real challenge to communicate and consult meaningfully with all sections of the community. Young people need to be taken seriously and not either ignored or assumed to have the same needs as older citizens. The police must be held to account for the service they deliver to young people. The Scottish Police Service has recently developed links with the Scottish Youth Parliament with a view to engaging in constructive dialogue about how services for young people might be improved and delivered. 'Midnight Football' is a good example of constructive consultation with young people in Dumfries and Galloway. Following numerous complaints from local residents about the behaviour of young people, a survey was conducted to establish what alternative activities would be attractive for the young people concerned. As a result, each Friday evening hundreds of girls and boys aged 12 to 18 take part in organised football training and competitions with input from Scottish Football Association coaches. This initiative has had a real impact on the number of complaints from residents and, more importantly, has provided a positive and constructive alternative activity for the young people of the region.

There are many good examples across Scotland of positive problem-solving initiatives, which have taken a radical approach to old problems and found new solutions. One such example is the establishment of 'dry' bars for young people under 18 years, which provide an attractive social setting for teenagers without the dangers of excessive alcohol consumption. Each of these has been founded on the principles of problem-solving and an attempt to tackle the root causes, a long-term commitment to resolving difficulties and an understanding that it is only through partnership working that lasting results can be achieved.

The police service in Scotland seeks to achieve appropriate and constructive engagement with all of Scotland's young people. This necessitates a graded or tiered approach to policing activity. There is still a role for a universal service, usually through schools when the police make a contribution to overall safety messages – personal safety, road safety, alcohol and drugs – and more constructively on active citizenship. The 'Police Box' is a well-designed programme for use in schools by community police officers, covering topics such as road safety, personal safety, drugs and citizenship. 'Leisure All Day' is a sports-based activity involving professional sports coaches communicating positive messages about healthy lifestyles and the dangers of drug misuse. Police officers want to help young citizens build up their confidence and their ability to make positive life choices.

A more focused approach is required for groups or individuals who merit greater direct police intervention. In particular there is a need to provide extra support to people identified as being at greater risk or vulnerable, whether as victims or offenders. These categories include looked-after children, children of parents who are in prison or misusing alcohol or drugs and children excluded from school. There are real benefits from the sharing of data and information between public-sector partners to identify at-risk young people and to ensure that adequate support is in place. This has not yet extended much beyond the field of child protection. The benefits from early and effective intervention with first-time offenders, such as warnings, letters to parents, restorative justice processes, are more than worth the investment when compared with the costs, both social and financial, of failure to prevent a slide into persistent offending.

Of course, the police have an enforcement role, and when faced with serious and persistent offending by young people, must be robust and relentless. No favours are done to either the communities harmed by persistent offenders or to the young offenders themselves if such behaviour is allowed to continue unchecked.

Policing of young people requires constructive engagement appropriate to the needs and behaviour of the those people. The police need to see young people as legitimate citizens in their own right and not some separate, marginalised section of society.

Youth justice

Age of offender

Given the inevitability of youth offending, we need to ask what should be society's response to offending behaviour? To what extent should the age of an offender be taken into account in determining the outcome of the judicial process? In the same way as the individual circumstances of adult offenders will affect the prosecution and sentencing decisions, the maturity and understanding of children and young people who offend should be important factors in determining outcomes. While only a tiny minority of children and young people are formally dealt with through the criminal justice system, a majority of young people will technically breach the criminal law, even if in only minor ways. Society's response to offending behaviour, therefore, needs to be much broader than simply the criminal justice system. Misbehaviour, rather than being seen as abnormal or deviant, is part of the transition from child to adulthood, which the majority of young people grow out of. This is particularly true in relation to minor offending and misdemeanours. Clearly, when serious offences are committed by persistent offenders, who are often out of control and at risk of highly damaging lifestyles, a much more robust and firm response is needed.

There is a question to be asked as to the age at which an individual can be held accountable for their actions. An infant or young child cannot be expected to know the difference between right and wrong or to form an independent view of their own actions. By adulthood an individual is considered to be responsible for his/her actions, but the age of criminal responsibility varies across western Europe from 8 to 14 years. Scotland tends to be at the lower end of this scale, at eight years of age. The challenge for the law is to identify an age at which young people can be held to be responsible and therefore criminally liable for their actions. The difficulty in this is that we know that each person is shaped by early experiences of the world around them, family environment and parental influences. Such experiences play a major part in determining the moral framework in which individual decisions are made. For young people who do offend there is a range of responses to their behaviour. At the very minor end of misbehaviour, inappropriate behaviour is normally dealt with informally by whichever adult is aware of it – such as a parent, teacher or youth worker. If a police officer is involved, it is likely to be dealt with by way of informal advice or guidance.

In recognition of the particular vulnerabilities of young people, police officers are specially trained to interview children, whether as witnesses or suspects. In some circumstances, training and interviewing are conducted with suitably qualified social workers. This combination protects the interests of justice in the broadest sense and the interests of the child.

Juvenile liaison schemes and police warnings

An early strand of policy in dealing with young offenders was the juvenile liaison schemes, which were introduced in the post-war period as a formal extension to the existing informal police warnings and discretion.

These schemes comprised an initial warning with a follow-up period of supervision by a police officer, known as a Juvenile Liaison Officer. A similar scheme had been in operation since 1936 in the city of Aberdeen working in conjunction with the local probation service, which carried out the supervisory role with the agreement of the chief constable. The juvenile liaison schemes involved visits to the children's homes, schools and minister or priest. Such schemes were fully established not only in Scotland, but throughout the UK.

Prior to the 1970s the police in Scotland had directed most of its energies and resources to a 'conception of police work which broadly excluded all methods of crime prevention which were not closely bound up with the protection of the persons and property of the public on the one hand, and the rapid detection and bringing to boot of malefactors on the other' (Ritchie and Mack 1974: 21). However, by the onset of the 1970s there was a considerable sea change in the way the police in Scotland viewed the wider aspects of crime prevention and its own role in the broader field of community involvement. The potential benefits for the community through the medium of effective crime prevention had dawned on the policing world and this new role of the police as facilitators and catalysts to community improvement through a multi-agency approach was gaining a foothold. The police officer became a key individual in the new system of social crime prevention and combating juvenile crime.

The idea of tackling juvenile delinquency at source in Scotland has always been based on encouraging local communities to support the police in identifying the hard core of young people responsible for much of the recurring crime and minor offences in their areas, seeking to prevent delinquency by interception and diversion at an early stage. It deals with both potential and petty offenders. The potential offender can be described as a young person whose anti-social behaviour is causing concern and may be an indicator that he or she is drifting into crime. Such offenders are dealt with by informal warning by a beat officer or officer from the community involvement branch. The warning usually takes place in the home, followed by counselling or supervision for a short period. Petty offenders who committed offences not serious enough to be referred to either the procurator fiscal or children's panel received formal warnings from a senior police officer, and counselling or a period of supervision by a member of the police community involvement branch could follow this when the circumstances warranted it.

This system of police warnings is essentially crime prevention in its broadest sense and generally dealt with children found in suspicious circumstances, unusual places, wandering late at night, exposed to moral danger, playing truant, associating with known criminals and experimenting with alcohol, solvents or drugs. The police normally bring behaviour of this kind to the notice of parents and this helps to make children more aware of their social responsibilities, and also serves as a reminder to parents of their own responsibilities.

Children's Hearings system

The Children's Hearings are a uniquely Scottish form of juvenile justice. They were established by the Social Work (Scotland) Act 1968 as a result of the recommendations of a report by a committee chaired by Lord Kilbrandon (Kilbrandon 1964). The system deals with children under the age of 16 who are either delinquent or in need of care and protection, and does not distinguish between the two. Its approach is a welfare, rather than a punitive one in which the interests of the child are paramount.

The Hearings do not act as a court of law – around 90% of cases of children and young people offending are not disputed (NCH Scotland 2004: 4) – although decisions about matters of fact can be referred to the Sheriff Court as necessary. The system works through lay children's panels consisting of trained volunteers, drawn from the local community and appointed by the Scottish ministers, who discuss what measures of care are appropriate to the children brought before them. A local panel of three members is assisted in each case by a Reporter who is a full-time professional official to whom referrals come for children prospectively in need of care. These referrals can come from a wide range of people, including the police, teachers and social workers, and the grounds for referral are many and varied. They include the committing of an offence or persistent truancy from school, but also cover instances where children are without parental control, are exposed to moral danger or are neglected. In recent years the majority of referrals have related to child-protection situations where a child is suspected of being a victim of physical or sexual abuse and this has necessitated changes in the system under the Children (Scotland) Act 1995. A panel operates by receiving background reports and involving itself in a conference with the child and its parents. The main outcomes are usually measures of supervision either at home or in a residential setting.

Children's Hearings have now been in operation for over 30 years. They have been much admired – though not replicated – by many other countries. It is a genuinely community-based system and provides real opportunities for inter-agency working. Interestingly, a study of the Children's Hearings System in 1974 showed that, prior to the introduction of children's panels, many police officers and social workers shared the conviction that their areas of work were incompatible and distinct from each other and should be kept apart. However, after 1971 attitudes changed on both sides, including new training approaches with an emphasis towards community work with a 'new sense of urgency' (Ritchie and Mack 1974: 70). There remains a public perception, however, that the move away from a punitive approach has represented a 'soft option', not helped by the fact that there has been a 'lack of imagination and investment in the range of disposals available to the panel' (NCH Scotland 2004: 8) and that there are too many cases where decisions simply are not implemented because of gaps in the service (Audit Scotland 2002). A sense of proportion about the extent of the problem dealt with by the Hearings has also to be maintained. The *Annual Report* of the Scottish Children's Reporter Administration (SCRA) showed that in 2001–02 fewer than four per cent of Scottish children were referred and less than half of these were referred on offence grounds (SCRA 2002).

Other interventions

In the case of serious offences, a child or young person will be reported to the procurator fiscal as well as the Reporter to enable a decision to be made in the public interest. However, no young person under the age of 16 may be prosecuted for any offence except on the instructions of the Lord Advocate (Criminal Procedure (Scotland) Act 1995 s.42). In those rare cases where a child is accused of the most serious offences such as murder or rape, prosecution proceeds through the High Court under special procedural rules.

In order to make an appropriate decision in an individual case it is necessary to have an understanding of the purpose of disposals in the criminal justice system. Three purposes are commonly quoted: punishment, deterrence and rehabilitation. While each has its place in the system, the most productive, yet at the same time most difficult to achieve, is the last – rehabilitation. It is notoriously difficult to change behaviours, which may be deeply ingrained from an early age. In response to these challenges there are a number of very successful, intensive intervention programmes in Scotland. Among them are the Freagarrach Project for persistent juvenile offenders run by Barnardo's in central Scotland, the NCH Renfrew Youth Crime Project and the Edinburgh Intensive Probation Project for young offenders on probation (Lobley *et al*. 2001; Audit Scotland 2002).

Adults know how difficult it is to change their lifestyles, for example to overcome an addiction to smoking or a change in diet. Yet there are some very unrealistic expectations of how young people are expected to change what are deep-rooted behavioural problems. Successful intervention programmes address a multitude of needs in the individual – not simply their offending behaviour, but including substance misuse, education, health and social issues. These are often delivered through multi-agency youth justice teams (in every local authority area in Scotland) overseen by youth justice strategy groups. The Scottish Executive has set targets to reduce the number of persistent young offenders by 10% by 2008 (Scottish Executive 2004c). In all of these initiatives there is police involvement and support. The turning point for young people who offend is often the establishment of a positive relationship with someone who is committed to their development, and who sticks with them no matter how badly they are treated. The impact of someone who believes in them and is willing to trust them is powerful.

Restorative justice

Recent research shows that victims of crime are attracted to the idea of being given an input into the criminal justice system where they can be given a 'voice' and obtain answers to their questions from offenders and other parties (Wemmer 2001: 43). The Scottish Executive has acknowledged this fact to an extent by allowing the introduction of 'victim statements' during the criminal justice process. The Executive, police and partnership agencies have been further prompted to introduce an element of restorative justice into the Scottish criminal justice process.

Although the restorative justice approach is a relatively new concept in Scotland, it has been in use in Australia, New Zealand, North America and a few European countries for a number of years. The thinking is now to introduce some of these processes into the toolkit of police responses in relation to various categories of youth offending. One major example has recently been piloted by Thames Valley Police and in other selected areas in England (Hahn 1998: 133–157; Miers 2001). Restorative warnings and conferences are currently operating in Scotland in a format where young offenders are made aware of the wider impact of their offending behaviour, particularly on the victims, and are given an opportunity for apology or other restitution. The scenario involves the victim and the perpetrator meeting to discuss the particular crime and its consequences on the victim and the community, in the presence of a facilitator or mediator. Any finalised form of warnings or cautioning has to be founded on the premise that there is a sufficiency of evidence to support a prosecution, if required. The offender must admit to the crime or offence and whenever relevant the parent or guardian must agree to the caution or warning being dispensed. The Scottish police has endorsed similar guidelines in the past within the children's hearings system, but it may prove to be more problematic when dealing with offenders over 16 years of age.

The pilot schemes are addressing a number of the issues, such as how best to meet the needs of victims and local communities, how to ensure an effective means of reducing re-offending, the development of best practice among the eight Scottish police forces, the production of national training guidelines, and an examination of the roles of the key agencies in the process. It is too early for a comprehensive evaluation of this new approach, but initial findings are encouraging.

The underlying principles of restorative justice are founded on the belief that victims and communities have limited access to and control in the criminal justice system, regardless of the individual's geographical location. A vital ingredient in the restorative process is to allow offenders to take responsibility for their actions, reintegrating them into the community in order to inhibit re-offending. Any credible restorative system must also ensure a rehabilitative role for the community. All indications are that the restorative cautioning approach for minor crimes and offences offers this. However, one essential issue which is critical to success is where the decision-making and power lie in the process – is it with the victim or the facilitator? Findings from Thames Valley and other projects reveal that police facilitators tend to play a dominant role during the proceedings, rather than that of a mediator encouraging all parties to play their equal share in achieving a successful outcome (Hoyle *et al.* 2002). On the other hand, experience shows that improved training programmes reduce the likelihood of this imbalance recurring regularly. Experience also suggests that the implementation of any new system in which the police have a key administration role will unfortunately add to the burgeoning bureaucracy within the service at a time when central government is committed to its reduction.

However, child-protection campaigners and opposition politicians are more critical of the new proposals, including the proposed national system of warnings for young offenders. They believe police forces should retain their power to take local and family circumstances into account when making decisions relative to police warnings and proceedings and consider that a 'one size fits all' system of juvenile justice is unnecessary and even 'counter-productive' (*Scotland on Sunday* 2003b: 11).

Research has also shown that any failure to blend and link up restorative justice initiatives with other programmes in the criminal justice system will relegate it to 'a marginal role in the administration of criminal justice' (Roche 2003: 224). Scottish developments are taking heed of this and restorative measures have to be seen alongside other policies. These include:

- the introduction of anti-social behaviour orders for children under 16 years old
- parenting orders that will require parents to fulfil their responsibilities in respect of their children's anti-social behaviour, with an ultimate imprisonment sanction for parents if they fail to do so
- the introduction of electronic tagging for those under 16 years

- the piloting of a Youth Court in Hamilton to target persistent 16- and 17-year-old offenders through fast-track procedures (McIvor *et al.* 2004).

An additional weakness is the poor turnout of victims willing to participate in the process of restorative cautioning. This 'raises important questions about the cultural and organisational challenges presented by attempts to integrate victims into the heart of criminal justice processes' (Crawford and Newburn 2003: 228), and planners and implementers will have to be mindful of such difficulties at an early stage.

Conclusion

This chapter has demonstrated the complexity of the role of the police officer in dealing with children and young people. That role is expanding and becoming more demanding. At the enforcement end, police officers require to take robust action against some of the most difficult people in communities. On the preventive side, police officers need to be educators, parents and youth workers, and their new role as problem-solvers in communities requires new skills as facilitators, analysts and community leaders.

The challenge for the service is to get the balance right between these competing demands and to integrate their approach to ensure that the police response is not fragmented. We need to be sure that both police officers and the wider community have a shared understanding of the police role and what is expected of them. Successful policing of young people is dependent on relationships, on communication and trust. The police have a crucial part to play in shaping the world for the young people of Scotland.

References

Alderson, J. (1979) *Policing Freedom – A Commentary on the Dilemmas of Policing in Western Democracies.* Plymouth: Macdonald and Evans.

Association of Chief Police Officers in Scotland (2004) *Youth Strategy.* Edinburgh: ACPOS.

Audit Scotland (2002) *Dealing with Offending by Young People.* Edinburgh: Stationery Office.

Brown, D. and Iles, S. (1985) *Community Constables – A Study of a Policing Initiative,* Research and Planning Unit Paper, No 30. London: Home Office.

Crawford, A. and Newburn, T. (2003) *Youth Offending and Restorative Justice – Implementing Reform in Youth Justice.* Devon: Willan Publishing.

Fielding, N. G. (1995) *Community Policing*. Oxford: Clarendon Press.

Friedmann, R. R. (1992) *Community Policing – Comparative Perspectives and Prospects*. Hemel Hempstead: Harvester Wheatsheaf.

Goldstein, H. (1990) *Problem-Oriented Policing*. New York: McGraw-Hill.

Hahn, P. H. (1998) *Emerging Criminal Justice – Three Pillars for a Proactive Justice System*. London: Sage.

HM Chief Inspector of Constabulary for Scotland (2003) *Annual Report 2002–2003*. Edinburgh: HMCICS.

Hoyle, C., Young, R. and Hill, R. (2002) *Proceed with Caution – An Evaluation of the Thames Valley Police Initiative in Restorative Cautioning*. York: Joseph Rowntree Foundation.

Kilbrandon, Lord (1964) *Report of the Committee on Children and Young Persons in Scotland*, Cmnd 2306. Edinburgh: HMSO.

Lobley, D., Smith, D. and Stern, C. (2001) *Freagarrach: An Evaluation of a Project for Persistent Juvenile Offenders*. Edinburgh: Scottish Executive Control Research Unit.

Mackay, R. E. (2003) 'Restorative justice and the children's hearings – A proposal', *European Journal of Crime, Criminal Law and Criminal Justice*, 11 (1): 1–17.

Marshall, T. F. (1999) *Restorative Justice – An Overview*. London: Home Office.

McIvor, G. *et al.* (2004) *The Hamilton Sheriff Youth Court Pilot: The First Six Months*. Edinburgh: Scottish Executive Central Research Unit.

Miers, D. (2001) *An International Review of Restorative Justice*, Crime Reduction Research Series No 10. London: Home Office.

NCH Scotland (2004) *Where's Kilbrandon Now?* Edinburgh: NCH.

Ritchie, M. and Mack, J. A. (1974) *Police Warnings*. Glasgow: Glasgow University.

Roche, D. (2003) *Accountability in Restorative Justice*. Oxford: Oxford University Press.

Scotland on Sunday (2003a) 'Does it really fit the crime?', 1 June: 15.

Scotland on Sunday (2003b) 'Two official warnings before referral to youth courts', 25 May: 11.

Scottish Children's Reporter Agency (2002) *Annual Report 2001/2002*. Edinburgh: Stationery Office.

Scottish Executive (2004) *Recorded Crime in Scotland 2003*. Edinburgh: Scottish Executive Statistical Bulletin.

Scottish Home and Health Department (1971) *Community Involvement Departments*. SHHD Police Circular No 6/71.

Smith, D. J. *et al.* (2004) *The Edinburgh Study of Youth Transitions and Crime: Key Findings*. Edinburgh: University of Edinburgh, Centre for Law and Society.

Sunday Herald (2003) 'Young offenders forced to make amends to victims', 24 August: 6.

Trojanowicz, R. and Bucqueroux, B. (1990) *Community Policing – A Contemporary Perspective*. Cincinnati: Anderson.

Weatheritt, M. (1987) 'Community policing now', in P. Willmott (ed.), *Policing and the Community*. London: Policy Studies Institute.

Wemmer, J. (2001) 'Restorative Justice – The Choice between Bilateral Decision-making Power and Third Party Intervention', in B. Williams (ed.), *Reparation and Victim-Focused Social Work*, Research Highlights in Social Work No. 42. London: Jessica Kingsley Publishers.

Willmott, P. (ed.) (1987) *Policing and the Community*. London: Policy Studies Institute.

Chapter 10

Scottish criminal justice and the police

Dale McFadzean and Kenneth Scott

Introduction

In his review of the criminal justice system in England and Wales, Lord Justice Auld suggested that the use of the expression 'Criminal Justice System' was misleading since there is no 'system' worthy of the name, only a criminal justice 'process' to which contribution is made by a number of different government departments and agencies, and other organisations (Auld 2001). The same comments could also be used in the Scottish context, where there is no unitary or consistent organisational structure of the justice system. The word 'system' is suggestive of a collective entity, serving a common purpose, whose many elements co-operate and work together. However, in Scotland, criminal justice is a public service delivered by a mixture of national and local organisations, central and local government bodies, non-departmental bodies and charitable organisations. These providers are only loosely related to one another and each has its own differing perspectives, views and policies. In fact, it has been suggested that perhaps the only real common links within the criminal justice system are crime and criminals (Young 1997).

The principal agencies of criminal justice in Scotland are the police, prosecution service and the courts. However, the system goes far wider than that. As is acknowledged elsewhere within the United Kingdom, it also covers the myriad of agencies that are responsible for offenders and victims, such as the Scottish Prison Service, local council social work departments and voluntary organisations. The system in Scotland does not, strictly speaking, include the Children's Hearings for dealing with juvenile offenders. This is a welfare-based system and is not a criminal court, although there has been a tendency in recent years to view it as a mechanism for juvenile justice and as part of the wider criminal justice process. The following overview looks at the principal agencies within the Scottish criminal justice system as well as those working in the wider context and seeks to relate these to the work of the Scottish police.

Prosecution

Public prosecution in Scotland is carried out by the Crown Office and Procurator Fiscal Service (COPFS). This is a department of the Scottish Executive. The head of the prosecution service is the Lord Advocate, assisted by the Solicitor General for Scotland. However, the day-to-day running of the service is devolved to the procurators fiscal. There are 48 procurator fiscal's offices which are organised into six regions corresponding to the six sheriffdoms in Scotland.

This structure is not unproblematic because of the nature of the appointments to the posts of Lord Advocate and Solicitor General, which are made by the First Minister as part of the Scottish Executive. In that sense, they are political appointments. The Lord Advocate sits as a member of the Scottish Cabinet and is expected to provide legal advice as required as well as running a department of the government. While such appointments will tend to be filled by lawyers who are not unsympathetic to the governing party of the day, they tend not to be active politicians or Members of the Scottish Parliament. However, undoubtedly the manner of appointment and duties of the law officers lie somewhat uneasily with the independent nature of the prosecution service, especially when law and order is seen as a high-profile political issue.

Unlike the police, the functions and responsibilities of the Crown Office and Fiscal Service cannot be found in any statutory form. Instead, they are based upon historical custom and practice, all derived from the authority of the Lord Advocate. The Service is reponsible for conducting prosecutions at all levels of court. However, the decision on whether or not to prosecute in the first instance is taken by the local procurator fiscal. In this respect, the fiscal is a crucial part of the criminal justice process. The Scottish system thus differs from that in England and Wales in that the police have never been involved in deciding on prosecutions. The fiscal makes the key decisions: whether or not to prosecute; in which court the prosecution will take place; and what type of procedure – summary or solemn, i.e. with or without a jury – will be followed (Jones and Christie

2003). The debate in England about the right to trial by jury does not apply in Scotland. That is a decision made by the prosecutor, largely on the basis of the seriousness of the crime. It would be unusual for a murder trial to be tried without a jury. Equally, it would be unlikely that a case involving, say, breach of the peace would be tried under solemn jurisdiction. However, in Scotland there is no 'right' to a jury trial.

Procurators fiscal also have powers to adopt alternatives to prosecution, including issuing fiscal fines and referring accused persons to social-work agencies for supervision, to health bodies for psychiatric or addiction treatment and an increasingly wide range of disposals. Under the Criminal Procedure (Scotland) Act 1995, the fiscal is also formally in charge of the investigation of crimes and is statutorily authorised to direct the police as to the reporting and investigation of offences. The creation of a Crown Prosecution Service (CPS) south of the border has moved some way towards this approach. However, as a more recently developed organisation, the dynamic of the CPS's relationship with the police is probably less clearly established than is the relationship between the fiscal and the police in Scotland.

The Crown Office and Procurator Fiscal Service is the sole public prosecution authority in Scotland. The Lord Advocate is responsible for prosecuting the most serious crimes in the High Court of Justiciary. However, with the exception of important or high-profile cases, such as the trial of those accused of committing the Lockerbie bombings held at Camp Zeist in the Netherlands, the actual prosecutions are led by advocates depute, known collectively as crown counsel. These experienced advocates take the decisions on whether to prosecute serious crimes such as murder, rape and armed robbery. They do so based on a report prepared by the police for the procurator fiscal, who will have made a recommendation on whether or not there is sufficient evidence to indicate that there is a case to answer.

The decision on whether to start criminal proceedings rests purely with the COPFS, whether or not a person has been arrested or charged by the police. There is a long-established practice that the Crown does not have to give any reasons for their decision to prosecute in any individual case or not. There is no law in Scotland which says that a crime must be prosecuted and the public prosecutor has considerable discretion over what action to take.

In the performance of their duties, procurators fiscal and staff of the Crown Office have regular contact with the police and the courts, as well as the wider legal community. The work of the Fiscal Service, in particular, has been subject to review by a Quality and Practice Review Unit. In the wake of a number of highly publicised cases, such as the Chokar case, in which the performance of the Fiscal Service was strongly criticised on both procedural and racial grounds, a new independent Inspectorate of Prosecution has been created, similar to those that exist for the police, prisons, social work and education (Scottish Executive 2004b). This Inspectorate does not investigate individual cases, but is concerned with the work of the prosecution service overall. Not surprisingly, the first area to be reviewed by the new Inspectorate is concerned with racial issues in prosecution.

The criminal courts

The Scottish Court Service (SCS), according to its corporate plan, is responsible for the 'administrative, organisational, and technical services required to support the judiciary' (SCS 2003). The Scottish Court Service is an executive agency of the Scottish Executive Justice Department and is accountable to the Justice Minister. It is split into three operational areas: the Supreme Courts, the Sheriff Courts and Agency Headquarters. In practical terms, the Scottish Court Service manages the court estates and provides the staff and computer systems required to administer the courts and give effect to the decisions of the judiciary. Typical activities of the Service include, *inter alia*, allocating judicial time; assisting with witness attendance; documenting court proceedings; and preparing court orders. Scottish Court Service staff are frequently in contact with a wide range of criminal justice organisations, most notably the COPFS.

The Supreme Courts consist of the Court of Session, the High Court of Justiciary, plus the Accountant of Court's Office and the Office of the Public Guardian. The High Court of Justiciary is the supreme criminal court of Scotland and sits as both a solemn trial and appeal court. The personnel of the High Court consists of 32 judges known as Lord Commissioners of Justiciary. The two most senior judges are the Lord Justice General and the Lord Justice Clerk. As a trial court, the High Court can sit in various locations throughout Scotland, using the local sheriff court as its base. The High Court deals with the most serious crimes, such as murder. In these cases it normally involves a judge sitting with a jury of fifteen persons. A verdict has to be agreed by a majority of the jury and in Scotland three possible verdicts exist: Guilty, Not Guilty and Not Proven. The sentencing powers of the High Court are unlimited in relation to both fines and imprisonment. As a court of criminal appeal, the High Court sits in Parliament House in Edinburgh as a bench of three judges. It hears appeals against both conviction and sentence on behalf of convicted persons, but now also hears appeals against leniency of sentence from the Crown. There is no further right of appeal in criminal cases in Scotland, as in England and Wales, to the House of Lords.

The sheriff courts are divided among six sheriffdoms. There are currently 49 such courts, each headed by a sheriff principal. The sheriff principal may give instructions to sheriffs and court staff in order to secure the administrative expediency of court business. Each sheriff court has one or more sheriffs who preside over both solemn and summary procedure courts, i.e. with or without a jury. The sentencing powers of the sheriff court vary depending on the procedure being used. When dealing with minor offences under summary procedure, a sheriff's powers are limited to three months' imprisonment and/or a fine up to £5,000.[1] More serious offences dealt with under solemn procedure carry a maximum sentence of three years' imprisonment and/or an unlimited fine. The sheriff courts are undoubtedly the main workhorses of the Scottish court system. It is here that the greatest number of cases are heard and that the greatest problems of managing the process arise.

The district courts were established by the District Courts (Scotland) Act 1975 (c 20) after the reorganisation of local authority areas. They replaced the Justice of the Peace Courts and the Burgh Police Courts in dealing with the most minor summary offences, of which the most common is the Scottish catch-all charge of breach of the peace. The personnel of the district courts, with the exception of Glasgow, consists of lay Justices of the Peace (JPs). JPs need not have any legal qualifications and are appointed by the First Minister on the recommendation of local advisory committees. Some JPs are councillors nominated for appointment by their local council. Up to one-quarter of a local authority's membership may be so appointed. Others come from various branches of community life. JPs are supported by legally qualified clerks of court who are local-authority employees. The sentencing powers of these courts reflect their lay role, being limited to 60 days' imprisonment and/or a fine not exceeding £2,500. In Glasgow, due to the amount of business to be conducted, salaried stipendiary magistrates sit in the district court. Such magistrates have the same sentencing powers as a summary sheriff. The district courts have no central administration. Each is an independent body which comes under the operational control of the relevant local authority. The District Courts Association is a body which organises membership for JPs and clerks. It has no statutory authority, but provides training and policy guidance for personnel and encourages good practice. It cannot bind local authorities in relation to district courts.

Specialist courts

In recent years the court system in Scotland has begun to move in the direction of some specialist courts dealing with particular types of cases. At present there are three examples of this type of court.

1. Drug courts

A drug court was first piloted in Glasgow in 2001 and extended to Fife in 2002. The objective is to reduce drug misuse and associated offending by offering treatment options outside of the normal disposals of criminal courts. The main example of this is the Drug Treatment and Testing Order (DTTO) by which the offender can gain access to treatment programmes quickly, but at the same time is subject to regular and random drug testing (McIvor *et al.* 2003).

2. Youth court

Scotland's first pilot youth court was established at Hamilton Sheriff Court in 2003. This scheme targets persistent young offenders in the 16–17 age group, the objective being to 'fast-track' them through the court system within ten days of being charged. A range of community sentences have been employed, including restriction of liberty orders involving electronic tagging, curfews and community service orders. Initial evaluation of the pilot has been quite positive (McIvor *et al.* 2004).

3. Domestic abuse court

This court was launched in 2004 and the two-year pilot scheme will target offenders from the Govan area of Glasgow, which has a high incidence of such crime. There is a dedicated team of fiscals and sheriffs who attend at this court and there is a very real attempt to deal with cases quickly, within six weeks. One of the main objectives of this court is to get the message across that the crime of domestic abuse is totally unacceptable and will not be tolerated (*The Herald* 2005).

One of the great strengths of all these new courts is the emphasis on multi-agency working. The police are closely involved in all three and the specialist nature of the courts allows close co-operation and planning with appropriate specialists. For example, in the drugs courts, medical and addictions staff are closely involved and in the domestic abuse court advocacy officers from a victims' organisation called ASSIST provide support and advice.

Bail

In Scottish criminal procedure, the question of whether or not an accused person should be granted bail is for the courts to answer. Prior to the incorporation of the European Convention on Human Rights into Scots law, all crimes except murder and treason were bailable. However, since the enactment of the Bail, Judicial Appointments etc. (Scotland) Act 2000, a person charged with *any* crime may legitimately apply to the court before which they are brought, seeking an order to be liberated on bail. Bail is an order of the court granted in terms of the Criminal Procedure (Scotland) Act 1995 and is defined as 'the release of an accused or an appellant on conditions'. It must be distinguished from what is commonly referred to as 'police bail'. The police, in fact, have no jurisdiction in relation to the granting of a bail order in Scotland. 'Police bail' is in fact liberation under very different terms and conditions and is restricted to ordering the accused to attend at a court at a given place and time; there are no other conditions attached and failure to attend is treated as a separate offence from the original.

In granting bail, the law differs depending on the stage of court proceedings at which the decision is made and whether the case has been brought under summary or solemn procedure. Under both procedures, the court must grant the application for bail unless it is of the opinion that, with regard to the public interest and securing the ends of justice, there is good reason why bail should be refused. Guidelines to assist judges in reaching their decisions were set out in a 1982 case where Lord Justice Clerk Wheatley held that appropriate grounds for refusal fell into two categories: the protection of public interest; and the administration of justice (*Smith* v *McC* 1982 JC 67). He also stated that previous convictions could be relevant, as could evidence that the offences committed amounted to a breach of trust on the part of the accused. This would involve circumstances where the accused was on bail or charged with another offence at the time the new offence was committed. Other possible grounds for refusal were noted as including the nature of the alleged offence, alleged intimidation of witnesses, absence of a fixed abode, or reasonable grounds for expecting that the accused would not turn up for trial. It is worth noting, however, that these grounds are merely provided as guidelines and in practice the courts do not rigidly apply them. Nonetheless, they provide some useful insight into judicial reasoning.

When granting bail, the courts are obliged to impose on the accused the standard bail conditions and any other conditions necessary to ensure that the standard conditions are met. The standard conditions are that the accused:

- appears at the appointed time at every diet relating to the offence with which s/he is charged of which s/he is given due notice
- does not commit an offence while on bail;
- does not interfere with witnesses or otherwise obstruct the course of justice whether in relation to self or any other person
- makes him/herself available for the purposes of enabling enquires or a report to be made to assist the court in dealing with him/her for the offence for which s/he is charged.

The discretion given to the courts relating to extra bail conditions allows greater flexibility as to the limitations which can be imposed on an accused's bail. There is no statutory or common-law list of such conditions, but some useful examples are that the accused should not approach any victims; the accused should adhere to a nightly curfew; or that the accused should reside in a bail hostel. The imposition of monetary bail will only be sanctioned by the courts if appropriate to any special circumstances of the case and it is up to the courts or the Lord Advocate to interpret such circumstances. Failure to accept any such bail conditions on the part of the accused is likely to result in the accused being remanded in custody by the court. Breach of bail remains a considerable problem for the courts which have to deal with the cases, for the police who have to apprehend the accused, and for the prisons where many in breach of bail end up.

Sentencing

The independence of the judiciary is a fundamental cornerstone of the Scottish legal system and Scottish ministers attach great importance to judicial discretion in sentencing. Apart from murder, for which there is a fixed penalty of life imprisonment by virtue of the Murder (Abolition of the Death Penalty) Act 1965, the Scottish courts are given a wide discretion to determine the most appropriate sentence within the maximum limits provided by Parliament. In recent years, the issue of sentencing has been particularly controversial. A spate of judicial review cases in England and Wales directly challenged the role of the Home Secretary in fixing a 'tariff' which has been higher than the recommendation of the trial judge. Consequently, the House of Lords found that the setting of such punitive tariffs by the Home Secretary was in conflict with Article 6 of the European Convention on Human Rights which enshrines the principles of a fair trial (*R (Anderson)* v *Secretary of State for the Home Department* [2003] HRLR 7). The basic constitutional principle that individual sentencing is a matter for the courts and not for politicians has already been long accepted in Scotland and there has been a notable lack of Executive interference in this area.

However, sentencing in Scotland comes replete with its own problems. Due to the lack of direct tariff guidance given by the Executive and the wide judicial discretion which is involved, there appears to be a high degree of inconsistency in Scottish sentencing. This has led to a very negative perception of the criminal justice system among the public. There have been many sentencing decisions made by the Scottish judiciary which have been perceived as unduly lenient and this has led to increased public scrutiny and debate over the future of the system. One such incident concerned the case of a man who was sentenced to five years in jail for the rape of a 13-month-old baby. Decisions such as this have led not only to public outcry, but also to unprecedented levels of comment and action by the Executive.

In an attempt to combat the inconsistency and alleged leniency of sentencing in Scotland, the Executive has set up a body known as the Sentencing Commission (Scottish Executive 2003). The Commission is chaired by Lord MacLean and the remaining membership has been drawn from the police, social work, and voluntary bodies. It has been vested with the task of reporting on how well public safety is protected by the Scottish courts and has a very wide remit which specifically includes an examination of the effectiveness of sentences in reducing re-offending and with scope to improve consistency in sentencing. So-called 'lenient' sentencing is one area on which the Commission will be focusing in particular (see www. scottishsentencingcommission.gov.uk). The final report of the Sentencing Commission is due to be submitted to the Scottish Executive by November 2005 for further consideration.

A further Executive initative is that of taking forward the development of a sentencing information system for the High Court of Justiciary (Hutton *et al.* 1996). This system is unique in the world as an implemented system which collects and provides information specifically intended for the use of judges when passing sentence. The system is computer based and provides users with information about the range of penalties which have been passed by the Court for similar cases in the past. The system allows a judge to enter certain information about the case which is under consideration and the range and quantum of penalties passed by the Court for similar cases is displayed. Formally, the system is descriptive rather than prescriptive in that it contains no guidance as to how a sentencer might use the information to assist in making the sentencing decision in a particular case. It can display the range of sentences for the particular combination of offence and offender characteristics selected, but the sentencer will have no guidance as to what extent and in what direction the appropriate sentence for- the case at hand should vary from the average. This is still at the discretion of the judge. It is hoped that the final version will help to eradicate the inconsistencies in sentencing caused by wide judicial discretion. Currently the project is being implemented and evaluated on a phased basis.

From the Scottish public's perspective, concern over sentencing is not only in the matter of consistency, but in the implementation of the sentence. In relation to custodial sentences there is from time to time considerable public complaint over the arrangements for release of offenders from prison. Under the Prisoners and Criminal Proceedings (Scotland) Act 1993 there are a number of arrangements for early release of different categories of prisoners. A short-term prisoner serving a sentence of less than four years is released unconditionally after serving half of the sentence. A long-term prisoner serving four years or more is released on licence after serving two-thirds of the sentence, but the Parole Board for Scotland may recommend an earlier release on licence after only half of the sentence is served. For discretionary life prisoners, whose sentence is not fixed by law, the judge specifies the period which should elapse before the prisoner is considered by the Parole Board for release on licence. Mandatory life prisoners are those convicted of murder because that is a sentence fixed by the Criminal Procedure (Scotland) Act 1995. However, even in such cases, a judge at time of sentence is entitled to recommend a minimum period, of not less than twelve years, before the offender may be released on licence (Stewart 1997: 227–231).[3]

What is not commonly understood in the case of long-term prisoners is that this licence continues over the entire period of the sentence and can be revoked at any time, with the prisoner being recalled to prison to serve the remainder of the sentence. It is popularly viewed as offenders being 'let off lightly' and, in the case of mandatory life prisoners, provokes in some quarters the demand that 'life imprisonment should mean for life'. This is fuelled by instances where prisoners on licence re-offend, although the number of instances of this in any one year is usually very small. In the case of short-term prisoners the situation causes greater concern because remission is automatic and, given the high re-offending rate of those who come out of Scottish prisons, the chances of further crimes being committed are relatively high.

Prisons in Scotland

The Scottish Prison Service (SPS) was created in 1993 and is an executive agency of the Scottish Executive, accountable to the Justice Minister. The Prison Service employs around 4,600 staff, runs sixteen prisons and is responsible for an average daily prison population of 6,500 prisoners, one of the highest in Europe. These prisoners are of various types: some are adults who have been convicted and sentenced by the courts and who are serving custodial sentences of varying lengths; some are on remand, either awaiting trial or waiting to return to court for sentence; some are under the age of 21 and are therefore officially classed as young offenders.

Prisons, too, come in varying types. Some, such as Barlinnie in Glasgow or Craiginches in Aberdeen, deal primarily with local, short-term prisoners serving less than four years; some, such as Shotts and Glenochil, house long-term prisoners including those who require maximum security conditions; Cornton Vale is the only all-female prison; there are two semi-open facilities, at Castle Huntly and Noranside; Polmont, near Falkirk, is the main Young Offenders Institution; Peterhead has a special unit for sex offenders; and several prisons have units to assist those who are about to be released. The most controversial is Kilmarnock, which is currently Scotland's only private prison, built under a private finance initiative contract. There has been much debate over this development and many people in Scotland are unhappy about a prison being run by a private company, arguing that the state alone should be responsible for dealing with those convicted of criminal acts. The counter-argument is that the prison remains part of the Scottish Prison Service estate and is ultimately controlled by SPS. However, with continuing problems in the standards of facilities in many of Scotland's older prisons – including the long-running 'slopping-out' controversy involving prisoners in emptying overnight chamber pots – and the high cost of building new prisons, the likelihood of more privately funded and privately managed prisons in the future is high and the Scottish Executive is committed to building two more.

The SPS has defined its mission in terms of four key activities: maintaining in custody those sent to it; maintaining order in its prisons; caring with humanity for those committed to it; and providing opportunities to exercise personal responsibility and prepare for release (www.scottishprisonservice. org.uk). The balance between 'punishment' and 'rehabilitation', which continues to be central to debates on imprisonment, is a difficult one. Certainly, in recent years the record of Scottish prisons on custody and order has been reasonable, with few prisoner escapes and only a small number of internal disorders that have made the headlines. While these matters are given the highest priority, a great deal of effort has also gone into policies and practices designed to assist the rehabilitation of prisoners through work, education, therapeutic programmes and training for return to the community. Drug dependency and continuing access to illegal drugs within prisons remain considerable problems within the system.

Criminal justice social work and community services

The role of social work relates to the criminal justice system at a number of different stages. Social workers provide a number of services to courts, especially before sentence is passed, by providing, for example, social enquiry reports on offenders' backgrounds and family circumstances. They are also involved with those committed to imprisonment, especially at the point when they are approaching release and may require continuing supervision in the community. Probably their key role is in providing supervision of community sentences for offenders. Community sentences include the following:

- a probation order with or without conditions, such as undertaking unpaid work

- a community service order which requires that a number of hours of unpaid work be carried out in the offender's own time

- a supervised attendance order which can be used for 16- and 17-year-olds in place of a fine

- a restriction of liberty order (RLO), which involves the use of electronic monitoring equipment, or 'tagging', so that track can be kept of the movements of offenders

- a drug treatment and testing order (DTTO), which is presently used on a pilot basis for referring offenders to the drug courts in Glasgow, Fife and Aberdeen.

Community sentences account for around 12% of all sentences in Scotland and have been increasing both in absolute terms and as a proportion of all court sentences (Scottish Executive 2004a). Probation is the most popular of these, but community service is also widely used. Such sentences may occur in cases where a custodial disposal is not appropriate, for example, with a first offender. In the light of prison overcrowding and debates over the effectiveness of imprisonment, community sentences are also increasingly favoured as an alternative to prison even in cases where a custodial disposal is available. In the case of community service orders, these can only be imposed in place of a custodial sentence.

Criminal justice social work services are provided primarily by the 32 local authorities in Scotland. In one instance of non-custodial disposal the police also have a role to play. The Sex Offenders Act 1997 established the setting up of a sex offenders' register. Anyone required to be named on the register must report basic information to the police within a specified time. The information includes place of residence and any movement from there and this is recorded on the Police National Computer (PNC). Once a year the police will carry out a check of those on the register. There appears to be a high level of compliance with the registration requirements in Scotland and there is a strong emphasis on communicating information across relevant agencies (Social Work Scotland Inspectorate 2005: 1).

Since its inception the electronic monitoring of offenders has been contracted out to a private company. Tagging was introduced in the Criminal Procedure (Scotland) Act 1995 to ensure offenders' compliance with RLOs, probation orders or DTTOs. This has since been extended in two directions: the Anti-Social Behaviour (Scotland) Act 2003 permits tagging of offenders under 16 as an alternative to secure accommodation;

and the Criminal Procedure (Amendment) (Scotland) Act 2004 provides for restricting a person's movement by electronic monitoring as a condition of bail. The Scottish Executive has made it clear that they believe this is an appropriate area to be operated by the private sector (Scottish Executive 2005: 1–2).

Voluntary agencies also play a role. For example, Safeguarding Communities, Reducing Offending (SACRO), a charitable organisation, provides mediation and other forms of diversion to offenders. Since the creation of social work in its modern form under the Social Work (Scotland) Act 1968, Scotland has taken a different road from England and Wales by establishing generic social work departments rather than having a dedicated probation service. The possibility of developing some specialisms in criminal justice gained some ground in the local government regions of the 1970s and 1980s because of their relatively large scale. However, since the creation of unitary local authorities in Scotland under the Local Government etc. (Scotland) Act 1994 there are many smaller social work departments who have found their resources stretched between the increasing demands of, on the one hand, a wide range of generic social work requirements and, on the other, the statutory nature of specialist criminal justice social work. Consequently, a number of authorities have created partnerships to provide these services in a more centralised form.

Worldwide, increasing attention is now being paid to the role of the victim in criminal justice processes and this is no less true of Scotland. At an official level, Victim Information and Advice (VIA) is part of the Crown Office and Procurator Fiscal Service. The service has been rolled out as part of the wider commitment to providing a prosecution service that is responsive to the public's needs and communicates openly and effectively. Victim Information and Advice offers advice to victims of crime, bereaved next-of-kin, and vulnerable witnesses. It also advises such people on the progress of cases which affect them and facilitates referral to other specialist agencies. Victim Information and Advice offices are located in several towns and cities throughout Scotland, including Glasgow, Edinburgh, Paisley, Kilmarnock and Hamilton.

Victim Support Scotland is a voluntary organisation with charitable status. It provides free emotional support, practical help and essential information to victims, witnesses and others affected by crime who are referred to it by statutory agencies, most commonly the police. The support offered is wide in range and covers such areas as understanding criminal justice procedures, supporting those giving evidence in court, acting as a witness, and dealing with youth crime.

Mental disorder

The main court disposals relating to psychiatric disorders are hospital orders under sections 58 and 59 of the Criminal Procedure (Scotland) Act 1995. In such cases two doctors have to certify that there is a mental disorder which requires detention in hospital for treatment. Where there is concern about public safety, the hospital order may have added to it an order restricting discharge. These orders are without limit of time, and authority for deciding on discharge lies with the First Minister in the Scottish Executive. In many instances these orders lead to admission to the State Hospital at Carstairs in Lanarkshire.

It is important to recognise that Carstairs is not part of the prison system, but of the National Health Service. It is a hospital which 'provides care and treatment in conditions of special security for around 240 patients ... with mental disorders who, because of their dangerous, violent or criminal propensities, cannot be cared for in any other setting' (www.show.scot. nhs.uk). About 62% of patients in the State Hospital are detained under a restriction order. They have usually committed an offence punishable by imprisonment, but are detained in hospital with the intention that through programmes of treatment and rehabilitation which deal with their mental disorder, re-offending will be prevented. Responsibility for the day-to-day management of restricted prisoners, including authorising leave of absence and transfers between hospitals, lies with the Scottish ministers, a responsibility which can cause acute political embarassment when matters go wrong, such as when a patient goes on the run (*Scotland on Sunday* 2004: 13).

On the recommendation of the MacLean Committee on serious violent and sexual offenders (2002), a new sentence has been introduced in the Criminal Justice (Scotland) Act 2003 called an Order for Lifelong Restriction (OLR). This is a lifelong sentence specifically designed to improve public safety by providing a framework under which high-risk offenders will be assessed and managed for the duration of their lives. This will be undertaken by a new statutory body, the Risk Management Agency, which is responsible for both the assessment of risk, based on sources such as police intelligence systems and court records, and the creation of a risk management plan for each offender. This arrangement is responding to the MacLean Report's conclusion 'that there is a lack of co-ordination of approach, guidance, and standards and a lack of adequate communication between all the relevant agencies' (Scottish Executive 2002: 2).

Criminal justice policy-making

The Scottish Executive Justice Department has lead responsibility for criminal justice policy in Scotland. It covers a wide range of duties, including substantial involvement with police matters. The Department, in partnership with chief constables and local police authorities, carries out the Scottish ministers' responsibilities for the administration of an efficient police service, including provision of central police services.

The traditional reticence in UK government about establishing a central, overarching 'ministry of justice' has been allayed somewhat by the mixed bag of responsibilities which the Justice Department has. It has responsibility for the police and the prisons, but it also oversees the fire services, the legal aid system, electoral procedures, emergency planning, land reform, freedom of information and royal and ceremonial matters in Scotland. Other parts of the Executive have responsibilities in relation to criminal justice matters, too. The Crown Office has responsibilities for court administration, some aspects of youth crime fall within the remit of the Education Department, and the recent high-profile legislation on anti-social behaviour was the responsibility of the Communities Department.

Within the Scottish Parliament there are two committees which deal with criminal justice-related policy and legislation. The committees are known as Justice 1 and Justice 2. As well as considering Executive proposals for legislation, these committees can also examine the need for reform of the law and, unlike the Westminster committee system, can initiate legislation in the form of Committee Bills. The committees' remit is to consider and report on matters relating to the administration of civil and criminal justice, the reform of the civil and criminal law and essentially to shadow all matters that fall within the responsibility of the Justice Minister.

With law and order high on the political agenda it is no surprise that both legislation and debates relating to the criminal justice system have played a very significant role in the work of the Scottish Parliament. The very first piece of legislation passed by the new Parliament related to criminal justice and, in the period since the Parliament's inception in 1999, no fewer than sixteen out of the 75 Acts enacted (over 20%) have been concerned with a wide range of matters falling under the criminal law.[3] This has included legislation on procedure in trials relating to sexual offences, the law banning fox hunting with dogs, the regulation of investigatory powers, the Anti-Social Behaviour etc. (Scotland) Act and an act dealing with vulnerable witnesses (www.scottishparliament.gov.uk).

The need to provide greater integration of the Scottish criminal justice system has clearly emerged as an issue. The diversity of bodies and interests that comprise the system has led to real doubts about the extent to which the various parts work in an integrated fashion. This is hardly surprising having regard to the separate responsibilities of the different parts of the system. The importance of cross-system liaison has been recognised as a continuing problem. Several groups have been set up by the Scottish administration in attempts to address the problem, include the Criminal Justice Liaison Group and the Criminal Justice Forum, whose memberships includes senior officials from the main criminal justice departments and agencies and from the Crown Office and Procurator Fiscal Service.

In March 2002 the Scottish Executive commissioned a review to be undertaken by the Crown Agent, Andrew Normand CB, with particular emphasis being placed upon integration. The report was published in March 2003 and contains a number of damning conclusions. Evidence taken from senior representatives within the various parts of the system overwhelmingly pointed to a lack of co-operation and integration in the approach to delivery of justice. The constituent components appear to work in relative isolation from each other with poor levels of communication, consultation and co-operation. As a result there are many different approaches to operations, targets and objectives throughout the country. Moving towards a harmonised system is no easy task. Each body within the system has its own statutory responsibilities and its own agendas. They are focusing upon their own targets and many are in competiton for increased resources and/or funding. There are also a number of existing conflict areas which would seriously hinder any move towards a unified approach, such as the requirement that procurators fiscal investigate complaints against the police. Indeed, most of the main agencies seem reluctant to embrace ownership of the justice process under a unified system. The current fragmented approach allows each agency to focus upon and protect its own interests and, insofar as 'the blame culture' is concerned, eases the impact of systemic incompetence.

Nonetheless, significant moves have been made towards a more integrated approach. A key recommendation put forward by the Normand Report (2003) suggested the creation of a Scottish National Criminal Justice Board. This Board was set up in December 2003 with a membership of senior criminal justice officials including sheriffs principal, prosecutors and agency representatives. The Board has responsibilty for overseeing the operation of the system and ensuring that greater levels of integration and co-operation exist between the relevant agencies. It is hoped that it will play a significant part in ensuring that legislative reforms are matched by effective, efficient and consistent action on the ground.

The Normand Report also recommended that there should be a system of local boards chaired by sheriffs principal. Consequently, two pilot local boards have been established in Fife and Lothian and Borders respectively. The local boards will address issues relating to the delivery of justice in their areas and will regularly report to the National Board.

A further initiative has been ongoing since the early 1990s to improve integration. It has long been recognised that efficiency could be improved significantly if information was more readily exchanged and shared among criminal justice organisations. This has resulted in the development of the Integration of Scottish Criminal Justice Information Systems Project. This is a joint programme by the major criminal justice agencies including the Scottish Executive, Crown Office and Procurator Fiscal Service, Scottish Prison Service, Scottish Criminal Record Office, Scottish police forces and local authorities. The project comprises a series of information technology links between the various systems of Scottish criminal justice organisations with the objective of allowing agreed information to be passed electronically from one organisation to another without sacrificing confidentiality. There are eight regional groups operating in Scotland to ensure the success of the project.

A more contentious move towards integration has been proposed by the Scottish Executive in the form some kind of national corrections agency. This proposes to bring together the parts of the system which particularly relate to re-offending, especially the prison service and criminal justice social work. Given the high rates in Scotland of crime committed by those who already have criminal convictions, the focus is on establishing a single national body which can tackle this problem by combining the responsibilities for both custodial and non-custodial sentences. The Scottish local authorities have been strongly opposed to this plan, arguing that community supervision needs a strong base in the local community in order to be successful and that social work services that relate to offenders cannot easily be disjoined from other services. The battle lines are clearly drawn and the outcome is not yet clear, although the signs are that the Executive is paving the way to back down on the creation of a fully integrated agency.

The role of the police

If criminal justice is a process, then the police are the gatekeepers to that process. Most people in Scotland who have anything to do with the criminal justice system encounter it in the first instance by way of the police. Anyone who appears in a criminal court does so as a result of being arrested and charged by the police; anyone who was taken to prison was escorted there by the police; anyone who breaches bail conditions or defaults on community sentences is followed up by the police; it is the police who check up on those registered as sex offenders; and most referrals to Children's Hearings relating to offending come from the police. Officially, of course, the involvement of the police goes no further than the initial investigation of a crime reported by the public, charging anyone suspected of the crime, and sending the necessary reports to the procurator fiscal. However, from the police perspective, the workings – and failings – of the criminal justice system produce considerable demands upon them. Prosecutors have the right to direct the police to investigate crimes; courts require police officers to attend to give evidence; in cases of prison escapes or disorders or absconding from the State Hospital the police are called in; and when known criminals are returned to the community because of the verdict of the court or after completing a sentence, it is the police who have to deal with any consequent re-offending. The symbiotic relationship between the police and other criminal justice agencies has traditionally been seen as a predominantly negative one for the police. There are some signs, however, that this is changing, partly because of attempts to respond to the problems created for the police by the system, and partly because the links between the police and other sectors of the system are becoming more organised.

The Police and COPFS

Under Scottish criminal law the responsibility not only for the prosecution, but also the investigation of crime, lies with the Crown Office and Procurator Fiscal Service. 'It is normally the role of the police to gather evidence and undertake enquiries on behalf of the procurator fiscal, but this should not obscure the fact that, whatever the degree of delegation, in practice the Fiscal retains primacy at all times' (HMICS 2000: 17). It is the Lord Advocate who issues instructions to a chief constable to report on alleged offences and it is the duty of chief constables to secure compliance. Indeed it is possible as a matter of law for investigation as well as prosecution decisions to be undertaken by the Crown with minimal or even no involvement on the part of the police (HMICS 2000: 18). Again, this is different from the situation south of the border where the CPS has no investigative role.

In March 2002, the Lord Advocate accepted the recommendation of the management review of the Crown Office and Procurator Fiscal Service that it should be restructured in such a way as to correspond largely with police force areas (Pryce-Dyer 2002). This measure was specifically intended to improve the quality of service provided to the public and to improve links with the police. This recommendation has now been put into practice and in July 2002, the new structure was implemented based upon eleven areas. Seven procurator fiscal areas (Central, Fife, Tayside, Grampian, Lothian and Borders, Dumfries and Galloway, and Highland and Islands) match the boundaries of the corresponding police force areas. The remaining four areas are within the force area of Strathclyde Police (Lanarkshire, Glasgow,

Argyll and Clyde and Ayrshire). This relatively simple realignment marks another step towards greater fostering of links between the police and the Crown Office and enhances operational effectiveness through increased liaison.

The police and warrants

Police officers have the power to arrest a suspect with or without a warrant. However, the warrant does give written authority to arrest a named person and can also permit entry and search of premises and vehicles and the seizure of property. A judge or JP can issue a warrant on application by the fiscal or a police officer. What is crucial is that the details contained in the warrant are fully accurate. In a number of instances warrants have been revoked because of errors in a person's name or address. Warrants should be executed as soon as possible and many are. However, at any given time there will be warrants outstanding because someone was not found or because other priorities on police time have overtaken them. This provides a relatively straightforward area for occasional 'purges' to take place, serving at one stroke to increase police activity levels and create huge problems for the courts which have to deal with the results.

The police and court attendance

Another move which has greatly assisted the role of the police has been the introduction of intermediate diets. In 1991 the Accounts Commission conducted a detailed study of the amount of time spent by police officers on witness duty in the Scottish courts. This suggested that approximately 250,000 citations were served annually on police officers in Scotland and that on any given day, 694 police officers were in court attendance and not on the streets. This evidence was made even more damning when it was found that only one in five of the officers attending court as witnesses were actually required to give evidence, since most trials did not proceed on the fixed date. This happened due to a variety of reasons: the accused did not appear; there was a plea of guilty; the fiscal accepted a reduced plea; witnesses failed to answer citations; the defence was ill-prepared; or the court had set down too many trials for a particular day in which pleas of not guilty were adhered to (Accounts Commission 1991).

In an attempt to reduce these problems, the Criminal Procedure (Scotland) Act 1995 was amended to include the scheduling of intermediate diets in most cases. These diets would allow courts to sort out most of the difficulties encountered well in advance of the trial date. Thus witnesses would not be required to attend trials needlessly and more importantly, police officers would be free to pursue their primary duties. However, the success of the intermediate diet has been questionable. Certainly, a sizeable reduction in the number of police personnel attending court per day has been evident. For example, a Lothian and Borders Police survey showed that, between 1991 and 1997, a drop of 289 was noted in the number of officers attending court per day (Lothian and Borders Police 2003). However, it has been shown that the success of intermediate diets varies from court to court depending upon the trial culture within that court (Summary Justice Review Committee 2004) and that the frequent use of plea bargaining has helped to thwart any gains made from the new procedure. There is evidence to suggest solicitors are waiting until the last moment to enter guilty pleas on behalf of their clients rather than at the earlier intermediate stage (Lothian and Borders Police 2003). This is being done in the hope that witnesses will ultimately still fail to show up or that a busy court schedule will allow them to plea-bargain for a lesser sentence. This has led the Executive to consider further reform of the system.

The police and prisoners

A further iniative designed to free up police time has focused upon the transporting of prisoners to court. The Scottish Prison Service was instructed by the Scottish ministers to set up a multi-agency team to put in place a central contract for prisoner escort and court custody services in Scotland. After the contract had been put out to tender, prisoner escort and court custody services were officially privatised and handed over to the security firm, Reliance Security Group, in 2004. In addition to the more general reasons for this privatisation, it was specifically regarded as necessary to free up police resources in the criminal courts and in the escort of prisoners. The project spectacularly backfired, with a prisoner escaping from court custody on the first day of the new arrangement being implemented, followed by a series of other mishaps. This led to a major row in the Scottish Parliament and an investigation of the management of the contract by one of the justice committees. However, the political storm identified that there had been a significant number of escapes from custody when the police ran the system. Perhaps more importantly, it highlighted that the potential for reallocating police officers from court and custody duties to frontline policing was quite limited, given that these duties were traditionally undertaken by constables in the later years of their service.

Conclusion

Traditionally in Scotland the police have been perceived not only as being at the front end of the criminal justice process, but also as being the dogged foot soldiers who carry out all the menial tasks created by the faults and weaknesses in the rest of the system. This is now beginning to change. The change comes partly from political considerations, namely that law and order, crime and punishment are key political concerns in post-devolution Scotland and Scottish ministers have identified many of these issues as priorities for new initiatives and policies. As a result, bodies such as ACPOS are extensively consulted on such matters and it is increasingly the case that chief constables are invited to sit on committees and commissions relating to criminal justice at a national level.

It has also become clear to Scottish ministers and others that a major weakness in Scottish criminal justice is the lack of effective co-ordination between the different agencies involved. A recurring theme of recent policy-making has been attempts to bring the different parts of the process together and to improve communication and interaction between them. The Scottish police have been very involved in this. More effective links with the Fiscal service, the courts, the prison service and social work services have been forged and the multi-agency model which has become very familiar in many other areas of police work has begun to operate in the criminal justice field as well. For example, when a Scottish criminal justice computerisation project was launched in the early 1990s it was a police team under an assistant chief constable who co-ordinated it.

At one time, what was happening throughout the world of criminal justice would not have been regarded as the business of the police, and that view was sometimes held within the police service itself. Now, the Scottish police is closer to the heart of the process of change and partnership that is moving through criminal justice in Scotland and is playing a central role within it.

Notes

1   Under the Criminal Procedure (Scotland) Act 1995, s.5(3), the maximum three-month period of imprisonment which can be imposed in a sheriff court under summary jurisdiction can be increased to a period of six months where a person is convicted of a second or subsequent offence of dishonesty or personal violence.
2   A new approach to early release is contained within the Crime and Punishment (Scotland) Act 1997. However, the relevant sections of this Act have not yet been implemented.
3   In addition, under a mechanism known as a Sewel motion, the Scottish Parliament may pass over to the Westminster Parliament the right to legislate on Scottish matters. Many of these 'Sewel motions' also relate to aspects of crime.

References

Auld, Lord Justice (2001) *Review of the Criminal Courts of England and Wales*. London: Department for Constitutional Affairs.

The Herald (2005) Society Supplement, 25 January.

HM Inspectorate of Constabulary for Scotland (2000) *A Fair Cop? The Investigation of Complaints Against the Police in Scotland*. Edinburgh: HMICS.

Hutton, N. *et al.* (1996) *A Sentencing Information System for the High Court of Justiciary of Scotland: Report of the Study of Feasibility*, Edinburgh: Scottish Office.

Jones, T. H. and Christie, M. G. A. (2003) *Criminal Law*, 3rd edn. Edinburgh: W. Green and Son.

Lothian and Borders Police (2003) *Silent Witness*. Edinburgh: Lothian and Borders Police.

MacLean, Lord (2002) *Report of the Committee on Serious Violent and Sexual Offenders*. Edinburgh: Scottish Executive.

McIvor, G., Eley, S., Malloch, M. and Yates, R. (2003) *Establishing Drug Courts in Scotland: Early Experiences of the Pilot Drug Courts in Glasgow and Fife*. Edinburgh: Scottish Executive Social Research.

McIvor, G. *et al.* (2004) *The Hamilton Sheriff Youth Court Pilot: The First Six Months*. Edinburgh: Scottish Executive Social Research.

Normand, A. (2003) *Criminal Justice System Objectives Review: Proposals for the Integration of Aims, Objectives and Targets in the Scottish Criminal Justice System*. Edinburgh: Scottish Executive.

Price-Dyer (2002) *Review of the Planning, Allocation and Management of Resources in the Crown Office and Procurator Fiscal Service*. Edinburgh: COPFS.

Scotland on Sunday (2004) 'The truth at Carstairs and why a patient went on the run', 12 December: 13.

Scottish Court Service (2003) *Corporate Plan*. Edinburgh: Scottish Court Service.

Scottish Executive (2002) *News Release on New 'Lifelong Restriction' Sentence*, 20 November (accessed at www.scotland.gov.uk).

Scottish Executive (2003) *News Release on Establishment of Sentencing Commission* (accessed at www.scotland.gov.uk).

Scottish Executive (2004a) *Criminal Proceedings in Scottish Courts 2002*. Edinburgh: Statistical Bulletin Criminal Justice Series.

Scottish Executive (2004b) *News Release on Appointment of First Inspector of Prosecution* (accessed at www.scotland.gov.uk).

Scottish Executive (2005) *News Release on Electronic Monitoring Contract*, 10 January (accessed at www.scotland.gov.uk).

Scottish Parliament website, www.scottishparliament.gov.uk.

Social Work Scotland Inspectorate (2005) *Managing the Risk: An Inspection of the Management of Sex Offenders Cases in Scotland*. Edinburgh: SWSI.

State Hospital website, www.show.scot.nhs.uk.

Stewart, A. L. (1997) *The Scottish Criminal Courts in Action*, 2nd edn. Edinburgh: Butterworth LexisNexis.

Summary Justice Review Committee (2004) *Report to Ministers*. Edinburgh: Scottish Executive.

Tata, C. *et al.* (2002) *A Sentencing Information System for the High Court of Justiciary: First Phase of Implementation, Enhancement and Evaluation.* Edinburgh: Scottish Executive.

Young, P. (1997) *Crime and Criminal Justice in Scotland.* Edinburgh: The Stationery Office.

Chapter 11

Police powers and human rights in Scotland

James D. Pennycook

Introduction

Scotland was the first part of the United Kingdom to introduce the European Convention on Human Rights (ECHR) into its system of laws. The Human Rights Act 1998 incorporated the Convention into Scots law with effect from 2 October 1998 and requires all public authorities, including the police, to act in conformity with Convention rights.

The maintenance of law and order by the police involves a delicate balance of operational efficiency and independence with accountability and responsibility to ensure that the police themselves are subject to that same law as the rest of the public. Berry *et al.* (1998) have identified two main reasons why human rights are of particular importance to policing. Human rights not only encompass the key principles which underpin the legal and moral accountability of the police in a democratic state, but also provide a practical control upon the conduct of the police in their everyday operations. At the most basic, street level, human rights can provide an antidote to the abuse of power by a powerful arm of the state by preventing arbitrary arrest and promoting the rule of law. Human rights can provide the bridge between the ethical dimension and the everyday world of policing and can provide a framework against which police policies and actions can be assessed. Neyroud and Beckley see the way forward for public policing as 'securing and reconciling human rights, balancing the rights of individuals and communities' (2001: 4).

It is often difficult to balance the rights of the individual with the rights of wider society. Gillespie (2000) argues that, if the police use this balance, then they will have nothing to fear from the Human Rights Act 1998. The Act confers additional protection on the police officer in the execution of his/her duties and makes actions less open to challenge in the courts. What the Act should also do is make police procedures more certain, open and transparent to the general public, thereby increasing accountability. Contrary to the received wisdom of both police and public, the Act offers the Scottish police the opportunity to become the guardians of civil liberties rather than being seen as the oppressors of them.

The interaction between policing and the Human Rights Act is new and evolving. This chapter seeks to draw out some of the implications for policing in Scotland both in terms of police forces and the individual police officer. Its focus is of necessity limited in view of the extensive and expanding nature of human rights legislation, the scope of human rights legislation and the judgements of the Scottish courts on these matters.

Police operations and use of force

The ECHR creates both positive obligations to take active steps to secure certain rights and also negative obligations to refrain from interfering with protected rights. The state may require to amend national laws to comply with ECHR standards. Article 2 (right to life) and Article 3 (prohibition against torture) are absolute rights which cannot be restricted in any circumstances. Some rights are limited and the state can opt out of these, for example in Article 5 on the right to liberty and security of the person and powers to fight terrorism. Others are qualified rights where the state can take the general public interest into account. Examples of this are Article 8 (respect for private life), Article 10 (freedom of expression) and Article 11 (freedom of assembly). A number of the guarantees contained in the Convention are particularly relevant to the proper performance of police duties.

Article 2 states that every person's right to life shall be protected by law and that no one shall be deprived of life intentionally save in the execution of a sentence of a court following conviction for a crime for which this penalty is provided in law. It imposes a duty on the state to provide a plausible explanation where a person, who was in good health prior to detention, dies while in police custody.

Consequently, the police are placed under two main duties. First of all, an effective investigation of crime must be conducted which is capable of identifying and punishing those responsible. There can be little doubt that, generally, the Scottish police do provide an effective system of investigation, although the growth in cases of alleged delay and miscarriage of justice give some cause for concern. Delay in police reporting of cases to the procurator fiscal has been subject to comment by judges in a number of cases. Lord Prosser observed that 'Scottish practice requires careful investigation and thought before a matter is reported to the Procurator Fiscal, and thereafter by him and where appropriate Crown Counsel, before any charge is brought by way of complaint or indictment. These careful procedures inevitably take some time' (*Gibson* v *HM Advocate* 2001 JC 125). On the other hand, a case involving a 22-month delay before a police report was sent to the fiscal in a straightforward case of embezzlement of a modest sum of money was held to be excessive and prejudicial. The McInnes Report on Summary Justice Review (2004) has proposed the use of abbreviated reports to allow the system to become more efficient and ECHR-compliant. While cases concerned with miscarriage of justice in Scotland have been less frequent than in England in recent years, there have been some, including the so-called 'ice cream murders' convictions against T.C. Campbell and Joseph Steele, which were overturned in 2004 by the High Court (2004 SLT 397).

Secondly, the police are required to take reasonable steps to protect the lives of individuals whom they believe to be at real and immediate risk. Wherever possible, police officers will use non-violent methods in carrying out their duties. Firearms are only used if there is no realistic alternative and it is absolutely necessary in order to save life or prevent serious injury. There are, therefore, relatively few cases of police firearms deaths in the UK, an average of four in each of 2002–03 and 2003–04 (Best and Quigley 2003). When they do occur the consequences are most serious, not only for the individual officers involved, but for police commanders as well.

There are three cases, all relevant to police officers, where deprivation of life may be permitted. One is when acting in self-defence against unlawful violence an officer uses force that is no more than 'absolutely necessary'. This strict test may result in a police officer who kills in the course of duty having a more limited scope for self-defence than is available to a civilian in corresponding circumstances. The second case is where effecting a lawful arrest or preventing the escape of a person lawfully detained and the third is where taking lawful action for the purpose of quelling a riot or insurrection. In Scotland there have been relatively few controversial deaths in police operations or custody. In 1989 an individual died of hypothermia, having been released in a drunken condition in an isolated place in wintry conditions (*Wilson* v *Chief Constable, Lothian and Borders Constabulary* 1989 SLT 97). Damages of £26,250 were awarded against two police officers who had exposed the deceased to unnecessary risk by failing to address their minds to the reasonably likely consequences of their actions. The issue of the use of proportionate force by the police, however, has been a source of some controversy in discussions over the use of non-lethal weapons such as CS gas spray and the Taser 50,000-Watt stun gun which temporarily disables muscles (*The Scotsman*, 2004).

Police detention and arrest

Article 3 of ECHR also touches on issues of police detention. For example, the use of force is not permitted during police interrogation and conditions of detention are regulated. Detention in a police cell is obviously an unpleasant experience, but has to be balanced against the interests of justice in detaining suspects. The leading Scottish case is *Napier* v *Scottish Ministers* (2004 SLT 555). Although a prison estate case in which press and public attention has concentrated on inadequate sanitary facilities and the problem of 'slopping out', expert evidence was led on adequate cell living space, natural and artificial lighting, ventilation and the risk of infection. The judge, Lord Bonomy, concluded that it amounted to degrading treatment:

> to detain a person along with another prisoner in a cramped, stuffy and gloomy cell which is inadequate for the occupation of two people, to confine them there together for at least 20 hours on average per day, to deny overnight access to a toilet throughout the week and for extended periods at the weekend and thus to expose Napier to both elements of the slopping out process [overpowering stench, spillage, contamination of skin and clothing and risk of infection; degrading practice], to provide no structured activity other than daily walking exercise for one hour and one period of recreation lasting an hour and a half in a week.
>
> (para. 75)

He concluded that this infringed Article 3 and the case led to an award of £2,400 compensation. Police detention in Scotland is short term, normally no longer than to the next available court day, unlike in England and Wales where police detention facilities have been used to alleviate prison overcrowding. While there are few Victorian police stations still in operation in Scotland, the little-publicised elements of this judgement may provide useful benchmarks for police detention facilities in future.

The strip search of a prisoner may constitute a breach of Article 3 if found to be inhumane and degrading. In pre-ECHR cases judgments differed: in *Gellatly* v *Heywood* (1998 SLT 287), where the accused was strip searched on arrest and placed in a cell, reasonable grounds for a justified search were found; in *Henderson* v *Chief Constable of Fife* (1988 SLT 361) the unlawful removal of an arrestee's brassiere was found to be an infringement of her liberty and privacy. The case of *Tolmie* v *Scottish Ministers* (2003 SLT 215) decided that the strip search of a prisoner constituted a visual examination of the external parts of the body permitted by prison rules. Nonetheless, an intimate search, particularly if disproportionate, not meeting a pressing need or by a member of the opposite sex, may well constitute a breach of Article 3.

Article 5 of the ECHR sets out the right to liberty and security of the person and is of vital importance to Scottish policing. At its heart lies the concept that a person may only be deprived of liberty if there is a reasonable suspicion of committing a crime. There are six permissible sets of circumstances, including conviction by a competent court, of a minor for educational supervision, for the prevention of spread of infectious diseases, or for unauthorised entry or with a view to deportation or extradition. Those of greatest significance for the police cover detaining a person, asking for a name and address or taking someone to a police station for questioning. Great importance is attached to arrest or detention being in accordance with a procedure prescribed by law and in all cases persons should be told, in a language that they understand, of the reasons for the arrest.

The issue of arrest is not straightforward and the Thomson Committee Report on Criminal Procedure in Scotland (1975) drew attention to the problems. Under Section 13 of the Criminal Procedure (Scotland) Act 1995, a general power is given to police officers, when they have reasonable cause to suspect that an offence has occurred or is in the course of commission, to demand information from certain members of the public. Section 14(1) of the same Act provides that where a constable has reasonable grounds for suspecting that a person has committed or is committing an offence punishable by imprisonment, the constable may detain that person. These powers are generally vague and ill defined with little relevant case law. Some guidance is offered in the case of *Houston* v *Carnegie* (2000 SLT 333), but even here it is contradictory. The accused had been detained by a police officer when standing in a public street at 10 p.m. in the company of a suspected drug dealer. The police officer did not know the accused, but were aware of suspicions about the person he was with. At the trial the defence objected to the admissibility of evidence obtained following the accused's detention on the ground that the detention was unlawful. The sheriff repelled the objection, holding that, while the officer had not applied his own mind to whether he had reasonable grounds for suspecting the accused of an offence, and had merely detained the accused on a superior officer's instructions, there were in fact reasonable grounds for suspecting the accused. The Appeal Court later quashed the conviction stating that, while detention could be lawfully effected by a constable who objectively had available reasonable grounds for suspicion without his ever having applied his mind to this, in this case there was insufficient material to justify that there were reasonable grounds for suspicion. The European Court of Human Rights (1992) has attempted to clarify what is meant by a 'reasonable suspicion' justifying arrest:

> Having a reasonable suspicion presupposes the existence of facts or information which would satisfy an objective observer that the person concerned may have committed the offence. What may be regarded as 'reasonable' will however depend upon all the circumstances.
>
> (1992 14 EHRR 108)

In England and Wales, under the Police and Criminal Evidence (PACE) Act 1984, codes of practice have been drawn up to protect the rights of individuals being questioned by the police. There are no such codes in Scotland. There are some safeguards in that a police officer must generally explain to a potential witness the nature of the alleged offence being investigated and tell the potential witness that the officer believes the witness may possess relevant information. Failure by a potential witness to provide personal particulars is an arrestable offence under the 1995 Act, but the use of force is not permitted to require a witness to remain at the scene. In regard to suspects, a police officer may demand a person's particulars and an explanation of the person's behaviour which has given rise to the constable's suspicions. However, the officer must first explain the nature of these suspicions and may then require the potential suspect to remain for a short, unspecified, period while the truthfulness of the information given is checked. The officer must only use 'reasonable force' to detain the suspect otherwise any evidence gathered may be declared inadmissible in court and the police officer may be exposed to charges of assault.

A police officer in Scotland does not have general powers to stop and question without reasonable suspicion that some criminal act has been or is being committed. The officer does not require to observe personally the alleged crime, but can rely on third-party information, previous knowledge of the suspect's habits and background, or a general knowledge of the area (*Woodward* v *Chief Constable of Fife* 1998 SLT 1342). Whether or not that suspicion subsequently proves to be justified is irrelevant, provided that the officer can reasonably justify his actions as part of the process of discretion. Strathclyde Police has carried out Operation Stance (targeting criminality among taxi drivers), Operation Eagle (targeting illegal drugs) and Operation Blade (targeting knife carrying). Lothian and Borders Police has carried out targeting operations at specific seasons of the year, such as Operation Festive Focus and Festival Watch. For many years all Scottish forces have run anti-drink-driving campaigns at Christmas and New Year, making extensive use of Breathalyser tests under the Road Traffic Acts. The common feature of all such operations is the mass targeting of large numbers of people, many of whom will be found not to be acting illegally. To what extent are the police always acting within their lawful powers in terms of having reasonable grounds for suspicion that an offence was being, or was about to be committed? Scots law already refers very clearly to the circumstances in which a person's liberty can be infringed. It may be, however, that it is cases brought under the ECHR that are most likely to succeed in influencing and changing police practices in these areas.

The 1995 Criminal Procedure (Scotland) Act also attempted to deal with another grey area, that of 'detention' at a police station. While this practice is not forbidden, the suspect is regarded as being in legal custody from the instant of detention and subject to the protection of a limited six-hour period. Only one such time period is permitted and the detention must end either when sufficient evidence is gathered or when six hours have passed. During this period the detainee has no right to see a solicitor, but is entitled to have a solicitor informed of the detention. The main problem is the exposure of the detainee to the control of the police over the six-hour period. The detainee has the right to remain silent, but will be alone, will probably be questioned by more than one police officer, and will be in an unfamiliar place. That process can be very intimidating.

The 1995 Act requires the detaining officer, and others who may later become involved in the detention process, to record certain vital facts such as the time and place detention began, the general nature of the suspected offence and the times at which the detainee was informed of the right to refuse to answer questions (other than give name and address) and the right to request that a solicitor or other person be informed. These requirements should provide an accurate and contemporaneous factual record that can be checked if any subsequent issue is raised by the detainee.

A further protection is the statutory caution which must be given prior to questioning the detainee further. However, Walker (1999: 330) sees this as weak protection, covering 'a crucial period in any interrogation', leaving the suspect open to many of the improper techniques which have been identified as common features of many miscarriages of justice, such as oppression in police custody, 'verbals' and hearsay evidence. The case of *Ucak* v *HM Advocate* (1999 SLT 392) provides an interesting application of these principles. In this case the detention of the person, a Turk who spoke no English, was held to be lawful although the interpreter was not available during the six-hour detention period. It was held that the police had done all they could to comply with procedure and that there was no unfairness or bias because both prosecution and defence used the services of the same interpreter. In relation to access to a solicitor, in the case of *Paton* v *Ritchie* (2000 SLT 239) it was held that there was no universal right of access before or during questioning by the police during the detention period.

In Scotland the right to remain silent under police questioning is of vital importance if there is to be a fair procedure and fair trial. However, even that right is not absolute. Where the suspect is subsequently charged under solemn procedure (i.e. on serious charges), a judicial examination is usually held at which the prosecutor can question the accused about relevant events. If the accused remains silent here, that silence can be adversely commented upon by either the prosecution or the trial judge if the accused subsequently raises matters at the trial which could have been revealed during the judicial examination, for example an alibi defence. While the ECHR recognises the right to silence as part of the right to a fair trial (Article 6), the court may permit such incursions into that right, subject to the test of overall fairness.

Is Scots law on detention and arrest compliant, then, with the European Convention on Human Rights? These matters have certainly been the subject of detailed consideration for over 30 years and have been the subject of two Criminal Procedure Acts, in 1980 and 1995. This has provided a rigorous framework, requiring the police officer to have reasonable grounds for suspecting that a detained/arrested person is committing or has committed an offence. The test evolved for 'reasonable suspicion' is partly subjective, in that the officer's suspicions must be genuine, and partly objective, in that there must be grounds for suspicion as judged by an objective bystander. It is likely that the ECHR does not pose a major threat to either Scots law or police practice in this area.

Stop and search

Although the issue of stop and search has been very controversial in England and Wales, there is little evidence that it has a particularly high profile in Scotland (Reid Howie Associates 2001). For many young people in urban areas of Scotland, stop and search has become almost a routine part of everyday life. The attitude and behaviour of police officers conducting stop and search appears to alienate many young people, from all communities, creates lack of trust in the police and feelings of being harassed and intimidated. It is clear that there are wide variations in police practice across Scotland (Reid Howie Associates 2001). There is widespread use of both statutory and voluntary stops and searches in the urban central belt of Scotland, whereas far fewer are carried out in rural areas. There are significant differences in the operational approaches of Scotland's eight forces. Only three engaged in 'active' stop-and-search operations and the overwhelming majority of these (87%) were described as 'voluntary'. The statutory bases for such operations – and the police must make it clear at the time that they are acting under specific statutory powers – most commonly related to road traffic offences, drugs, stolen property and weapons, but also included poaching and possession of alcohol at sporting events.

Reid Howie Associates (2001) studied nearly 7,000 stops in Glasgow, Edinburgh and Dundee. Most stops involved people under 25 years of age; most were of young men between 15 to 19; only 11% were on females, with over 800 of those under 16. Overall, articles were recovered in 9% of searches. While the vast majority of police officers discharged their duty in a competent and professional manner, the research also identified poor practice by a minority of officers, such as intimidatory tactics, abusive language and overall lack of respect, which gave stop-and-search procedures a bad reputation. This research also detected a change in police culture, moving towards the identification and marginalisation of those officers with poor practice and poor people skills with the general public. It did, however, question how widespread and how effective this tendency was. In their recommendations to the Scottish Executive, Reid Howie Associates (2001: 88) suggested a number of useful matters to be pursued, such as setting up a system of recording stops, better collection of relevant data on stops, and improved guidance to officers on the legal, civil liberties and practical issues involved.

One of these issues may be the difficulty identified by Mead (2002), namely that in Scotland there is currently no positive legal duty on the police to seek informed consent before a search, nor to inform the subject of a search that s/he has the right to refuse consent to search. Mead calls such searches 'acquiescence searches' to denote the absence of informed consent. Police officers in Scotland are entitled to search anyone they have lawfully arrested with or without warrant. The search can be carried out at the locus of the suspected crime (*Jackson* v *Stevenson* (1897) 2 Adam 255) or at the police station (*Henderson* v *Chief Constable of Fife* 1988). The police have a legal duty to search a suspect for any evidence which might support the initial suspicion against the arrested person (*Adair* v *McGarry* 1933 SLT 482), but a 'fishing expedition' search to decide whether or not to arrest the suspect is not permissible, unless carried out within the powers to search a detained person under section 14 of the 1995 Act. The right to search includes the visual examination of physical injuries and the taking of fingerprints, but only to investigate the offence for which the suspect has been arrested (*Namyslak* v *HM Advocate* 1994 SCCR 980). The suspect can be required to take part in an identification parade. Section 18 of the Criminal Procedure (Scotland) Act 1995 also enables the police to take samples and prints from arrested persons.

To what extent are these stop-and-search provisions likely to be compliant with the ECHR? Mead (2002) argues that stop and search engages the protection of Article 5 as the suspect is deprived of liberty, albeit even temporarily. As such, the invasion of the suspect's rights must be 'prescribed by law' and 'lawful', that is, the action must be taken lawfully under a domestic power which is both accessible and foreseeable (*Sunday Times* v *United Kingdom* 1979 2EHRR 245). On that basis the powers exercised by the police in Scotland probably are ECHR-compliant. However, Mead further argues that there may be additional problems under Article 8, which protects against arbitrary interference by public authorities. As judicial intervention is not practically possible before search, the minimum safeguard of an information-giving duty on police officers before conducting a search, coupled with effective record keeping, would enable a court to later assess the validity of that search and the best test of such validity would be where informed consent is given. Mead concludes that the present lack of police duty to inform citizens of their right to refuse 'voluntary' searches is 'weighted too heavily against the privacy and liberty rights of individuals' (ibid.: 803). Mead also doubts whether simple legal regulation would effectively alter police practice on the streets, but believes that a change to informed consent would 'signify a minor but crucial rebalancing of the equilibrium in power between the State and the citizen' (ibid.: 803)

The arguments about informed consent and the precondition of 'reasonable suspicion' may act as warnings to the police to be circumspect in the use of search powers. The low success rate in converting stops into arrests, and the fact that those arrested usually face conviction only on minor offences, suggest that in many cases there may be no reasonable grounds for conducting searches and that police officers may then be in danger of acting illegally. In order to become ECHR-compliant, police practice on stop and search would require to change to a more targeted, intelligence-led approach. The recording of all stops, whether or not a search follows, would provide an audit trail that would be available for subsequent review by a court and might be a deterrent, by way of additional paperwork, to the oppressive use of stop and search.

Surveillance and entrapment

In accordance with Article 6 of the ECHR everyone accused of a criminal offence has the right to a fair trial. Arguably, from the time that the police treat a person as a suspect, s/he is entitled to be treated 'fairly'. Lord Bonomy observed that:

> it has perhaps been a surprising feature of Scottish criminal procedure that in the past the strict timetable for bringing those in custody to trial, including the renowned 110-day rule should not be complemented by rules designed to ensure that those not in custody, who are subject to serious criminal charges but not active proceedings, and who are presumed innocent, should have their fate determined within a reasonable time. The introduction of such a right under the Convention must be welcomed.
>
> (*HM Advocate* v *Hynd* 2000 JC 552)

Article 6 requires that, while the overall fairness of a criminal trial should not be compromised, the constituent parts of a fair trial are not always prescribed or absolute. An individual's rights may be encroached upon if the state can demonstrate a clear and proper public objective which strikes a fair balance between the rights of the individual and the wider public interest. For example, in the case of *Stott* v *Brown* (2000 JC 328; 2001 SLT 59) the court accepted that the state had a legitimate public interest and duty to minimise the death and personal injury brought about by increased use of cars through the Road Traffic Acts, which did not undermine an accused's right to a fair trial overall.

The police must allow defence lawyers to prepare clients' cases properly because the accused and his/her solicitor must have proper access to, and time to investigate, the evidence, particularly the police investigation. The European Court of Human Rights has already found against the United Kingdom in a case where a suspect was denied access to a solicitor during the first 24 hours of detention (*Averill* v *United Kingdom* (2001) 31 EHHR 36). Solicitor and client also need to be able to communicate freely and privately with each other when the accused is in police custody or on remand in prison awaiting trial, and this out of hearing of any third party. In 2001 the European Court, in *Khan* v *United Kingdom* (31 EHRR 45), held that, because at the relevant time there was no statutory system to regulate the use of such devices by the police, state interference in the accused's rights by using covert listening devices was not 'in accordance with the law'. The secrecy of lawyer–client communications is a cornerstone of a fair process and is guaranteed by ECHR Articles 6(3) and 8, the right to privacy, and covert surveillance flies directly in the face of these.

A number of high-profile cases have contributed to the debate about the limits on covert police operations. In *Connor* v *HM Advocate* (2002 SLT 671) people seen entering and leaving the accused's home during the course of a police surveillance operation were detained and questioned. The issue at stake was whether or not the surveillance went beyond mere observation. The court held that the procedures involved in speaking to those entering and leaving involved third parties and did not breach the rights of the accused under ECHR Article 8. In *McGibbon* v *HM Advocate* (2004 SLT 588) the Court found that a breach of Article 8 had occurred through covert audio and video recordings, but that the accused had nevertheless received a fair trial. In *Rose* v *HM Advocate* (2003 SLT 1050), the destruction of a CCTV videotape, which may or may not have enabled an accused to defend an assault charge, was also found not to be in breach of the right to a fair trial.

The Regulation of Investigatory Powers (Scotland) Act 2000 (RIP(s)A), however, now legislates for covert human intelligence sources and covert surveillance in Scotland, including on police premises. The Scottish Act differs from the provisions in England and Wales in one important respect, namely the absence of a 'catch-all' clause permitting Scottish ministers to authorise surveillance. Three types of surveillance are covered: directed surveillance, to obtain information about or to identify a particular person or to determine who is involved in a matter under investigation; intrusive surveillance in relation to residential premises or a private vehicle; and covert human intelligence sources, defined as 'a person who establishes or maintains relationships in order to covertly use the relationship to obtain and disclose information covertly' (section 1(7)). Intrusive surveillance must be authorised by the chief constable for buildings within the force area and must also be approved by a Surveillance Commissioner before the operation commences. The Act also places limitations on some aspects of intelligence-led policing, such as eliminating the use of informants with criminal records. Some forces have introduced new guidelines to prevent informants from using police officers to investigate and arrest criminal rivals, often on false grounds. Specially trained officers now handle all informants.

Another difficult line to tread is the matter of incitement to commit a crime. Does Article 6 introduce into Scots law for the first time a defence of entrapment? Entrapment occurs where the accused has committed a criminal act, artificially created by agents of the state (police or otherwise) and which, but for that pressure, would never have happened. The case of *Brown* v *HM Advocate* (2002 SLT 809), concerning the theft of motor cars, adopted into Scots law the principles laid out in a previous House of Lords case (*Regina* v *Loosley* [2001] 1 WLR 2060), namely that entrapment is an abuse of state power and that the prosecution of anyone induced to commit crimes in this way amounts to an abuse of process of which the courts should have no part. In the Scottish case, however, the court found no evidence that the state, through its police agents, had misused its powers in luring citizens into committing acts forbidden by law and had then sought to prosecute them for doing so. While certain police practices, such as secret surveillance by audio or video technology and entrapment, may be seen in some quarters as unprofessional and underhand, they may be justified as proportionate steps in the fight against serious crime, as long as the use of undercover police officers does not actively incite the commission of crime. Otherwise any evidence gathered may be rendered inadmissible in court.

Another potentially controversial area is the apparently straightforward action of obtaining samples from detained or arrested persons. The aim here is to harness modern technologies in the fight against crime, but even the older science of fingerprinting has recently been brought into disrepute, following the case of Shirley McKie, the Strathclyde police officer found not guilty on a perjury charge following alleged contamination of a murder crime scene. This case raised serious, as yet unresolved, issues about fingerprint identification in Scotland and the requirement for sixteen points of similarity on which it is based. Even the built-in safeguards for taking samples may not be sufficient. The authority of a senior officer of the rank of inspector or above is required before a non-invasive sample is taken, such as head hair, mouth saliva, fingernail or toenail clippings. However, that officer need not be independent of the investigation.

Further controversy centres on even newer technologies such as DNA databases and the lack of judicial authority on whether or not DNA sampling is 'invasive'. Invasive samples, which involve penetration of the suspect/detainee's body, such as blood or semen samples, dental impressions or internal physical examinations, require a warrant from a sheriff who will balance the public interest against individual rights. These samples are obtained by police surgeons. Such decision-making processes usually have a built-in proportionality test, so, for example, the grant or refusal of a warrant requires an assessment of the seriousness of the alleged offence and the availability of other less intrusive methods to obtain the evidence. In England a number of cases have robustly supported interference with privacy on the grounds of proportionality (*Regina* v *Chief Constable of South Yorkshire*, 2002; *Marper* v *Chief Constable of South Yorkshire*, [2002] EWCA Civ 1275). The point remains to be tested in court in Scotland.

In Scotland all samples and all information derived from such samples must be destroyed as soon as possible following a decision not to prosecute or at the conclusion of such prosecution. However, difficulties can arise in respect of co-accused where samples obtained from suspect A, against whom charges are later dropped, could be used in evidence against suspect B. In those circumstances there is no requirement for the police to destroy A's samples. Further, there is a growing view that, in the interests of effectively catching criminals, a national DNA database should be established. Walker and Starmer (1999) have clearly demonstrated the dangers of DNA profiling and its selective applications. Pannick (2002) has argued, however, that, if a DNA database is created in the public interest, then all citizens should be included. By excluding those citizens who have never been charged with a criminal offence, the principles of equal treatment enunciated in ECHR Article 14 are in danger of being breached without adequate justification. With no clear Scottish judicial authority available, the matter has to revert to the first principles of triangulation: to be justified in taking samples the aim must be the prevention of crime, but the collection methods must be proportionate. Thus, while the testing of local males of a restricted age range may be permissible in a rape case, the taking of DNA samples at birth for a national database may not be ECHR-compliant.

Firearms

Article 6 of the ECHR applies to the administrative functions of the police as well as to their criminal investigations and this includes the licensing of firearms. Section 27 of the Firearms Act 1968, which applies equally on both sides of the border, directs the chief constable for the area where the applicant resides to renew a firearm certificate if satisfied: (1) that the applicant has good reason for the possession, purchase or acquisition of the specified firearm or ammunition; and (2) that the applicant's possession of the firearm ammunition will not involve danger to the public safety or peace. Thus the legislation imposes a positive duty to grant a licence unless certain conditions apply and the chief constable has to make relevant enquiries into the applicant's character, known associates and previous convictions. A certificate will, unless previously revoked or cancelled, then normally continue in force for three years or a shorter specified period.

In recent years the most notorious and difficult Scottish case involving firearms licensing was that of Thomas Hamilton, who perpetrated the 1996 Dunblane Primary School shootings in which a teacher and sixteen pupils died. Lord Cullen's Report (1996) on these events found weaknesses in the system used by Central Scotland Police to carry out firearms licensing enquiries and to make decisions on applications. As a result, Hamilton was in possession of four handguns and 743 rounds of ammunition on that fatal day. The documents, which may cast light on why the authorities failed to prevent Hamilton's gun licence being renewed, despite a number of previously expressed concerns about his suitability, remain closed to public access under a 100-year ruling.

In England the Crown Court may review the reasoning and decision of the chief constable and may substitute its own decision. However, the Scottish courts have been reluctant to so interfere. Until recently there was conflicting legal authority as to whether a sheriff was acting in an administrative or judicial role when considering appeals against a chief constable's decision. *Rodenhurst* v *Chief Constable of Grampian Police* (1992 SLT 104) has now resolved that in favour of the judicial capacity. This allows for a more rigorous and transparent examination of firearms decisions, as in the case of *Meikle* v *Chief Constable of Strathclyde* (scotcourts.gov. uk/opinions/b55_00.html), where the court found insufficient evidence to support the revocation of the appellant's shotgun certificate. This is a much more ECHR-compliant position.

Admissibility of evidence

The Human Rights Act has introduced new dimensions to the familiar issue as to whether or not 'improperly' obtained evidence should be excluded from trials. The very broad protection included in ECHR Article 8 has been held to include protection against state interference in a range of circumstances, including entry to private premises without apparent lawful authority, the search of premises including business premises, the interception of telephone calls including business calls, and the photographing by the police of suspects during a demonstration in a public place. Certainly unlawful entry and search without justification would breach Article 8, but in Scotland the granting of a warrant by a Justice of the Peace has been regarded as an effective safeguard against possible abuse of police powers (*Birse* v *HM Advocate* 2000 SLT 869). The police may normally only search premises either with the consent of the occupier freely given or with a clearly specified warrant which sets out the place(s) to be searched and the material sought. Otherwise, there is a possibility that any additional material obtained during the search may be excluded from evidence.

Even before the advent of the Human Rights Act, Scots law had long recognised the discretion of a court to admit or exclude evidence which might be improperly obtained in order to protect the citizen from illegal invasion of liberty by the authorities. Duff considers the justification for this rule to be that 'exclusion is necessary or desirable in order to control the police and other law enforcement agencies' (2004: 160). However, Duff rejects this hypothesis, partly because a minor breach of procedure can allow an (otherwise guilty) accused to go free, partly because the motives of the police officer have to be examined – and motivation is a difficult matter to ascertain in law – and partly because the rationale has little influence on police behaviour. The pressure to solve crime considerably outweighs possible exclusion at some distant future date. In Europe, many of the Article 8 challenges have arisen in the context of covert policing operations and the rise of intelligence-led policing aimed at specified offenders and crimes. Police conduct which ensnares people into future crime is not permitted. While each case has to be considered on its merits, where, for example, the police comply with Regulation of Investigatory Powers (Scotland) Act (RIP(S)A) Codes the supervision of an undercover operation is likely to be in accordance with the law and thus permissible (Ashworth 2002).

Disclosure and freedom of information

The law concerning data protection is both complex and open to subjective interpretation. Section 4 of the Data Protection Act 1998 requires that personal data – defined as information that affects the individual's privacy, whether in personal or family life, business or professional capacity – must be 'adequate, relevant and not excessive' and be processed by the police accurately, kept up to date and retained for no longer than necessary. The Scottish police intelligence-gathering model has received favourable mention in official reports (Bichard 2004), but the process does pose a number of searching questions with regard to criminal intelligence held on individual citizens:

- Why is this information held? Clearly the prevention and detection of crime will justify the collection of data on persons suspected of criminal activity, in terms of the ECHR criterion of pursuing 'a legitimate purpose'.

- For what purposes will this information be used? Bichard (2004) identified a range of purposes from child protection issues through sexual offences to employment recruitment and vetting, all of which meet ECHR criteria. In the case of M v *Chief Constable of Strathclyde Police* (2003 SLT 1007), the disclosure to an employer, in strictest confidence, that M had been questioned by police and subsequently charged with illegal sexual conduct with three young girls was justified on the grounds of the risks towards other children presented by the character of M's work. The court found no breach of ECHR articles.

- Where does the balance lie between public interest and private interest? Parliament did not intend that data-protection legislation should impede the effective investigation of crime. The Human Rights Act allows a 'proportionate' response to the harm to be prevented. The collection and retention of sensitive personal data can therefore be justified particularly in the case of serious crimes. This justification may also stand even with minor crimes where the retention of rumour and hearsay may later prove important, for example, in identifying the whereabouts of a person at a particular time in relation to a crime.

The recording, retaining, interpretation and distribution of sensitive personal information on members of the public were examined in great detail by the Bichard Inquiry into the background of the Soham murderer, Ian Huntley. Sir Michael Bichard conceded that the judgment about relevance for the disclosure of intelligence is 'a distraction from "normal" policing duties that a hard-pressed police service can ill afford' (ibid.: 4.105.2). While recognising the particular relevance of ECHR Article 8 in protecting individual privacy, he also recognised the risk that 'the police will blur the decisions about whether information should be retained and whether it should be disclosed. These are different issues ...' (ibid.: 4.105.3). For example, it may be justifiable for a police force to interfere with a person's private and family life by retaining confidential information on her/him, but not justifiable to communicate that information to an employer.

The Freedom of Information (Scotland) Act 2000, which came into force in Scotland on 1 January 2005 and extends the personal access provisions under the Data Protection Act 1988, requires all police forces to provide a 21-day response to the new public right of access to information which they hold about persons. While there are exemptions under the Public Interest Test, such as investigation of crime, law enforcement and court records, each force is required to establish and maintain a publication scheme designed to encourage proactive publication of material and promote an increased culture of openness and accountability. Only sensitive core data should be withheld. The normal presumption will be towards disclosure.

The appointment of a Scottish Information Commissioner is of over-arching importance to the new regulatory regime and should enable the necessary consultation and training processes to be speeded up. Based on the English experience already, the Act will have a substantial impact on public right of access to data held by the police. Essex Constabulary fell foul of ECHR Article 8 when a convicted thief successfully obtained an injunction against his proposed 'naming and shaming' on display posters in railway stations and restaurants (*Ellis* v *Chief Constable of Essex* ([2004] EWCA Civ 1068). Similarly, in *Regina* v *Chief Constable of West Midlands Police* ([2004] 2 All ER 1), the court held that disclosure to an employer was not compliant with ECHR Article 8 even where the disclosed information was such that a responsible employer would want to know, namely that in a previously discontinued case a person employed as a social worker was charged with indecent exposure, although the victim failed to identify the accused in a covert identification parade.

The non-disclosures which had such tragic effects in the Soham murder case, as Bichard (2004) concluded, are a constant reminder of the weak guidance available on the creation, retention and deletion of police computer files as well as the poor communication at times of police intelligence and the erroneous belief that human rights legislation prohibits exchange of such information. The balancing of confidentiality against the public interest in disclosure requires the police to look at each case on its merits and to decide where the balance lies – to protect the person who supplies information or evidence, or to make such information or evidence available to be challenged in public or tested in the courts. It is not an easy balance to strike, but that way alone lies the remedy for the problems involved in disclosure of information which may be wrong or inaccurate.

Public order

Perhaps the scenarios which have most potential to damage public confidence in the Scottish police are public-order situations such as demonstrations or industrial disputes. Article 10 of the ECHR imposes a positive obligation to protect freedom of expression of a wide range of opinions and Article 11 protects the twin rights of peaceful assembly and association with others in private and public meetings. Article 11 includes a right to protest, not restricted to those whose views accord with the majority. The right to public assembly and procession may be restricted in certain circumstances, but it is for the police and public authorities to show that it is both lawful and necessary to curtail the basic right before any restriction can be justified. For example, in *Whaley* v *Lord Advocate* (2004 SLT 425), the court decided that Article 10 did not confer any right to carry out fox hunting and that Article 11 did not cover the prohibition on fox hunting because the Protection of Wild Mammals (Scotland) Act 2002 does not prevent the assembly of the hunt, it merely regulates the activities in which the hunt might engage.

These freedoms impose positive obligations on the police, firstly to enable a peaceful demonstration to take place, and secondly to protect that demonstration from any counter-demonstration by taking appropriate and reasonable measures. Even if the assembly is unlawful, the police obligations still apply, though not if the meeting or assembly seeks to promote violence. Considerations such as traffic management and public order, problems of damage to property and routeing issues are all clearly relevant matters for the police to consider and generally the courts have supported police actions which pursue public safety and prevention of disorder and are proportionate to a legitimate aim. The case of *Jones* v *Carnegie* (2004 SLT 609) concerned five separate charges of breach of the peace, three of which involved public-order offences at either a military base or the Scottish Parliament, but no breaches of ECHR Articles 10 or 11 were found.

Scots law has long recognised the right to restrict public procession or demonstration, stretching back to a case in 1882 banning parades by the Salvation Army (*Deakin* v *Milne* 1882, 5 Couper 174). The police role in advising local councils as to whether or not to permit a proposed procession or demonstration requires a delicate balancing judgement between allowing the event and the scale of any likely disorder. A procession can be banned altogether or restrictions can be imposed for a legitimate purpose, such as modifying the route to avoid potential flashpoints. In addition, the Public Order Act 1984 permits the senior police officer present during a procession to impose conditions upon the place, time and conduct of the procession in order to prevent serious public disorder, serious damage to property, serious disruption to the life of the community or intimidation. These powers are also available in respect of public assemblies, i.e. 20 or more persons in a public place wholly or partly open to the air, and industrial action by pickets (Public Order Act 1984, section 14).

These decisions are often controversial because they tend to touch on many of the big political and social issues of the day, such as anti-war protest, religious belief, animal rights, anti-nuclear protest, anti-poll tax protest, immigration and asylum. Hence the Executives decision to appoint an independent review of parades and marches in Scotland and to make it available for public consultation (Scottish Executive 2005). While the reasons for public assembly and meetings may vary considerably, the critical questions about whether or not interference with these rights is likely to be ECHR-compliant remain consistent: Does it meet a legitimate aim? Is the action proportionate? Is it justified by relevant and sufficient reasons?

Conclusion

The 1998 Human Rights Act requires all public authorities in Scotland, including the courts and the police, to act in conformity with Convention rights. However, such rights are not always as clearly enunciated as popular opinion perceives them to be and they often require judicial clarification and interpretation. By emphasising the principle of proportionality, European jurisprudence attempts to balance the competing interests of the state and the citizen, debated in the rational and considered atmosphere of the courtroom. Police officers, on the other hand, face the difficult task of applying such principles fairly and instantly to the often confused situations which confront them. It is also still early in the implementation of the Act for a substantial body of precedent and experience to have been built up to guide police actions. Thus it is not a straightforward task for the police to apply a simple and clear 'code of rights' to the exercise of their powers.

The ECHR appears to offer both opportunities and threats to the Scottish police. On the positive side, if the police follow the spirit and detail of the Convention jurisprudence, then they will be less vulnerable in court to damaging cross-examination. The public will have greater confidence in the probity and integrity of the police, hopefully leading to increased co-operation and support. As a by-product, the Act will also apply fairness to the conduct of internal police disciplinary proceedings and will extend to police officers certain rights as enjoyed by other citizens.

The growing interest in ethical approaches to policing may also be assisted by the Act. Mills (2002: 25) recognises 'significant reluctance or at best apathy within the Police Service, as an institution, to embrace the ethical challenges facing it'. The Act, with its emphasis on effective promotion and protection of human rights, provides an ethical framework within which fair and practical solutions to everyday policing problems can be based. The introduction of a code of ethics based on the Human Rights Convention, similar to that not only introduced, but effectively implemented by the Police Service of Northern Ireland, would be a major step forward for both police and public in Scotland.

On the negative side, the Act will undoubtedly entail additional work for police officers in the proper planning and execution of police operations and the increased openness of information disclosure. In some quarters it may be seen as yet another demand on the time and energy of officers and on forces in the provision of training and awareness raising. The ECHR also provides an environment within which the public may be encouraged to scrutinise more closely the use of police powers and, if necessary, to invoke their right to pursue these concerns in a court of law.

A recent Scottish Executive report on *The Use of Human Rights Legislation in the Scottish Courts* (Greenhill *et al.* 2004) concluded that the Act had made a moderate impact on practice in the legal system. Human-rights points had been deployed at a steady rate, but few challenges to public policy had been successful. There had been notable clusters of successful cases on immigration control, prison conditions and children. In several instances, the Executive has pre-empted potential challenges by introducing amending legislation. The Report confirmed that Article 6 issues (fair trial, etc.) predictably dominated, but no primary legislation had been invalidated. Thus it has been very much 'business as usual' for the Scottish criminal justice system as a whole (Greenhill *et al.* 2004). Many of the principles behind the Act were already incorporated as principles of natural justice, such as the presumption of innocence, the right to challenge witnesses, and time and facilities to prepare a defence, all essential requirements of Article 6. The prison statistics do not reveal either a substantial decrease in convictions, with guilty men walking free as the more sensational critics suggested (McCluskey 2000), nor do they show undue leniency in sentencing. The balance between privacy under Article 8 and the sharing of information between agencies in the public interest under Article 10 has been recognised (Ellis and Soham).

The Scottish Police Service appears to have divided itself into three camps over the incorporation of the European Convention on Human Rights into Scots law. The first view is that the Human Rights Act has made no difference to the exercise of police powers in Scotland. The second view is that the Act will have a massive negative effect on policing by preventing the service from doing its job properly. The third and 'middle' view is that the Act is bound to have an effect, but that it is a challenge to which the service can adapt. It is perhaps still too early to fully assess the impact on Scots law and police procedures. The signs so far are that neither the early fears of the pessimists, who predicted the creation of a compensation culture and a collapse of the criminal justice and legal systems (McCluskey 2000), nor the optimistic hopes of those who foresaw a 'new culture of rights' (Klug 1996; Cheney et al. 1999) with a plethora of revolutionary cases being upheld, appear to have been fulfilled. As with most aspects of Scots law and policing, wrongs and injustices are remedied and improvements made at an evolutionary, rather than revolutionary, pace.

References

Ashworth, A. (2002) 'Redrawing the boundaries of entrapment', *Criminal Law Review*, March: 161–179.

Berry, G., Izat, J., Mawby, R. and Walley, L. (1998) *Practical Police Management*. London: Police Review Publishing Co.

Best, D. and Quigley, A. (2003) 'Shootings by the police: what predicts when a firearms officer will pull the trigger?' *Policing and Society*, 13 (4): 349–364.

Bichard, Sir M. (2004) *Inquiry Report to House of Commons on Soham Murders*. London: HMSO.

Cheney, D., Dickson, L., Fitzpatrick, J. and Uglow, S. (1999) *Criminal Justice and the Human Rights Act, 1998*. Bristol: Jordan Publishing.

Cullen, Lord (1996) *Public Inquiry into Shootings at Dunblane Primary School*. Edinburgh: HMSO.

Duff, P. (2004) 'Admissibility of improperly obtained physical evidence in the Scottish criminal trial: the search for principle', *Edinburgh Law Review*, 8: 152–176.

Gillespie, A. (2000) 'Clause for concern', *Police Review*, 12 May: 29–30.

Greenhill, P., Mullen, T., Murdoch, P., Craig, S. and Miller, A. (2004) *The Use of Human Rights Legislation in the Scottish Courts* (accessed at http:///www.scotland.gov.uk/socialresearch).

Klug, F. (1996) 'A Bill of Rights as secular ethics?' in R. Gordon and R. Wilmot-Smith (eds), *Human Rights in the United Kingdom*, 1st edn. Oxford: Oxford University Press, pp. 37–57.

McCluskey, Lord (2000) 'Trojan horse at the gates of our court?', *Scotland on Sunday*, 6 February.

McInnes, Sheriff Principal J. (2004) *The Summary Justice Review Committee: Report to Ministers*. Edinburgh: Scottish Executive.

Mead, D. (2002) 'Informed consent to police searches in England and Wales: a critical re-appraisal in the light of the Human Rights Act', *Criminal Law Review*, October: 791–804.

Mills, A. (2002) 'Ethics and the police: facing the challenge', *Policing Today*, 8 (3): 25–27.

Neyroud, P. and Beckley, A. (2001) *Policing, Ethics and Human Rights*. Devon: Willan Publishing.

Pannick, D. (2002) 'Some fingerprints are more equal than others', *The Times*, 1 October.

Reid Howie Associates (2001) *Police Stop and Search among White and Minority Ethnic Young People in Scotland*. Edinburgh: Scottish Executive Central Research Unit.

The Scotsman (2004) 'Neo-lethal weapons', 2 December.

Scottish Executive (2005) *Supporting Police, Protecting Communities: Proposals for Legislation*. Edinburgh: Scottish Executive.

Starmer, K., Strange, M. and Whitaker, Q. (2001) *Criminal Justice, Police Powers and Human Rights*. London: Blackstone Press.

Thomson, Lord (1975) *Criminal Procedure in Scotland*, 2nd Report. Edinburgh: HMSO.

Walker, C. (1999) 'Miscarriages of justice in Scotland', in C. Walker and K. Starmer (eds), *Miscarriages of Justice: A Review of Justice in Error*. London: Blackstone Press.

Walker, C. and Starmer, K. (eds) (1999) *Miscarriage of Justice: A Review of Justice in Error*. London: Blackstone Press.

Chapter 12

Semper Vigilo: the future of Scottish policing

Daniel Donnelly and Kenneth Scott

Introduction

The motto of the Scottish Police Service – *Semper Vigilo* – implies a constant watchfulness for the safety and protection of Scottish society over the past 200 years or so. During that time society has undergone significant change in all sorts of areas of people's lives and the police has sought to adapt to these changes while trying to maintain its constant basic functions and ultimate purposes. In this book we have traced these purposes, functions and changes in order to better understand the present nature and workings of Scotland's police forces. In this chapter eight themes arising from the various contributions are discussed in order to identify some of the issues and challenges which lie ahead for the Scottish police service in the 21st century.

The future of traditional Scottish policing in the local community

Historically, Scottish policing developed in relation to two important characteristics: concern for the public good and a close association with government at the local level. At the core of the traditional model of Scottish policing is an ever-present interaction with the local community in terms of public well-being, the welfare of the community and policing which always went beyond mere law enforcement. Social change has transformed that community with the increased use of new technologies, higher levels of public education and awareness, increased expectations of public standards, and a greater element of multiculturalism. At the same time, from outside Scotland have come the influences first of a European context and, then, of globalisation. Scottish policing has sought to respond positively to these changes, but it is obvious that the necessary upheavals of continually adjusting over the years have placed exceptional pressures on the traditional model of Scottish policing to a point where its very survival may be in doubt.

Ample evidence exists that the community in Scotland wishes the traditional style of policing to continue and this will be difficult with the high and increasing level of demands on present police resources. All indications point to a future policing model that is quite dissimilar to the traditional one. A future model is likely to involve a greater mixture of types of police operating at different levels: community support officers; wardens and auxiliary support; paid special constables; local partnerships, with some being funded directly from the Scottish Executive; increased civilian roles; and the private and voluntary sector having a greater part to play than before. All parties, particularly the community, will be expected to embrace new working practices that will impact on age-old traditions and attitudes to ensure success. Some examples of these changing practices and systems that are already emerging include:

- expanding use of call centres
- non-emergency police telephone numbers
- problem-solving policing
- non-attendance of police at low-level incidents
- increased use of civilian staff in and outside of police offices
- less direct interface between police officers and the public than before
- communities wardens, support officers and voluntary workers being expected to solve local community problems without police assistance.

A level of adjustment of this new 'mosaic' of policing will have to be negotiated between the community and the police in order to make it acceptable, and that will not be easy. There are also major questions about how such a system will be managed – by the police, by local government, by the private sector – and how it will be integrated. There are likely to be more complex arrangements for funding these new systems, and decisions on accountability will also have to be made. Central to this future scenario is how the relationship between the Scottish police and its community, embodied in the cornerstone of 'policing by consent', can be effectively maintained.

Developing future leadership in Scottish policing

The present review shows that the police in Scotland has a history of bringing about change, but only at its own pace and on its own terms. This is no longer sufficient against a political backdrop of finding instant solutions to problems. The end result has been a change in attitude and mindset in police circles and the introduction of a more positive approach to the management of policing. This approach is based on a belief that action must be taken, problems can be solved and difficulties can be eradicated. The means of achieving this is through a strategic approach to tasks, better management, higher educational qualifications, increased performance monitoring, more professional development, the introduction of additional professional support staff, and, as a particular priority, the development of a robust leadership strategy for taking the service forward. This book bears witness to evidence of the currency of all of these ideas in modern Scottish policing.

The key management focus continues to be on the organisational response to change and fresh challenges in this respect are forever on the horizon. For example, the Scottish police are not exempt from the important demographic changes in Scotland that are beginning to have an effect and which will have increasing effects in the future. This process will have a major impact on recruitment, civilianisation and the burden on pension provision. With an ageing population and fewer young people available for police work, pressures on recruitment will increase. The Scottish Police Service prides itself on the care taken to select the most suitable candidates for the job and, if public expectations are to be met, care will have to be taken to ensure standards are maintained. Already there is a small, though growing, number of older recruits, and there has been a noticeable increase in the number of women in the police service in recent decades. However, the number of females at chief officer level is still very low and even in the senior promoted ranks is still disproportionately small. Equally, there is also pressure to increase recruitment from across the cultural range within the community. The number of officers in Scottish police forces from ethnic communities is still low, although some Commonwealth citizens are already working as police officers in Scotland as a result of direct recruitment. The police may also benefit from the Scottish Executive's 'Fresh Talent' policy of attracting incomers to Scotland and there has been some recruitment advertising carried out by the police aimed at areas of Europe.

Scottish policing will be competing in the same ring as other public-sector and private employers as never before, not only for quality police personnel, but also for the increasing number of civilian roles to be filled. Some police commentators believe that the police officer–support staff balance might rise to a 50/50 mix before too long. Such a goal in Scotland would certainly generate a loss of considerable experience at the operational and command levels at a period of major staff turnover. At the same time, increased civilianisation throughout the police organisation is necessary if the support functions are going to be effectively and efficiently managed.

In addition, the organisation will have to find new ways of retaining existing experienced personnel. With the age profile of existing police officers moving towards the retirement peak, the potential negative effects of pensions on police operational budgets is considerable. In common with other areas of work, ways of extending the retirement age beyond 30 years of police service is requiring urgent attention in order to stem the flow of experience out of the organisation. The introduction of new police pension regulations from 2006 will increase the minimum full pensionable service for new recruits from 30 to 35 years. One potential consequence of this that has received less attention is the impact of lack of experienced staff on ensuring a universal quality of service across Scotland. This may mean encouraging experienced police and civilian staff to be more flexible in work practices and to display a willingness to apply for jobs and promoted posts in different parts of Scotland. Such flexibility has existed in most areas of the public sector for the past 50 years, while localism in the Scottish Police Service has meant that it has lagged behind.

An ageing population in society and a growing diversity within the police organisation will present their own unique challenges in acquiring new skills in managing a wider mix of employees and, from an operational policing stance, necessitating changes to frontline policing. The development of leadership at all levels becomes crucial to facing up to these challenges. At the highest levels the leadership has to become more proactive in demonstrating its own expertise as the managers of Scotland's police organisations.

Future tasking of Scottish policing to tackle crime

Evidence from crime surveys and opinion polls indicates that, even when the overall crime statistics show a decline, crime is still a matter of great concern to the Scottish public. Crime also features high on the agenda of the politicians and is likely to remain there for the foreseeable future. Scottish Executive legislation and policies give considerable prominence to the fight against crime, with anti-social behaviour strategies, targeting and partnership initiatives. The key issues for policing in the future tend to be less the idea of crime as a generality, but increasingly specific types of crime which are particularly related to public perceptions and 'fear of crime'. In Scotland these include violent crime and low-level 'quality of life' offences.

Continued rises in violent crime, especially in the west of Scotland, are a matter of huge public concern, matched only by criticism of the police for apparently failing to curb this tendency. Not only do the crime statistics show that violent crime, especially serious assaults, is continuing to rise, but the two national targets on reduction in violent crime and clear-up rates for violent crime have never been met by Scottish police forces. The police, of course, are not solely responsible for this problem. Some parts of the country have a lengthy tradition of association with violence, the role of alcohol in generating violent behaviour has been clearly identified, and links between violence and deep-rooted social problems such as poverty and deprivation are well established. Nonetheless, the perceived failure of the police to stem the flow of violent crime is a major issue which will require to be successfully addressed if public support is to be maintained.

At the other end of the crime scale, there is also a problem with those high-volume offences which, although low level in nature, affect people in the quality of their everyday lives and surroundings, such as graffiti being sprayed on walls or minor harassment on local streets. Here it has been recognised that the police are no longer the sole combatants against disorder. The Scottish Executive is making it clear that there is a major role for other stakeholders such as local government, the private sector, auxiliaries and volunteers. Local authorities are increasingly being given powers and responsibilities to tackle low-level offences through prevention and enforcement, for instance, by the use of community wardens. The private security industry is rapidly expanding throughout Scotland and is likely, subject to regulation, to have a key role in crime prevention and investigation in the future. Communities themselves are being encouraged to exercise responsibility for their own safety to a greater extent than before.

The issue for the police is how to co-ordinate these developments. One way forward is through partnership policing at the neighbourhood level. For example, it would be possible to develop a neighbourhood policing concept within local authority electoral wards whereby community police officers are given an enhanced leadership role and responsibility to co-ordinate and lead the mix of police and non-police resources within the ward boundaries. This is already being piloted in some parts of the UK at present. Senior police managers at the divisional or command unit level will also have to become more directly involved in strategic planning by striking up community safety partnerships and service level agreements with their local authorities, even to the extent that funding comes direct to that level and bypasses police headquarters.

The future of Scottish policing in the war on drugs

The position of the Scottish police in relation to tackling drugs is a complex and difficult one because of the many, often incompatible, vested interests involved. In policy terms, policing is a Scottish Parliament responsibility, but drugs are a matter reserved to Westminster. In operational terms, drug crime is an aspect of local policing and is often interrelated with other types of crime, but there is also a national agency, SDEA, whose remit is specifically dealing with drug crime. In combating drug crime, there are major global networks which require both international and national co-operation between a range of other agencies, but there is also a local face to drug crime which requires action on the ground in local neighbourhoods. Increasingly the organised criminals who run drug crime are being pursued by methods that involve financial and legal measures, but these take time and patience and do not always provide quick solutions that the public can see. Meantime, local communities are faced with the scourge of drugs and drug dealers and rightly demand a police response of some sort, irrespective of the niceties of political and police diplomacy.

There is little evidence in drugs policing of a substantially cohesive and workable corporate policy or of adequate performance measurement systems. There is a tendency for too many masters making decisions within a heavily bureaucratic policy-making framework. The ubiquitous world supply of drugs makes it difficult to quantify and ascertain success to date and indications are that the future does not appear to offer the prospect of better immediate results. The British answer that is emerging is the creation of the so-called 'FBI style' Serious and Organised Crime Agency, with SDEA as its Scottish arm. However, within this context there is still a need for a rethink of how Scotland can deal more effectively with its drugs problem in the 21st century.

The future of Scottish policing in tackling youth crime

It would be easy to suggest, as politicians and certain sections of the public do, that there is an almost inevitable gulf in relationships between the police and young people in Scotland. However, that would not only be oversimplistic, it would also be untrue. The community involvement approach characteristic of the Scottish police tradition, whereby many police officers are involved with schools and youth organisations, coupled with the fact that the large majority of young people are never in any kind of formal trouble with the police supports the view that there is much common ground between young people and the police. The problem is dealing with the minority of youths who go beyond being occasional mischief-makers to becoming persistent young offenders, those who by the time they reach adulthood already have a lengthy criminal record to their names and have almost exhausted every available form of corrective treatment.

The police does have an enforcement role which society expects it to fulfil, but it should not be at the expense of creating continual conflict between the police and the young, nor of permanently alienating them. The way forward appears to have been recognised in some quarters, for example by ACPOS in its youth strategy. An approach is needed based on medium- to long-term problem-solving and the appropriate use of newer forms of restorative justice for young people. The future role of policing youth in Scotland will be complex and will require new policing skills at all levels. It is also important that the eight forces adopt a common approach to the problem to ensure an equitable level of service across the country.

The future police role in an integrated Scottish criminal justice system

With major reforms throughout the Scottish criminal justice system, the major shift in recent years has been to recognise the core role which policing plays. There is now a greater willingness by all parties to work together in order to improve the system and while, the police service feels the impact of virtually every change, it is happy to play its part if it is treated as an equal partner. It is also being recognised that many of the types of developments of which the police service has experience can be shared and built upon by the other criminal justice agencies, such as inter-agency working, partnerships and strategic planning. Communication and interaction within the system are crucial and increasingly policies are being implemented with the aim of creating a more integrated system. The role of new technology in this process is central and again police experience has been invaluable. For example, the police service and COPFS staff have been working on integrative computer projects since the early 1990s. There has also been a marked change in emphasis towards the role of the victim in the Scottish system and in supporting and informing victims throughout proceedings, although this approach is still not without its problems. Because it is police officers who have most to do with victims, at least in the early stages of an investigation, it is likely that they will play a greater role in this respect as the victim focus expands. Similarly, as new concepts such as 'community justice' and 'community prosecution' are developed, those with the closest contact with communities, namely the police, will probably be relied upon to make a significant contribution.

A related issue is the impact of human-rights legislation on the working of the Scottish criminal justice system, including policing. The Human Rights Act has the potential to affect many aspects of public and private life although, as the contribution in this volume indicates, negative impact has so far been more feared than actual. Nonetheless, many of the recent Acts of the Scottish Parliament relating to enforcement and the governance of law-and-order issues, such as the anti-social behaviour legislation, have had as part of their purpose the establishment of a legal framework which will ensure compliance with the ECHR. The police may not like the proliferation of legislation which leads to increased workloads, but the Executive knows it has no choice; otherwise it could face criticism for non-compliance.

There is no doubt that the Human Rights Act has influenced Scottish policing. So far the embodiment of any given police power in law and the proportionate use of that power by the police in any given situation have been sufficient, by and large, for the Scottish courts to interpret actions as ECHR-compliant. No doubt, as human-rights law evolves and its interpretation is brought to bear on a range of new and different situations, the impact of the ECHR dimension may become greater. Ironically, its effects may well prove more immediate on police work than on police powers because the Human Rights Act has been instrumental in initiating secondary legislation in the field of employment law covering matters such as disability, shift-working and working time regulation. These raise important issues for police employers which add to the growing complexity of the management of police forces simply as work organisations, irrespective of their wider functions within society.

Future impact of devolved government and police accountability

Devolution has greatly decreased the distance between politics and the police in Scotland and has greatly increased the amount of scrutiny and monitoring of the police which now takes place. The net result is a definite weakening of constabulary independence and an imbalance in the relative strengths of the three legs of the tripartite system of governance and accountability. The role of local government is becoming more equivocal: on the one hand, it is destined to play a bigger role in combating low-level crime and disorder through community safety initiatives; on the other hand, its capacity to operate, especially through joint police boards, as an effective local element in police accountability is dubious. As the new political and constitutional settlement evolves over time, there are likely to be further changes to which both national and local politicians and senior police officers will have to accommodate themselves. The growing web of scrutiny, audit and inspection as means of holding the police to account is likely to continue and to expand, creating even more pressure from various layers of politicians. As it is, police forces are less part of a tripartite system and more at the core of a multi-tiered system which demands cooperation and compliance on all sides:

- local municipal enforcement (wardens, support officers, volunteers)
- general policing (eight independent forces)
- national agencies, such as SDEA, SOCA, Special Branch, MI5, NIM
- common police services
- national policy- and strategy-making bodies
- public-sector multi-agency partnerships
- private security industry.

The *ad hoc* growth of this multi-tiered structure is in danger of obscuring key principles on which Scottish policing has traditionally been based, including a clear structure of responsibility within the police organisation and defined areas of accountability by the police to representatives of the public. Arguably there is now an increased degree of political ambiguity and fuzziness, with Scottish policing being required to respond to a plethora of masters at local, central and national levels.

In two areas of accountability in particular there is a need for greater clarity in the future. One of these is the lack of any mechanism by which the common police services can be held publicly to account. Among the many important issues which the Shirley McKie case has highlighted, the black hole of accountability that surrounds these centrally run services is one of the most important and is one that still remains to be resolved. Attempts have been made to improve the oversight of these services by police and central government interests, and there was at one time a suggestion that the common services, including the SDEA, might form a 'ninth force' with its own chief constable and police board. However, the question of how to establish a third leg of public representation to properly oversee Scotland's central police services still remains unanswered, although future legislation may provide a start.

The second outstanding issue is that of public complaints against the police. Despite some occasional debate on this in the Scottish Parliament and an Executive consultative paper, the final verdict on the direction that the police complaints system will take has still to be decided. The crux of the matter is whether the police should continue to investigate complaints against officers internally or whether some kind of independent complaints body should be set up. There is a continuing acceptance in some quarters

National Operational Influences

Community Safety and Planning
Community Wardens' Schemes
Special Constabulary
Emergency Planning & Counter Terrorism
Crimestoppers
Criminal DNA database
Scottish Road Policing Strategy
Scottish Drug Enforcement Agency
Scottish Money Laundering Unit
Scottish Intelligence Database
Scottish Witness Liaison Unit
Scottish HI-Tech Crime Unit
Scottish Police Technical Support Unit
Scottish Tactical Tasking &
    Co-ordination Group
Automatic Number Plate Recognition
National Restorative Justice Cautioning
National Intelligence Model
National Crime Intelligence Service
Special Branch & Security Services
HM Customs and Excise
Immigration Service & Asylum Issues

National Policy/Strategy Influences

Scottish Crime Recording Standard — Scottish Domestic Violence Strategy
National Drugs Strategy for Scotland — ACPOS People Strategy
National Single Non-Emergency Telephone Number — Scottish Victims Strategy
National Customer Service Centre Users' Group — Child Protection Strategy
Scottish Police Qualifications — Scottish Police Diversity Strategy
ACPOS Youth Strategy — Scottish Police Information Strategy

**Delivering
Effective Policing
to the
Scottish Community**

LOCAL POLICE FORCES

*Central Scotland Police
Dumfries and Galloway Constabulary
Fife Constabulary
Grampian Police
Lothian and Borders Police
Northern Constabulary
Strathclyde Police
Tayside Police*

National Management/Support Influences

ACPOS / ASPS / SPF
Police Support Staff Council (Scot.)
Scottish Police College
National Conditions of Service
National Discipline & Efficiency Regs.
Scottish Police Promotion Exams.
National Appraisal System
National police uniform
National Professional Standards
National Senior Command Module
Accelerated Promotion Scheme
National Criminal History System
National Fingerprint Database
Airwave Communication Project
Common Services Programme Bd.
Forensic Science Lab Service
Police Info & Co-ordination Centre
Scottish Business Crime Centre
Integrated Criminal Justice Info
System
Legal Info Network for Scotland

National Political/Monitoring Influences

Justice Minister & Department — Scottish Police Grant Funding
Lord Advocate/Crown Office — Scottish Best Value Group
National Police Targets — Scottish Police Authorities Forum
Audit Scotland — Police Advisory Board (Scotland)
Accounts Commission for Scotland — Police Negotiating Board (UK)
HM Inspectorate of Constabulary — Scottish Crime Surveys

Figure 12.1 Scottish Policing System Model

of the arguments that police officers are best placed to identify malpractice in the activities of other police officers, and that the system, backed up by the role of the procurator fiscal where criminal proceedings are involved, has generally worked well. However, the tide of practice elsewhere, both in other parts of the UK and throughout the police world, is flowing in a contrary direction. Independent and external investigations of complaints against the police exist in many places and are capable of working effectively. Sooner or later, Scotland is going to have to follow in the same direction, driven by future legislation.

The future of Scottish policing: a national force?

If anyone was given a blank sheet of paper and asked to plan a police system for a small country the size of Scotland, it is highly unlikely that what we have at present would be the outcome. Many of the contributions to this book will help to provide answers as to how and why Scottish policing has evolved in the way it has, but whether or not the Scottish police should be reorganised and restructured towards a national force remains one of the key questions for the future.

This is not the first time that the question has been raised. In 1962 the Royal Commission on the Police considered the same issue and came down on the side of the present system of partnership between central government, local authorities and the chief constable to run local police forces. The Commission was not opposed to a national police service for Scotland, or indeed for England and Wales. The *Final Report* commented that there was a robust argument for central control of the police and discounted 'any suggestion that a unified police service would endanger liberty or facilitate the overthrow of lawful government' (Royal Commission 1962). The Commission simply believed that a national set-up was inappropriate at that time.

From time to time other prominent police and political figures have lent their support to the idea of a single Scottish police force or, at least, to some form of restructuring. Sir Leslie Sharp, Chief Constable of Strathclyde Police, did so in a *Police Review* article in 1995 (Sharp 1995: 28–29), but appeared to be out of step with his fellow chief constables in favouring such a development. In 1998 Donald Dewar, then Secretary of State for Scotland, speculated in a speech to the annual conference of the Scottish Police Federation about a reduction in the number of Scottish forces, largely on grounds of efficiency of scale and cost-effectiveness. However, he specifically discounted an immediate move to a national police service (Dewar 1998). More recently, an appeal by Paddy Tomkins, Chief Constable of Lothian and Borders Police, for an open and wide-ranging debate on

Scottish policing centred on the idea of a 'Scottish national police service' (*The Herald* 2004: 1).

Out of public view, a comprehensive review into the structure of the Scottish police was carried out by the Scottish Executive over the period from 1999 to 2000. This recommended changes in the organisation of the common police services provided on a national basis already, but did not propose any change to the existing eight police forces and indicated no movement towards a national police service. Unfortunately, the report of the review group and the case for and against its proposals did not see the light of day and so its arguments and discussions remain relatively unknown to the Scottish public.

Many of the reasons why this debate about a national force needs to take place are to be found throughout this book. Firstly, the demands made on Scottish policing in recent years have stretched resources beyond what is comfortable and the situation is unlikely to improve. Further demands on the police keep arising in the form of anti-terrorist measures, expanding the war on drugs, dealing with organised crime, assisting with the problems of asylum seekers, responding to new initiatives from the Parliament and Executive, creating new policing agencies, and the continuing flow of government policies that have policing at the centre of their strategies.

Secondly, as there are approximately 15,500 police officers and 6,200 civilian support officers in Scotland to police a population of five million people, it is essential to ensure a uniformity of training, experience, conditions of service and career structures. There is also the requirement in changing times of a more flexible workforce with free movement of personnel between forces to facilitate integration, to bring greater cross-fertilisation of experience across the nation, and thus ensuring a more equal delivery of service to the Scottish public.

Thirdly, Scotland's police gross expenditure budget for 2002–2003 was approximately £955 million. Over half of this amount went to cover the costs of Strathclyde Police alone, because it is responsible for at least 50% of Scotland's policing needs. Merely at face value, there is an apparent inequality when a single police force has this massive responsibility while seven others cover the rest of Scotland. At operational level, a divisional commander in Strathclyde can have up to 1,000 police and civilian personnel under his/her command. The full complement of resources for the four smallest forces in Scotland is 789, 1,072, 1,122 and 1,349, respectively, yet each is managed by a hierarchy of chief, depute and assistant chief constables.

Fourthly, because of new legislation from the Scottish Parliament, the Scottish police are now more statutorily accountable to national strategic and community planning partnerships, along with a variety of elected politicians and non-elected officials in other agencies. Furthermore, as a result of devolution, the 129 MSPs are regularly in touch with their local senior police officers, probably just as much as with local councillors. Democratic control of policing is greatly assisted by the fact that a large number of MSPs can be on the doorsteps of their local police commanders very quickly and are inclined to do so, given their increasing accountability to the local electorate and their willingness to taking on board many of the police-related problems of their constituents.

Fifthly, some would argue that, in reality, Scotland is already very close to having a national police service headed by a corporate board of eight chief executives under the title of ACPOS. The corollary of our initial question provides an interesting perspective: what in Scottish policing is now not national? Since devolution a Justice Minister and department have been introduced with one of their main responsibilities being to oversee the police service. A national Police Advisory Board and a UK Police Negotiating Board govern police conduct and efficiency and conditions of service. A Scottish Police Authorities Forum facilitates the role of elected members in carrying out the work of police boards: the Association of Chief Police Officers in Scotland, the Association of Scottish Police Superintendents, the Scottish Police Federation and the civilian Police Support Staff Council (Scotland) look after the interests of their members throughout Scotland.

There is national training at the Scottish Police College; national Criminal Records Office and Fingerprinting services; and a Scottish Business Crime Centre, partly sponsored by Scottish companies. A national stolen-property database exists along with the Disclosure Scotland Bureau, which offers a national service of criminal-history information to both police and non-police customers, as well as a criminal DNA database. In addition, there is a Scottish Police Information Strategy; a Scottish Road Policing Strategy; National Airwave Communication Project; Integrated Scottish Criminal Justice Information System; Legal Information Network for Scotland; Automatic Number Plate Recognition; National Restorative Justice Cautioning; and Scottish Crime Recording Standard.

There is also a National Drugs Strategy for Scotland with the national Scottish Drug Enforcement Agency (SDEA) playing a vital role along with its component national groups, such as the Scottish Money Laundering Unit, Scottish Intelligence Database, Scottish Witness Liaison Unit, Scottish Hi-Tech Crime Unit and Scottish Police Technical Support Unit. The SDEA also monitors the use of the National Intelligence Model and chairs the Scottish Tactical Tasking and Co-ordination Group.

Moreover, the SDEA liaises with other national forces and departments outside Scotland and interfaces with European policing groups and the UK National Crime Intelligence Service, National Crime Squad, HM Customs and Excise and the Immigration Service. It is anticipated that the SDEA will have an important role as the Scottish contact for the new Serious and

Organised Crime Agency soon to be introduced in England and Wales. Scotland still retains a national Special Branch network, mainly overseen from London, and in answer to the growing threats of terrorist attack, the Scottish police have introduced the Scottish Police Information and Co-ordination Centre. In addition, a recently constituted Programme Board will be responsible for overseeing the introduction of a National Services Authority, which will include the National Forensic Science Laboratory Service in Scotland and will examine the potential for including additional central support services under its umbrella.

The model of Scottish policing which most people have in mind of eight territorial police forces assisted by a small number of common service organisations proves to be oversimplistic. The actual model, shown in Figure 12.1, shows a system of eight police forces delivering policing at a local level, but in co-operation with and strongly constrained by a wide range of national influences affecting management and support, police operations, policy and strategy, politics and monitoring – what is to all intents and purposes a national police service in embryo.

There is, of course, another side to this argument. There are a number of concerns about abolishing the present eight-force structure. The financial costs of restructuring could be potentially high and might risk diverting more of the available funds for policing away from providing key resources where the public most want them, on the streets. The benefits to the public of such a major change to Scottish policing may not be fully obvious and experience of large-scale restructuring in other services has created a degree of scepticism among the Scottish public for such changes. Above all, it is believed that there is a great risk of losing local democratic control of the police and the much-valued police links with the local community, although the example of Strathclyde Police does not suggest that bigger scale necessarily means a weakening of local community relations. Undeniably, close community contact is essential to the maintenance of traditional Scottish policing and any move towards a national police service would have to ensure its continuance.

Conclusion

Devolution has undoubtedly increased the tendency towards centralisation in Scottish policing. It has enabled the Scottish Executive to routinely seek national solutions to national problems, to introduce new statutory responsibilities on a national level, and to create its own brand of performance management involving setting targets and objectives for policing from the centre, backed up with constant monitoring, auditing and inspection. Like it or not, there is a national flavour to policing in

Scotland and a continuing drive from central government to influence and control policing policy. This process of creeping centralisation and political control of Scottish policing has taken place stealthily, within an increasingly national framework, but continuing to highlight the important links with the community. However, the situation is somewhat fuzzy and complex and for everyone's benefit, particularly the public, is in need of clarification. Reorganisation and restructuring, it is argued, would provide opportunities to introduce a more accountable system, which is easier to organise, manage, oversee, and audit in a more transparent manner with public confidence.

It is not the purpose of this book to advocate a national police service for Scotland nor to blindly support the status quo. Our contribution is to present information, explanation and analysis about policing in Scotland which can sustain and support an open debate on police structures and their appropriateness for modern Scottish policing. Indeed, there is a need for a great deal more open and transparent public discussion of the issues raised here and on the changes required to equip Scotland's police to meet effectively the challenges of the future. The Scottish Parliament was founded on the principles of transparency, openness and accountability and these qualities need to inspire a full and proper review and debate on the future of policing in Scotland, with a focus on redefining concepts of 'policing' and the roles of the 'police constable' for the 21st century. In face of what lies before it, the Scottish police service will require to maintain that constant vigilance which has served it so well in the past.

References

Dewar, D. (1998) *Secretary of State's Speech to Scottish Police Federation Annual Conference*, 22 April.
Royal Commission on the Police (1962) *Final Report*, Cmnd 1728. London: HMSO.
Sharp, L., Sir (1995) 'Sharp's vision', *Police Review*, 28 April: 28–29.
The Herald (2004) 13 September, pp. 1–2 (accessed at www.theherald.co.uk).

Bibliography

Abel, R. (1995) 'Contested communities', *Journal of Law and Society*, 22: 118.

Advisory Council on the Misuse of Drugs (1994) *Drug Misusers and the Criminal Justice System Part II: Police, Drug Misusers and the Community*. London: HMSO.

Alderson, J. (1979) *Policing Freedom – A Commentary on the Dilemmas of Policing in Western Democracies*. Plymouth: Macdonald and Evans.

Alderson, J. and Stead, J. C. (eds) (1973) *The Police We Deserve*. London: Wolf Publishing.

Allan, D. L. (1989) *How Do the Police Measure Up? – A Study of Efficiency and Effectiveness in the Police Service*. University of Strathclyde, Glasgow: Unpublished MPhil thesis.

Anderson, S. (1999) 'Crime statistics and the "problem of crime" in Scotland', in P. Duff and N. Hutton (eds), *Criminal Justice in Scotland*. London: Ashgate, pp. 38–55.

Arrestee Drug Abuse Monitoring (ADAM) (2000) *1999 Annual Report on Drug Use Among Adult and Juvenile Arrestees*. Washington, DC: National Institute of Justice.

Ashworth, A. (2002) 'Redrawing the boundaries of entrapment', *Criminal Law Review*, March: 161–179.

Association of Chief Police Officers (1990) *Strategic Policy Document: Setting the Standards for Policing, Meeting Community Expectations*. London: ACPO.

Association of Chief Police Officers in Scotland (1998) *Policing the Future – Statement of Common Purpose and Values*. Edinburgh: ACPOS.

Association of Chief Police Officers Scotland (2003a) *Statement of Ethical Principles and Code of Ethical Practice*. Edinburgh: ACPOS.

Association of Chief Police Officers In Scotland (2003b) *Drug Strategy*. Edinburgh: ACPOS.

Association of Chief Police Officers in Scotland (2003c) *Policing Priorities for Scotland 2003–2006*. Edinburgh: ACPOS.

Association of Chief Police Officers Scotland (2004a) *Annual Report 2003–2004*. Edinburgh: ACPOS.

Association of Chief Police Officers in Scotland (2004b) *People Strategy*. Edinburgh: ACPOS.

Association of Chief Police Officers in Scotland (2004c) *Youth Strategy*. Edinburgh: ACPOS.

Association of Scottish Police Superintendents website: www.scottishsupers.org. uk

Atkinson, R. (2003) 'Domestication by cappuccino or a revenge on urban space? Control and empowerment in the management of urban spaces', *Urban Studies*, 40: 18–43.

Audit Commission (1990) *Effective Policing – Performance Review in Police Forces,* Paper No 8. London: HMSO.

Audit Commission (1996) *Streetwise – Effective Street Patrol.* London: HMSO.

Audit Scotland (2002) *Dealing with Offending by Young People.* Edinburgh: Stationery Office.

Audit Scotland (2004) *Police and Fire: Performance Indicators 2003–04* (Prepared for the Accounts Commission) (accessed at www.audit-scotland.gov.uk).

Auld, Lord Justice (2001) *Review of the Criminal Courts of England and Wales.* London: Department for Constitutional Affairs.

Babington, A. (1969) *A House in Bow Street.* London: Macdonald.

Bailey, V. (ed.) (1981) *Policing and Punishment in Nineteenth Century Britain.* London: Croom Helm.

Banton, M. (1964) *The Policeman in the Community.* London: Tavistock.

Barr, A. (1996) *Practising Community Development – Experience in Strathclyde.* London: Community Development Foundation.

Bayley, D. (1996) 'What do the police do?', in W. Saulsbury *et al.* (eds), *Themes in Contemporary Policing.* London: Police Foundation/Policy Studies Institute, pp. 29–41.

BBC News Release (17 October 2004) *Agencies to Get Organised Over Crime.*

Bennett, T. (ed.) (1983) *The Future of Policing.* Cambridge: Institute of Criminology.

Bennett, T. (1998) *Drug Testing Arrestees.* London: Home Office.

Bennett, T. (1992) 'Themes and variations in Neighbourhood Watch', in D. Evans, N. Fyfe and D. Herbert (eds), *Crime, Policing and Place: Essays in Environmental Criminology.* London: Routledge, pp. 272–285.

Benyon, J. *et al.* (1995) *Police Co-operation in Europe.* Leicester: University of Leicester Centre for the Study of Public Order.

Berry, G., Izat, J., Mawby, R. and Walley, L. (1998) *Practical Police Management.* London: Police Review Publishing Co.

Best, D. and Quigley, A. (2003) 'Shootings by the police: what predicts when a firearms officer will pull the trigger?' *Policing and Society*, 13 (4): 349–364.

Bichard, Sir M. (2004) *Inquiry Report to House of Commons on Soham Murders.* London: HMSO.

Blair, A. (2004) *Speech on Public Service and Welfare State Reform*, 3 December. Edinburgh: Napier University.

Bland, N. and Coope, S. (2003) *Reducing the Impact of Local Drug Markets: A Research Review.* Scottish Executive Drug Misuse Research Programme. Edinburgh: Stationery Office.

Bourne, D. (1999) 'Results driven', *Police Review*, 1 January: 14–16.

Bowling, B. and Foster, J. (2002) 'Policing and the police', in M. Maguire, R. Morgan, and R. Reiner (eds), *The Oxford Handbook of Criminology*, 3rd edn. Oxford: Clarendon Press, pp. 980–1033.

Bradley, D., Walker, N. and Wilkie, R. (1986) *Managing The Police: Law Organisation and Democracy.* Sussex: Wheatsheaf.

Brake, M. and Hale, C. (1992) *Public Order and Private Lives: The Politics of Law and Order*. London: Routledge.

Bramley-Harker, E. (2001) *Sizing the UK Market for Illicit Drugs*. RDS Occasional Paper No 74. London: Home Office Research, Development and Statistics Directorate.

Bratton, W. (1997) 'Crime is down in New York City: blame the police', in N. Dennis (ed.), *Zero Tolerance: Policing a Free Society*. London: IEA, pp. 29–42.

British Crime Survey (2001/2002) London: Home Office.

Brodeur, J. P. (ed.) (1995) *Comparisons in Policing – An International Perspective*. Aldershot: Avebury.

Brown, D. and Iles, S. (1985) *Community Constables – A Study of a Policing Initiative*, Research and Planning Unit Paper, No 30. London: Home Office.

Bryson, J. M. (1995) *Strategic Planning for Public and Non Profit Organisations – A Guide to Strengthening and Sustaining Organisational Achievement*. San Francisco: Jossey Bass.

Bunyan, T. (1977) *The History and Practice of the Political Police in Britain*. London: Quartet.

Butler, D., Adonis, A. and Travis, T. (1994) *Failure in British Government – Politics of the Poll Tax*. Oxford: Oxford Paperbacks.

Button, M. (2002) *Private Policing*. Devon: Willan Publishing.

Cairnie, J. (1999) 'The politics of crime prevention: the safer cities experiment in Scotland', in P. Duff and N. Hutton (eds), *Criminal Justice in Scotland*. London: Ashgate, pp. 74–93.

Cameron, H. R. G. (1991) *The Management of Change in Police Organisation*. University of Strathclyde, Glasgow: Unpublished MPhil thesis.

Carson, W. G. (1984) 'Policing the periphery: the development of Scottish policing 1795–1900 (1)', *Australian and New Zealand Journal of Criminology*, 17 (4): 207–232.

Carson, W. G. (1985) 'Policing the periphery: the development of Scottish policing 1795–1990 (2)', *Australian and New Zealand Journal of Criminology*, 18 (1): 3–16.

Carson, W. and Idzikowska, H. (1989) 'The social production of Scottish policing 1795–1900', in D. Hay and F. Snyder (eds), *Policing and Prosecution in Britain 1750–1850*. Oxford: Oxford University Press.

Chatterton, M., Gibson, G., Gilman, M., Godfrey, C., Sutton, M. and Wright, A. (1995) *Performance Indicators for Local Anti-Drugs Strategies: A Preliminary Analysis*. Police Research Group Crime Detection and Prevention Series, Paper 62. London: Home Office.

Checkland, O. and Lamb, M. (eds) (1982) *Health Care as Social History – The Glasgow Case*. Aberdeen: Aberdeen University Press.

Cheney, D., Dickson, L., Fitzpatrick, J. and Uglow, S. (1999) *Criminal Justice and the Human Rights Act, 1998*. Bristol: Jordan Publishing.

Chief Surveillance Commissioner (2004) *Annual Report to the Prime Minister and Scottish Ministers for 2003–2004*. London: Stationery Office.

Clark, M. and Crawford, C. (eds) (1994) *Legal Medicine in History*. Cambridge: Cambridge University Press.

Colquhoun, P. (1797) *A Treatise on the Police of the Metropolis of London*. London.

Cope, S., Leishman, F. and Starie, P. (1997) 'Globalisation, new public management and the enabling state: futures of police management', *International Journal of Public Sector Management*, 10 (6): 444–460.

Council of Europe (2002) *The European Code of Police Ethics*. Strasbourg: Council of Europe.

Craig, G. and Mayo, M. (eds) (1995) *Community Empowerment – A Reader in Participation and Development*. London: Zed Books.

Crawford, A. (1996) 'The spirit of community – Rights, responsibilities and the communitarian agenda', *Journal of Law and* Society, 23 (2): 250.

Crawford, A. (2003) 'The pattern of policing in the UK: policing beyond the police', in T. Newburn (ed.), *Handbook of Policing*. Devon: Willan Publishing, pp. 136–168.

Crawford, A. and Newburn, T. (2003) *Youth Offending and Restorative Justice – Implementing Reform in Youth Justice*. Devon: Willan Publishing.

Critchley, T. A. (1978) *A History of Police in England and Wales*. London: Constable.

Crowther, M. and White, B. (1988) *On Soul and Conscience – The Medical Expert and Crime, 150 years of Forensic Medicine in Glasgow*. Aberdeen: Aberdeen University Press.

Cullen, Lord (1996) *Public Inquiry into Shootings at Dunblane Primary School*. Edinburgh: HMSO.

Cummings, A. J. G. and Devine, T. M. (eds) (1994) *Industry, Business and Society in Scotland since 1700*. Edinburgh: John Donald.

Daly, M. (2004) 'Passing out parade', *Druglink*, January/February: 6–7.

Das, D. K. (ed.) (1994) *Police Practices – An International Review*. London: Scarecrow Press.

Davies, H. (1992) *Fighting Leviathan – Building Social Markets That Work*. London: Social Market Foundation.

Dennis, N. (ed.) (1997) *Zero Tolerance: Policing a Free Society*. London: IEA.

DETR (Department of the Environment, Transport and the Regions) (1998) *Modernising Local Government – Improving Local Services through Best Value*. London: DETR.

Devine, T. M. (1994) 'Urbanisation and the civic response: Glasgow 1800–1830', in A. J. G. Cummings and T. M. Devine (eds), *Industry, Business and Society in Scotland since 1700*. Edinburgh: John Donald.

Dewar, D. (1998) *Secretary of State's Speech to Scottish Police Federation Annual Conference*, 22 April.

Ditton, J., Short, E., Phillips, S., Norris, C. and Armstrong, G. (1999) *The Effect of Closed Circuit Television on Recorded Crime Rates and Public Concern about Crime in Glasgow*. Edinburgh: Scottish Office.

Donnelly, D. (2002a) 'New community', *Police Review*, 3 May: 26–27.

Donnelly, D. (2002b) *New Police Management – The Strategic Management of Community Policing in the Strathclyde Police*. Glasgow Caledonian University: Unpublished PhD thesis.

Donnelly, D. (2002c) 'A communal approach to crime', *Police Review*, 20 September: 14.

Donnelly, D. (2003) 'Pioneering Scots', *Police Review*, 3 January 2003: 25.

Donnelly, D. (2004a) 'A national service?', *Police Review*, December: 26–27.

Donnelly, D. (2004b) *Local Perspectives on Community Policing in the West of Scotland*, Occasional Paper 1. Hamilton: Scottish Centre For Police Studies.

Donnelly, D. (2005) 'Community policing', in G. Kurian (ed.), *World Encyclopedia of Police Forces and Correctional Systems*. New York: Gale.

Donnelly, D. and Scott, K. B. (2002a) 'Police accountability in Scotland – (1) The "new" tripartite system', *The Police Journal*, 75 (1): 1–12.

Donnelly, D. and Scott, K. B. (2002b) 'Police accountability in Scotland – (2) "New" accountabilities', *The Police Journal*, 75 (1): 56–66.

Donnelly, D. and Scott, K. (2003) 'Journey on a moving landscape: the effects of Scottish devolution on policing', *Policing Today*, 8 (2): 25–26.

Donnelly, D. and Wilkie, R. (2002a) 'Scottish colonisation', *Police Review,* 110 (5703): 20–21.

Donnelly, D. and Wilkie, R. (2002b) 'States of Scotland: policing the police', *The Scottish Review*, 2 (6): 45–54.

Dorn, N., Murji, K. and South, N. (1992) *Traffickers: Drug Markets and Law Enforcement*. London: Routledge.

Dorn, N., Jepsen,. J. and Savona, E. (eds) (1996) *European Drug Policy and Enforcement*. Basingstoke: Macmillan.

Dorn, N., Oette, L., and White, S. (1998) 'Drugs importation and the bifurcation of risk: capitalisation, cuts out and organised crime', *British Journal of Criminology*, 38 (4): 537–560.

Duff, P. (2004) 'Admissibility of improperly obtained physical evidence in the Scottish criminal trial: the search for principle', *Edinburgh Law Review*, 8: 152–176.

Duff, P. and Hutton, N. (eds) (1999) *Criminal Justice in Scotland*. London: Ashgate.

The Economist (1992) 'Embattled Bobbies', 8 February: 31–32.

Edmunds, M., Hough, H. and Urqua, N. (1996) *Tackling Local Drug Markets in London*. Home Office Police Research Group Paper 80. London: Stationery Office.

Edwards, C. J. (1999) *Changing Policing Theories for the 21st Century Societies*. NSW: Federation Press.

Emsley, C. (1983) *Policing and its Context 1750–1870*. London: Macmillan.

Emsley, C. (1991) *The English Police – A Political and Social History*. Hemel Hempstead: Wheatsheaf.

Emsley, C. (1995) 'Preventive policing – the path to the present', in J. P. Brodeur (ed.), *Comparisons in Policing – An International Perspective*. Aldershot: Avebury, pp. 135–144.

Emsley, C. and Weinberger, B. (eds) (1991) *Policing Western Europe: Politics, Professionalism and Public Order, 1850–1940*. Connecticut: Greenwood Press.

Englander, D. (1991) 'Police and public order in Britain 1914–1918', in C. Emsley and B. Weinberger (eds), *Policing Western Europe: Politics, Professionalism and Public Order, 1850–1940*. Connecticut: Greenwood Press.

Erskine, J. (1773) *An Institute of the Law of Scotland*. Edinburgh.

Etzioni, A. (1993) *The Spirit of Community*. London: Fontana Press.

Evans, D., Fyfe, N. and Herbert, D. (eds) (1992) *Crime, Policing and Place: Essays in Environmental Criminology*. London: Routledge.

Evening Times (2004) 'Wardens will walk city streets in bid to beat anti-social behaviour' (accessed via www.eveningtimes.co.uk/print/news).

Farnham, D. and Horton, S. (eds) (1996) *Managing the New Public Services*, 2nd edn. London: Macmillan Press.

Fielding, N. G. (1991) *The Police and Social Conflict*. London: Athlone Press.

Fielding, N. G. (1995) *Community Policing*. Oxford: Clarendon Press.

Fine, B. and Millar, R. (eds) (1985) *Policing the Miners' Strike*. London: Lawrence and Wishart.

Finer, C. J. (1998) 'The new social policy in Britain', in C. J. Finer and M. Nellis (eds), *Crime and Social Exclusion*. Oxford: Blackwell, pp. 154–170.

Finer, C. J. and Nellis, M. (eds) (1998) *Crime and Social Exclusion*. Oxford: Blackwell.

Fitzgerald, M. and Hough, M. (2002) *Policing for London*. Devon: Willan Publishing.

Fitzpatrick, S. and Kennedy, C. (2000) *Getting By: Begging, Rough Sleeping and the Big Issue in Glasgow and Edinburgh*. Bristol: Policy Press.

Friedmann, R. R. (1992) *Community Policing – Comparative Perspectives and Prospects*. Hemel Hempstead: Harvester Wheatsheaf.

Fyfe, N. (1995) 'Law and order policy and the spaces of citizenship in contemporary Britain', *Political Geography*, 14: 177–189.

Fyfe, N. and Bannister, J. (1996) 'City watching: closed circuit television surveillance in public spaces', *Area*, 28: 37–46.

Fyfe, N. and Bannister, J. (1999) 'Privatisation, policing and crime control: tracing the contours of the public-private divide', in P. Duff and N. Hutton (eds), *Criminal Justice in Scotland*. London: Ashgate, pp. 335–354.

Garland, D. (1996) 'The limits of the sovereign state: strategies of crime control in contemporary societies', *British Journal of Criminology*, 36: 445–471.

Giddens, A. (1997) 'Anomie of the people', review of Etzioni, A. 'The New Golden Rule – Community and Morality in a Democratic Society', *The Guardian (G2)*, 31 July: 11.

Gillespie, A. (2000) 'Clause for concern', *Police Review*, 12 May: 29–30.

The Glasgow Herald, 18 December 1932.

The Glasgow Herald, 22 October 1932.

The Glasgow Herald, 3 May 1932.

Goldberg, R. (2004) 'Single issue campaigns for the Scottish Parliament', *Scottish Affairs*, 49, Autumn: 1.

Goldsmith, A. (2002) *The Development of the City of Glasgow Police 1800–1939*. University of Strathclyde, Glasgow: Unpublished PhD thesis.

Goldstein, H. (1987) 'Toward community-oriented policing – Potential, basic requirements and threshold questions', *Crime and Delinquency*, 33: 6–30.

Goldstein, H. (1990) *Problem-Oriented Policing*. New York: McGraw-Hill.

Gordon, P. (1980) *Policing Scotland*. Glasgow: Scottish Council for Civil Liberties.

Gordon, R. and Wilmot-Smith, R. (eds) (2000) *Human Rights in the United Kingdom*, 1st edn. Oxford: Oxford University Press.

Graham, R. (1895) 'Description of expedition into Glasgow City', in J. Russell (1895) *The Evolution of the Function of Public Health Administration*. Glasgow.

Grant, D. (1973) *The Thin Blue Line – The Story of the Glasgow Police*. London: John Long.

Greenhill, P., Mullen, T., Murdoch, P., Craig, S. and Miller, A. (2004) *The Use of Human Rights Legislation in the Scottish Courts* (accessed at www.scotland.gov. uk/socialresearch).

The Guardian (1992) 'Clarke calls for sacking of lazy police', 23 September 1992: 18.

Hahn, P. H. (1998) *Emerging Criminal Justice – Three Pillars for a Proactive Justice System*. London: Sage.

Hale, C. and Uglow, S. (2000) *The Police and the Public in Scotland: An Analysis of Data from the British and Scottish Crime Surveys 1982–96*. Crime and Criminal Justice Research Findings No. 33. Edinburgh: Central Research Unit.

Harcourt, B. E. (2001) *Illusion of Order – the False Promise of Broken Windows*. Cambridge, Mass.: Harvard University Press.

Hassan, G. and Warhurst, C. (2001) 'New Scotland? Policy, parties and institutions', *The Political Quarterly*, 72 (2): 213–226.

Hay, D. and Snyder, F. (eds) (1989) *Policing and Prosecution in Britain 1750–1850*. Oxford: Oxford University Press.

Hay, G., Gannon, M., McKeganey, N., Hutchinson, S. and Goldberg, D. (2005) *Estimating the National and Local Prevalence of Problem Drug Misuse In Scotland*. University of Glasgow: Centre for Drug Misuse Research.

Hay, G., McKeganey, N. and Hutchison, S. (2001) *Estimating the National and Local Prevalence of Problem Drug Use in Scotland*. Edinburgh: ISD.

Henry, H. (2004) *Speech by the Deputy Justice Minister Hugh Henry MSP*, 3 December. Glasgow: National Conference of Community Wardens.

Henry, K. I., Painter, C. and Barnes, C. (eds) (1997) *Management in the Public Sector – Challenge and Change*, 2nd edn. London: International Thomson Business Press.

The Herald (2001) 'Role of bobbies on the beat reviewed. Review of community policing in the Strathclyde Police', 5 May: 4.

The Herald (2005) 'Police fears on political neutrality', 20 January: 6.

HM Chief Inspector of Constabulary for Scotland (1859) *Annual Report for the Year Ending 15 March 1859*. Edinburgh: HMSO.

HM Chief Inspector of Constabulary for Scotland (1994) *Report for the Year Ended 31 December 1993*. Edinburgh: HMSO.

HM Chief Inspector of Constabulary for Scotland (1995) *Thematic Inspection on Community Policing*. Edinburgh: HMSO.

HM Chief Inspector of Constabulary for Scotland (1997) *Annual Report 1996–97*. Edinburgh: HMSO.

HM Chief Inspector of Constabulary for Scotland (1998a) *Annual Report 1997–98*. Edinburgh: HMSO.

HM Chief Inspector of Constabulary for Scotland (1998b) *Grampian Police Primary Inspection*. Edinburgh: HMSO.

HM Chief Inspector of Constabulary for Scotland (2002) *Narrowing the Gap – Police Visibility and Public Reassurance: Managing Public Expectation and Demand*. Edinburgh: The Stationery Office.

HM Chief Inspector of Constabulary for Scotland (2003) *Annual Report 2002–2003*. Edinburgh: The Stationery Office.

HM Chief Inspector of Constabulary for Scotland (2004a) *Annual Report 2003–2004*. Edinburgh: The Stationery Office.

HM Chief Inspector of Constabulary for Scotland (2004b) *Local Connections: Policing with the Community*. Edinburgh: The Stationery Office.

HM Inspectorate of Constabulary for Scotland (2000) *A Fair Cop? The Investigation of Complaints against the Police in Scotland*. Edinburgh: HMSO.

HM Government (1995) *Tackling Drugs Together: A Strategy for England 1995–1998*. London: HMSO.

Home Office (1919) *Desborough Committee of Enquiry into Policing in England, Wales and Scotland*, Cmnd 253 and 574. London: HMSO.

Home Office (1949) *Oaksey Committee on Police Conditions of Service*, Cmnd 7674. London: HMSO.

Home Office (1962) *Royal Commission on the Police Final Report*, Cmnd 1728. London: HMSO.

Home Office (1978) *Committee of Enquiry on the Police (Edmund Davis Enquiry) – Report on Negotiating Machinery and Pay*, Cmnd 7283. London: HMSO.

Home Office (1983) *Manpower, Effectiveness and Efficiency in the Police Service*. Home Office Circular: No 114/83.

Home Office (1993a) *Report of Enquiry into Police Responsibilities and Rewards*, Cmnd 2280. London: HMSO.

Home Office (1993b) *Police Reform – A Police Service for the Twenty-First Century*, White Paper, Cmnd 2281. London: HMSO.

Home Office (1995) *Review of Police Core and Ancillary Tasks*, Final Report. London: HMSO.

Home Office (1998) *Tackling Drugs To Build A Better Britain*. London: HMSO.

Home Office (2001) *Policing a New Century – A Blueprint for Police Reform*, White Paper, Cmnd 5326. London: Home Office.

Home Office (2004a) *Building Communities, Beating Crime – A Better Service for the 21st Century*, Police Reform Policy Paper. London: Home Office.

Home Office (2004b) *Drug Seizure and Offender Statistics 2001 and 2002*. Home Office Statistical Bulletin 08/04. London: Stationery Office.

Home Office (2004c) *Serious and Organised Crime*. Government White Paper. London: Stationery Office.

Hood, C. (1991) 'A public management for all seasons?', *Public Administration*, 69 (1): 3–19.

Hope, T. and Shaw, M. (eds) (1998) *Communities and Crime Reduction*. London: HMSO.

Horton, C. (1995) *Policing Policy in France*. Dorset: Policy Studies Institute.

Hough, M. (2002) 'Missing the target: police performance measurement', *The Stakeholder*, May/June: 29–30.

Hoyle, C., Young, R. and Hill, R. (2002) *Proceed with Caution – An Evaluation of the Thames Valley Police Initiative in Restorative Cautioning*. York: Joseph Rowntree Foundation.

Hutton, N. *et al.* (1996) *A Sentencing Information System for the High Court of Justiciary of Scotland: Report of the Study of Feasibility*. Edinburgh: Scottish Office.

Innes, M. (1999) '"An iron fist in an iron glove?" The zero-tolerance policing debate', *The Howard Journal*, 38: 397–410.

Johnston, L. (1996) 'Policing diversity', in F. Leishman *et al.* (eds), *Core Issues in Policing*. Harlow: Longman, pp. 54–70.

Johnston, L. (2000) *Policing Britain – Risk, Security and Governance*. Harlow: Pearson Education.

Johnstone, C. (2004) 'Crime, disorder and the urban renaissance', in C. Johnstone and M. Whitehead (eds) *New Horizons in British Urban Policy: Perspectives on New Labour's Urban Renaissance*. London: Ashgate, pp. 75–94.

Johnstone, C. and Whitehead, M. (eds) (2004) *New Horizons in British Urban Policy: Perspectives on New Labour's Urban Renaissance*. London: Ashgate.

Joint Consultative Committee (1990) *Operational Policing Review*. Surbiton: Joint Consultative Committee.

Jones, J. H., Sir (1993) *Trouble Shooter 2*. London: Penguin.

Jones, T. H. and Christie, M. G. A. (2003) *Criminal Law*, 3rd edn. Edinburgh: W. Green and Son.

Jones, T. and Newburn, T. (1995) 'How big is the private security sector?', *Policing and Society*, 5: 221–232.

Jones, T. and Newburn, T. (1997) *Policing After the Act – Police and Magistrates Court Act*. London: Policy Studies Institute.

Jones, T. and Newburn, T. (2002) 'The transformation of policing?: Understanding current trends in policing systems', *British Journal of* Criminology, 42: 129–146.

Joyce, P. (1999) *Strategic Management for the Public Services*. Bucks: Open University Press.

Joyce, P. (2000) *Strategy in the Public Sector – A Guide to Effective Change Management*. Chichester: John Wiley & Sons.

Judge, T. (2002) 'Change Mr Blunkett – We've been changing for years!', *Police*, September: 28–29.

Kelling, G. L. (1987) 'Acquiring a taste for order – The community and the police', *Crime and Delinquency*, 33 (1): 90–102.

Keogh, A. (2004) 'The oldest profession or an age-old injustice?', *New Law Journal*, 17 September: 1350–1351.

Kerley, R. (2003) 'Public performance: targets can have a positive effect', *Holyrood*, 100, 1 December: 27.

Kilbrandon, Lord (1964) *Report of the Committee on Children and Young Persons in Scotland*, Cmnd 2306. Edinburgh: HMSO.

Kirkpatrick, I. and Lucio-Martinez, M. (eds) (1995) *The Politics of Quality in the Public Sector*. London: Routledge.

Kleinig, J. (1996) *The Ethics of Policing*. Cambridge: Cambridge University Press.

Klug, F. (1996) 'A Bill of Rights as secular ethics?', in R. Gordon and R. Wilmot-Smith (eds), *Human Rights in the United Kingdom*, 1st edn. Oxford: Oxford University Press, pp. 37–57.

Kurian, G. (ed.) (2005) *World Encyclopedia of Police Forces and Correctional Systems*. New York: Gole.

Law, J. (2001) 'Accountability and annual reports: the case of policing', *Public Policy and Administration*, 16 (1): 75–90.

Lee, M. (1996) 'London: community damage limitation through policing', in N. Dorn, J. Jepsen and E. Savona (eds), *European Drug Policy and Enforcement*. Basingstoke: Macmillan.

Leishman, A., Cope, S. and Starie, P. (1995) 'Reforming the police in Britain – New public management, policy networks and a "Tough Old Bill"', *The International Journal of Public Sector Management*, 8 (4): 26–38.

Leishman, F., Loveday, B. and Savage, S. (eds) (1996) *Core Issues in Policing*. Harlow: Longman.

Leishman, F., Loveday, B. and Savage, S. P. (eds) (2000) *Core Issues In Policing*, 2nd edn. England: Pearson Education.

Lobley, D., Smith, D. and Stern, C. (2001) *Freagarrach: An Evaluation of a Project for Persistent Juvenile Offenders*. Edinburgh: Scottish Executive Central Research Unit.

Lothian and Borders Police (2003) *Silent Witness*. Edinburgh: Lothian and Borders Police.

Loveday, B. (1991) 'Police and government in the 1990s', *Social Policy and Administration*, 25 (4): 311–328.

Loveday, B. (1997) 'Management and accountability in public services: a police case study', in K. I. Henry, C. Painter and C. Barnes (eds) *Management in the Public Sector – Challenge and Change*, 2nd edn. London: International Thomson Business Press.

Loveday, B. (1998) 'Improving the status of police patrol', *International Journal of the Sociology of Law*, 26: 161–196.

Lustgarten, L. (1986) *The Governance of Policing*. London: Sweet and Maxwell.

McCluskey, Lord (2000) 'Trojan horse at the gates of our courts?', *Scotland on Sunday*, 6 February.

McConnell, J. (2003) *First Minister's Address to the Annual Conference of Chief Police Officers in Scotland*, 29 May.

McFadden, J. and Lazarowicz, M. (2002) *The Scottish Parliament: An Introduction*, 2nd edn. Edinburgh: T & T Clark.

McInnes, Sheriff Principal J. (2004) *The Summary Justice Review Committee: Report to Ministers*. Edinburgh: Scottish Executive.

McIvor, G. *et al.* (2004) *The Hamilton Sheriff Youth Court Pilot: The First Six Months*. Edinburgh: Scottish Executive Central Research Unit.

McKeganey, N., Connelly, C., Knepl, J., Norrie, J. and Reid, L. (2000) *Interviewing and Drug Testing of Arrestees in Scotland: A Pilot of the Adam Methodology*. Crime and Criminal Justice Research Findings No 48. Edinburgh: Central Research Unit.

McKevitt, D. (1992) 'Strategic management in public services', in L. Willcocks and J. Harrow (eds), *Rediscovering Public Services Management*. London: McGraw-Hill.

McKinnon, G. (2004) 'Police performance in England and Wales', *Justice of the Peace*, 168.

McLaughlin, E. (1994) *Community, Policing and Accountability*. Aldershot: Avebury Gower.

McLaughlin, E. and Murji, K. (1995) 'The end of public policing? Police reform and "the new managerialism"', in L. Noaks *et al.* (eds), *Contemporary Issues in Criminology*. Cardiff: University of Wales Press, pp. 110–127.

MacLean, Lord (2002) *Report of the Committee on Serious Violent and Sexual Offenders*. Edinburgh: Scottish Executive.

Macleod, G. (2002) 'From urban entrepreneurialism to a revanchist city? On the spatial injustices of Glasgow's renaissance', *Antipode*, 34: 602–624.

Maguire, M., Morgan, R. and Reiner, R. (eds) (1997) *The Oxford Handbook of Criminology*, 2nd edn. Oxford: Clarendon Press.

Morgan, R. and Reiner, R. (eds) (2002) *The Oxford Handbook of Criminology*, 3rd edn. Oxford: Clarendon Press.

Manning, P. K. (1984) 'Community policing', *American Journal of Police*, 3 (2): 205–227.

Mark, Sir R. (1977) *Policing in a Perplexed Society*. London: Allen and Unwin.

Marshall, G. (1973) 'The government of the police since 1964', in J. Alderson and J. C. Stead (eds), *The Police We Deserve*. London: Wolf Publishing.

Mastrofski, S. D. (1993) 'Varieties of community policing', *American Journal of Police*, 12 (3): 65–77.

Mawby, R. I. (1990) *Comparative Policing Issues*. London: Unwin Hyman.

May, C. (1997) *Citizens' Democracy – Theory and Practice*. Glasgow: Scottish Local Government Information Unit, Discussion Paper 5.

May, T., Edmunds, M. and Hough, M. (1999) *Street Business: Links between Sex and Drug Markets*. Crime Prevention and Detection Series Paper. London: Home Office Policing and Reducing Crime Unit.

Mead, D. (2002) 'Informed consent to police searches in England and Wales: a critical re-appraisal in the light of the Human Rights Act', *Criminal Law Review*, October: 791–804.

Melrose, M. (2003) 'Street prostitution and community safety: a case of contested meanings', *Community Safety Journal*, 2 (1): 21–31.

Metcalfe, L. and Richards, S. (1987) 'The efficiency strategy in central government: an impoverished concept of management', *Public Money*, June: 32.

Miers, D. (2001) *An International Review of Restorative Justice*, Crime Reduction Research Series No 10. London: Home Office.

Miller, W. (1989) 'Party politics, class Interest and reform of the police 1829–1856', *International Review of Police Development*, 10: 1 (Spring 1989).

Mills, A. (2002) 'Ethics and the police: facing the challenge', *Policing Today*, 8 (3): 25–27.

Milne, B. (2002) 'Higher learning', *Policing Today*, 3 (1): 42–44.

Monaghan, B. (1997) 'Crime prevention in Scotland', *International Journal of the Sociology of Law*, 25: 21–44.

Morris, T. (1989) *Crime and Criminal Justice since 1945*. Oxford: Basil Blackwell.

Muir, W. K. (1977) *Police – Streetcorner Politicians*. Chicago: University of Chicago Press.

Muncie, J. (1999) 'Institutionalised intolerance: youth justice and the 1998 Crime and Disorder Act', *Critical Social Policy*, 19 (2): 147–176.

MVA (2002) *The 2000 Scottish Crime Survey Overview Report*. Edinburgh: Scottish Executive.

National Audit Office (1991) *Promoting Value For Money in Provincial Police Forces*. London: HMSO.

National Criminal Intelligence Service (2004) *United Kingdom Threat Assessment*. London: Home Office.

NCH Scotland (2004) *Where's Kilbrandon Now?* Edinburgh: NCH.

Newburn, T. (ed.) (2003) *Handbook of Policing*. Devon: Willan Publishing.

Newburn, T. and Jones, T. (1995) 'The future of traffic policing', *Policing*, 11 (2): 131–132.

Neyroud, P. W. and Beckley, A. (2001) *Policing, Ethics and Human Rights*. Devon: Willan Publishing.

Noaks, L., Levi, M. and Maguire, M. (eds) (1995) *Contemporary Issues in Criminology*. Cardiff: University of Wales Press.

Normand, A. (2003) *Criminal Justice System Objectives Review: Proposals for the Integration of Aims, Objectives and Targets in the Scottish Criminal Justice System*. Edinburgh: Scottish Executive.

ODPM (2004) *Neighbourhood Wardens Scheme Evaluation*. London: Office of the Deputy Prime Minister.

Oliver, I. (1997) *Police, Government and Accountability*, 2nd edn. Basingstoke: Macmillan Press.

Orr, J. (1997) 'Strathclyde's spotlight initiative', in N. Dennis (ed.), *Zero Tolerance: Policing a Free Society*. London: IEA, pp. 104–123.

Oster, S. (1995) *Strategic Management for Non-Profit Organisations*. New York: Oxford University Press.

O'Toole, B. J. and Jordan, G. (eds) (1995) *Next Steps – Improving Management in Government*. Aldershot: Dartmouth.

Painter, C. (1995) 'The next steps reform and current orthodoxies', in B. J. O'Toole and G. Jordan (eds), *Next Steps – Improving Management in Government*. Aldershot: Dartmouth, pp. 17–36.

Pannick, D. (2002) 'Some fingerprints are more equal than others', *The Times*, 1 October.

Pasquino, P. (1978) 'Threatrum politicum: the genealogy of capital, police and the state of prosperity', *Ideology and Consciousness*, No 4, cited in W. G. Carson (1984) 'Policing the periphery: the development of Scottish policing 1795–1900 (1)', *Australian and New Zealand Journal of Criminology*, 17 (4): 207–232.

Patten, J. (1998) 'Foreword', in T. Hope and M. Shaw (eds) *Communities and Crime Reduction*. London: HMSO, pp. v–vi.

Patten, C. (1999) *A New Beginning for Policing in Northern Ireland: The Report of the Independent Commission on Policing in Northern Ireland*. Belfast: HMSO.

Pearson, G. (2001) 'Normal drug use: ethnographic fieldwork among an adult network of recreational drug users in inner London', *Substance Use and Misuse*, 36 (s1): 167–200.

Peele, G. (2004) *Governing The UK*, 4th edn. Oxford: Blackwell.

Pilkington, A. (1995) 'Measuring crime', *Sociology Review*, November: 15–17.

Police Review 100 Years of Service, 1893 – 1993 (Centenary Edition), 3 January 1993.

Police Review and Parade Gossip, 22 January 1932.

Police Review and Parade Gossip, 28 October 1932.

Pollitt, C. and Harrison, S. (eds) (1992) *Handbook of Public Services Management*. Oxford: Blackwell.

Popham, G. (1989) 'The management of law and order', in I. Taylor and G. Popham (eds), *An Introduction to Public Sector Management*. London: Unwin Hyman, pp. 150–175.

Price-Dyer Report (2002) *Review of the Planning, Allocation and Management of Resources in the Crown Office and Procurator Fiscal Service*. Edinburgh: COPFS.

Radzinowicz, L. (1948–1969) *A History of English Criminal Law, Vols. 1–4*. London: Stevens.

Rallings, C., Temple, M. and Thrasher, M. (1994) *Community Identity and Participation in Local Democracy*, Research Report No 1. London: Commission for Local Democracy.

Rawlings, P. J. (2002) *Policing – A Short History*. Devon: Willan Publishing.

Reid Howie Associates (2001) *Police Stop and Search among White and Minority Ethnic Young People in Scotland*. Edinburgh: Scottish Executive Central Research Unit.

Reid, G. (2002) 'The Scottish Parliament: how it works', in M. Spicer (ed.), *The Scotsman Guide to Scottish Politics*. Edinburgh: Scotsman Publications.

Reiner, R. (1991) *Chief Constables*. Oxford: Oxford University Press.

Reiner, R. (1992) *The Politics of the Police*, 2nd edn. Hemel Hempstead: Harvester Wheatsheaf.

Reiner, R. (1995) 'Community policing in England and Wales', in J. P. Brodeur (ed.), *Comparisons in Policing – An International Perspective*. Aldershot: Avebury, pp. 161–165.

Reiner, R. (1997) 'Policing and the police', in M. Maguire, R. Morgan and R. Reiner (eds), *The Oxford Handbook of Criminology*, 2nd edn. Oxford: Clarendon Press, pp. 997–1049.

Reith, C. (1956) *A New Study of Police History*. Edinburgh: Oliver and Boyd.

Renwick, R. (ed.) (1912) *Extracts form the Records of the Burgh of Glasgow with Charters and Other Documents, Vol. V11. 1760–1780*. Glasgow: Scottish Burgh Records Society.

Riechers, L. M. and Roberg, R. R. (1990) 'Community policing: a critical review of underlying assumptions', *Journal of Police Science and Administration*, 17 (2): 105–114.

Ritchie, M. and Mack, J. A. (1974) *Police Warnings*. Glasgow: Glasgow University.

Robertson, W. A. (1996) *Creating an Excellent Police Force – A Guide for Chief Police Officers*. University of Strathclyde, Glasgow: Unpublished MPhil thesis.

Roche, D. (2003) *Accountability in Restorative Justice*. Oxford: Oxford University Press.

Rogerson, P. (1995) 'Performance measurement and policing: police service or law enforcement agency?', *Public Money and Management*, 15 (4): 25–30.

Royal Commission on the Police (1962) *Final Report*, Cmnd 1728. London: HMSO.

Ruggiero, V. and South, N. (1995) *Eurodrugs, Drug Use Markets and Trafficking in Europe*. London: UCL Press.

Russell, J. (1895) *The Evolution of the Function of Public Health Administration*. Glasgow.

Salmon, H. (1995) 'Community, communitarianism and local government', *Local Government Policy Making*, 22 (3): 4.

Saulsbury, W., Mott, K., and Newburn, T. (eds) (1996) *Themes in Contemporary Policing*. London: Policy Foundation/Policy Studies Institute.

Savage, S. (2001) 'Forces of independence', *Police Review*: 20–21.

Savage, S. P. and Leishman, F. (1996) 'Managing the police – a force for change', in D. Farnham and S. Horton (eds), *Managing the New Public Services*, 2nd edn. London: Macmillan Press, pp. 242–256.

Savage, S., Charman, S. and Cope, S. (2000) *Policing and the Power of Persuasion*. London: Blackstone Press.

Schaffer, E. (1980) *Community Policing*. London: Croom Helm.

Scotland on Sunday (2003a) 'Two official warnings before referral to youth courts', 25 May: 11.

Scotland on Sunday (2003b) 'Does it really fit the crime?', 1 June: 15.

Scotland on Sunday (2004a) 'Security firms' ties to crime revealed by police', 24th October (accessed via www.scotlandonsunday.scotsman.com).

Scotland on Sunday (2004b) 'The truth at Carstairs and why a patient went on the run', 12 December: 13.

The Scotsman (1998) 'Police not a law unto themselves', 13 February, 1998.

The Scotsman (2004a) 'Non-lethal weapons', 2 December.

The Scotsman (2004b) 'Scotland and England go their separate ways', 25 November.

Scott, K. (2003) 'Smash and grab', *Holyrood*. 100, 1 December: 24–25.

Scott, K. and Wilkie, R. (2001) 'Chief constables: a current "crisis" in Scottish policing?', *Scottish Affairs*, 35: 54–68.

Scottish Children's Reporter Administration (2002) *Annual Report 2001/2002*. Edinburgh: Stationery Office.

Scottish Court Service (2003) *Corporate Plan*. Edinburgh: Scottish Court Service.

Scottish Drug Enforcement Agency (2003) *Annual Report (2002–2003)*. Edinburgh: Stationery Office.

Scottish Drug Enforcement Agency (2004) *Annual Report (2003–2004)*. Edinburgh: Stationery Office.

Scottish Executive (2000a) *Iain Gray Targets Scotland's Drug Misery*. News Release SE3101/2000, 1 December. Edinburgh: Scottish Executive.

Scottish Executive (2000b) *Drug Action Plan*. Edinburgh: HMSO.

Scottish Executive (2000c) *The Active Communities Initiative*. Edinburgh: Scottish Executive.

Scottish Executive (2001a) *The Stephen Lawrence Inquiry – An Action Plan for Scotland* (accessed at www.scotland.gov.uk/library2/docoi/sli-02.htm).

Scottish Executive (2001b) *Wallace Announces New Targets for Police to Tackle Racist Incident* (accessed at www.scotland.gov.uk/news/2001/05/se1179.asp).

Scottish Executive (2001c) *Complaints Against the Police: A Consultation Paper*. Edinburgh: HMSO.

Scottish Executive (2002a) *Scottish Crime Survey 2000*. Edinburgh: HMSO.

Scottish Executive (2002b) *'New CCTV System Launched in Fife'* (accessed via www.scotland.gov.uk/pages/news).

Scottish Executive (2002c) *News Release on New 'Lifelong Restriction' Sentence*, 20 November (accessed at www.scotland.gov.uk).

Scottish Executive (2003a) *News Release on Establishment of Sentencing Commission* (accessed at www.scotland.gov.uk).

Scottish Executive (2003b) *A Partnership for a Better Scotland*. Edinburgh: HMSO.

Scottish Executive (2003c) *Building Strong, Safe and Attractive Communities: a consultation document on other community based initiatives to tackle anti-social behaviour*. Edinburgh: Scottish Executive.

Scottish Executive (2003d) *Annual Report on Drug Misuse*. Edinburgh: HMSO.

Scottish Executive (2004a) *Common Police Services* (accessed at www.scotland.gov.uk/Topic/Justice/Police/17).

Scottish Executive (2004b) *Criminal Proceedings in Scottish Courts 2002*. Edinburgh: Statistical Bulletin Criminal Justice Series.

Scottish Executive (2004c) *Building a Better Scotland – Spending Proposals 2005–2008: Enterprise, Opportunity, Fairness* (accessed at www.scotland.gov.uk/library5/finance/srtn04-01.asp).

Scottish Executive (2004d) *News Release on Appointment of First Inspector of Prosecution* (accessed at www.scotland.gov.uk).

Scottish Executive (2004e) *Recorded Crime in Scotland 2003*. Edinburgh: Scottish Executive Statistical Bulletin.

Scottish Executive (2004f) *More Help For Drug Addicts*. Press Release October 2004. Edinburgh: Scottish Executive.

Scottish Executive (2005) *News Release on Electronic Monitoring Contract*, 10 January (accessed at www.scotland.gov.uk).

Scottish Executive (2005) *Supporting Police, Protecting Communities: Proposals for Legislation*. Edinburgh: Scottish Executive.

Scottish Home and Health Department (1971) *Community Involvement Departments*. Edinburgh: SHHD Police Circular: No 6/71.

Scottish Home and Health Department (1983) *Consultation between the Community and the Police*. Edinburgh: SHHD Police Circular: No 2/83.

Scottish Home and Health Department (1984) *Manpower, Effectiveness and Efficiency in the Police Service*. SHHD Police Circular No 3/84.

Scottish Home and Health Department (1985) *Manpower, Effectiveness and Efficiency in the Police Service – Objectives and Priorities*. SHHD Police Circular No 2/85.

Scottish Home and Health Department (1986) *Civilianisation in the Police Service*. SHHD Police Circular 5/86.

Scottish Home and Health Department (1993) *Civilianisation in the Police Service*. SHHD Police Circular 11/93.

Scottish Office (1994) *Drugs in Scotland – Meeting the Challenge* (Drugs Task Force Report, Lord Fraser). Edinburgh: HMSO.

Scottish Office (1999) *Tackling Drugs in Scotland: Action in Partnership*. Edinburgh: HMSO.

Scottish Parliament website, www.scottishparliament.gov.uk.

Scottish Police Federation (1969) *Scottish Police Federation Golden Anniversary Brochure*. Edinburgh.

Scottish Population Census 1901. Edinburgh.

Seneviratne, M. (2004) 'Policing the police in the United Kingdom', *Policing and Society*, 14 (4): 329–347.

Shanks, N. J. (1980) *Police Community Involvement in Scotland*, Scottish Office Central Research Unit Paper. Edinburgh: HMSO.

Shapland, J. and Vagg, J. (1988) *Policing by the Public*. London: Routledge.

Sharp, L., Sir (1995) 'Sharp's vision', *Police Review*, 28 April: 28–29.

Shearing, C. D. and Stenning, P. C. (1987) (eds) *Private Policing*. Thousand Oaks, CA: Sage.

Shields, J. V. M. and Duncan J. A. (1964) *The State of Crime in Scotland*. London: Tavistock Publications.

Shirley McKie website: www.shirleymckie.com.

Short, C. (1983) 'Community policing beyond slogans', in T. Bennett (ed.), *The Future of Policing*. Cambridge: Institute of Criminology.

Short, E. and Ditton, J. (1996) *Does Closed Circuit Television Prevent Crime? An Evaluation of the use of CCTV surveillance cameras in Airdrie*. Edinburgh: Scottish Office.

Sinclair, J. *et al.* (1995) 'Market driven reform in education: performance, quality and industrial relations in schools', in I. Kirkpatrick and M. Lucio-Martinez (eds), *The Politics of Quality in the Public Sector*. London: Routledge.

Smith, A. D. (1931) *City of Glasgow Police Criminal Returns 1930*. Glasgow.

Smith, D. and Young, P. (1999) 'Crime trends in Scotland since 1950', in P. Duff and N. Hutton (eds), *Criminal Justice in Scotland*. London: Ashgate, pp. 14–37.

Smith, D. J. *et al.* (2004) *The Edinburgh Study of Youth Transitions and Crime: Key Findings*. Edinburgh: University of Edinburgh, Centre for Law and Society.

Smith, P. T. (ed.) (1985) *Policing Victorian London*. Connecticut: Greenwood Press.

Smout, T. C. (1986) *A Century of the Scottish People 1830–1950*. London: Fontana.

Social Work Scotland Inspectorate (2005) *Managing the Risk: An Inspection of the Management of Sex Offenders Cases in Scotland*. Edinburgh: SWSI.

South, N. (1988) *Policing for Profit*. London: Sage.

South Lanarkshire Council (2004) *South Lanarkshire – Joint Problem Solving Model*. Hamilton: South Lanarkshire Council.

Spicer, M. (ed.) (2002) *The Scotsman Guide to Scottish Politics*. Edinburgh: Scotsman Publications.

Spitzer, S. and Scull A. (1977) 'Privatization and capitalist development: the case of the private police', *Social Problems*, 25: 18–29.

Spurgeon, P. (ed.) (1998) *The New Face of the NHS*, 2nd edn. London: The Royal Society of Medicine Press.

Squires, P. (1997) 'Consumer agenda', *Policing Today*, 3 (1): 46–50.

Starmer, K., Strange, M. and Whitaker, Q. (2001) *Criminal Justice, Police Powers and Human Rights*. London: Blackstone Press.

State Hospital website, www.show.scot.nhs.uk

Stead, P. J. (1983) *The Police of France*. London: Macmillan.

Steedman, C. (1984) *Policing the Victorian Community – The Formation of English Provincial Police Forces 1856–1880*. London: Routledge and Kegan Paul.

Stephens, M. (1994) 'Care and control: the future of British policing', *Policing and Society*, 4: 237–251.

Stevens, J., Sir (2004) quoted in *The Herald*, 20 December (accessed at www.theherald.co.uk).

Stewart, A. L. (1997) *The Scottish Criminal Courts in Action,* 2nd edn. Edinburgh: Butterworth Lexis Nexis.

Storch, R. D. (1975) '"A plague of the blue locusts": police reform and popular resistance in Northern England, 1840–1857', *International Review of Social History*, 20: 61–90.

Storch, R. D. (1976) 'The policeman as domestic missionary: urban discipline and popular culture in Northern England, 1850–1880', *Journal of Social History*, 9 (4): 481–509.

Strathclyde Police (2001) *Review of Community Policing*. Strathclyde Police: unpublished report.

Summary Justice Review Committee (2004) *Report to Ministers*. Edinburgh: Scottish Executive.

Sunday Herald (2001) 'Politics infecting police "like aids"', 10 June: 6.

Sunday Herald (2003) 'Young offenders forced to make amends to victims', 24 August: 6.

Tata, C. *et al.* (2002) *A Sentencing Information System for the High Court of Justiciary: First Phase of Implementation, Enhancement and Evaluation.* Edinburgh: Scottish Executive.

Taylor, D. (1998) *Crime, Policing and Punishment.* London: Macmillan.

Taylor, I. and Popham, G. (eds) (1989) *An Introduction to Public Sector Management.* London: Unwin Hyman.

Thomson, Lord (1975) *Criminal Procedure in Scotland*, 2nd Report. Edinburgh: HMSO.

Tilley, N. (2003) 'Community policing, problem-oriented policing and intelligence-led policing', in T. Newburn (ed.), *Handbook of Policing*. Devon: Willan Publishing.

Tobias, J. J. (1972) *Nineteenth-Century Crime – Prevention and Punishment.* Devon: David & Charles.

Tobias, J. J. (1979) *Crime and Police in England 1700–1900.* Dublin: Gill & Macmillan.

Tomkins, P. (2004) quoted in *The Herald*, 13 September: 1–2 (accessed at www.theherald.co.uk).

Trojanowicz, R. and Bucqueroux, B. (1990) *Community Policing – A Contemporary Perspective.* Cincinnati: Anderson.

United Nations Office on Drugs and Crime (2004a) *World Drug Report by the United Nations Office on Drugs and Crime.* United Nations: UNODC.

United Nations Office on Drugs and Crime (2004b) *Afghanistan Opium Survey.* United Nations: UNODC.

United Nations Office on Drugs and Crime (2004c) *Farmers' Intention Survey.* United Nations: UNODC.

Vestri, P. and Fitzpatrick, S. (2000) 'Scotland's councillors', *Scottish Affairs*, 33: 62–81.

Villiers, P. and Adlam, R. (eds) (2004) *Policing a Safe, Just and Tolerant Society – An International Model.* Winchester: Waterside Press.

Vine, J. D. (2003) *Why So Few Women Supervisors? What Can Be Done to Enhance the Prospects of Promotion for Women in the Scottish Police Service?* University of Abertay, Dundee: Unpublished MSc thesis.

Walker, C. (1999) 'Miscarriages of justice in Scotland', in C. Walker and K. Starmer (eds), *Miscarriages of Justice: A Review of Justice in Error.* London: Blackstone Press.

Walker, C. and Starmer, K. (eds) (1999) *Miscarriages of Justice: A Review of Justice in Error.* London: Blackstone Press.

Walker, N. (2000) *Policing in a Changing Constitutional Order.* London: Sweet & Maxwell.

Walker, N. (2003) 'The pattern of transnational policing', in T. Newburn (ed.), *Handbook of Policing*. Devon: Willan Publishing, pp. 111–135.

Warwickshire Police (2004) *Policy on Drug Testing – Alcohol, Drugs and Substance Abuse.* Warwickshire Police.

Wasserman, G. (2004) 'A lesson from America', *Policing Today*, 10 (3): 25–27.

Weatheritt, M. (1987) 'Community policing now', in P. Willmott (ed.), *Policing and the Community*. London: Policy Studies Institute, pp. 7–20.

Wemmer, J. (2001) 'Restorative justice – the choice between bilateral decision-making power and third party intervention', in B. Williams (ed.), *Reparation and Victim-Focused Social Work*. Research Highlights in Social Work No. 42. London: Jessica Kingsley Publishers.

White, B. (1994) 'Training medical policemen: Forensic medicine and public health in nineteenth century Scotland', in M. Clark and C. Crawford (eds), *Legal Medicine in History*. Cambridge: Cambridge University Press.

White, R. M. (1998) 'Disciplining chief constables', *Scots Law Times*, 11: 77–80.

Wilkie, R. (1992) 'The organisational structure of the police', in C. Pollitt and S. Harrison (eds), *Handbook of Public Services Management*. Oxford: Blackwell.

Willcocks, L. and Harrow, J. (eds) (1992) *Rediscovering Public Services Management*. London: McGraw-Hill.

Williams, B. (ed.) (2001) *Reparation and Victim-Focused Social Work*, Research Highlights in Social Work No. 42. London: Jessica Kingsley Publishers.

Williams, B. *et al.* (2004) *The Interface between the Scottish Police Service and the Public as Victims of Crime: Victim Perceptions* (accessed at www.scotland.gov.uk/socialresearch).

Willmott, P. (ed.) (1987) *Policing and the Community*. London: Policy Studies Institute.

Willmott, P. (1989) *Community Initiatives – Patterns and Prospects*. London: Policy Studies Institute.

Wilson, J. Q. and Kelling, G. (1982) 'Broken windows: the police and neighborhood safety', *The Atlantic Monthly*, March: 29–38.

Woodcock, J., Sir (1992) Speech given at IPEC Conference. London: HMCIC.

Young, P. (1997) *Crime and Criminal Justice in Scotland*. Edinburgh: The Stationery Office.

279

Index